Reforming the Federal Judiciary

Reforming the Federal Judiciary

My Former Court Needs to Overhaul
Its Staff Attorney Program and
Begin Televising Its Oral Arguments

Richard A. Posner

ISBN 978-1976014796

Contents

Preface

When I resigned as a law professor at the University of Chicago, and became a member of the U.S. Court of Appeals for the Seventh Circuit, lo these many years ago (December 4, 1981, to be exact), I had never heard the terms "staff attorney" or "staff attorney program," nor was I aware that there was a desire in some quarters that judicial proceedings be televised. I learned soon enough that my court had a staff attorney program, but it was small and distinctly marginal. It is larger today, as I'll explain in this book, which is concerned with the program (but also with the staff attorney programs of the other federal courts of appeals) and its personnel, but is also concerned with the unrelated question of whether to allow the televising of judicial proceedings, a question ignored by my court until quite recently. The staff attorney program remains marginal, unfortunately, and the question of televising unanswered. Both subjects have generated considerable controversy within the court, and controversy is at the forefront of this book. I argue that allowing the televising of oral arguments is long overdue and that the staff attorney program is ripe for a major overhaul. My discussion of the television issue, which constitutes Part Two of the book, is brief, but only because the issue is straightforward. The court's staff attorney program, and its counterparts in the other federal courts of appeals, are complex (and there is considerable variance among the different courts' programs—see, for a compact summary, the spreadsheet in Appendix One to Part One), and therefore occupy the bulk of the book.

Regrettably my views on these issues do not at present command any support in the court, primarily because of the opposition of the current chief judge to my endeavors to improve the staff attorney program. That opposition is necessarily a theme of the book, but it is also a source of regret as I had never before quarreled with another member of the court. But I emphasize that my disagreements with the chief judge are not tinged by personal animosity. I performed her marriage ceremony some years ago.

In part because ideas that are important to me have failed to command the support of the other judges, in part because I was a member of the court for 35 years and am now approaching my 79th birthday, and in part because I have writing commitments that my work for the court has prevented me from completing, I recently decided to retire (having been eligible to retire since I was 65), and have now done so, effective September 2 of this year.

I wish to acknowledge Chief Judge Wood's gracious announcement of my retirement: "It is with great regret that I announce the retirement of Judge Richard A. Posner after nearly thirty-six years on the Seventh Circuit. For more than 50 years Judge Posner has been one of the leading public intellectuals in the United States—indeed, in the world. He is one of the most distinguished people to ever sit on the federal bench. His opinions have had an impact around the world. He has produced an unparalleled body of scholarship—books, articles, and public commentary—covering virtually every legal topic that can be imagined. The impact Judge Posner has had on this Court is immeasurable, and it is with the deepest gratitude that we wish him well." To which I responded that "It has been a tremendous honor to serve on this Court. I thank my colleagues, past and present, for the opportunity to work with them."

Although the primary focus of this book is on staff attorney programs and the television issue, there is more. Inevitably the analytic focus falls partly on me, not because I'm a fascinating person eager to write autobiographically but because the positions I take in this book represent a change, beginning some months ago, in my outlook on the downtrodden, who include most of the litigants who interact with staff attorneys, and also because that change in outlook engendered an unfortunate conflict between the chief judge and me. That conflict, though now amicably resolved, requires attention, as does the evolution of my attitude toward the downtrodden—the pro se's, which is to say *litigants* who have no lawyers, many of whom moreover have the further handicap of being prison inmates. My evolving attitude toward these unfortunates is central to my analysis of staff attorney programs and my disagreements with my judicial colleagues.

On August 20, 2017, I thought the book was finished. But deciding on a last-minute skimming of the voluminous files that I had assembled concerning the staff attorney programs of the 13 federal courts of appeals, I discovered that the following statement in this Preface was inaccurate: "I started to engage with the core issues intensively in the late winter of 2017, as their importance finally sunk into my mind. I did not begin to write this book until June 9 but once I began I completed a first draft in three weeks, and have since spent a great deal of time expanding and revising the manuscript. The book is long enough to be a reference work— but that's fine, because there's never been a book on staff attorneys or staff attorney programs, even though such programs have existed for the last half century and are a significant component of the judiciary." What I discovered in the files was that June 9 was not the beginning of this book project—the beginning took place on April 13 of this year, when I composed the first of a long series of memos, all concerned with what I regarded and regard as essential improvements in my court's staff attorney program. The memos had gradually morphed into book-length documents culminating in the present book. The April 13 memo consisted of a single page listing eight modest suggestions. By May 2 it had grown to 23 pages, entitled "Improving the Seventh Circuit's Staff Attorney Program," by May 8 to 38 pages, by May 23 to 98 pages (a draft coauthored with Michael Fridkin, the director of the staff attorney program), and from there it grew in successive versions to its present size. The May 30 version (also 98 pages), incidentally, had a nice abstract at the beginning, which I take the liberty of quoting:

> Staff attorneys employed by courts of appeals provide advice to judges of their court on the disposition of appeals, motions, and other filings by pro se litigants (often prison inmates). But frequently the judges and the staff attorneys

who advise them fail to issue orders or opinions disposing of the pro se's appeal or other motion that are likely to be intelligible to pro se's, thereby depriving them of potentially vital information relating to their situation and possible future avenues of legal relief. The main thrust of this memorandum is, emphasizing the importance of providing reasoned orders in all pro se decisions, to encourage our judges and staff attorneys always to provide lucid, fully intelligible rulings resolving cases brought by pro se's, bearing in the mind the frequent educational and intellectual handicaps under which such litigants labor.

My reason for recounting the chronology of my engagement with the staff attorney program is to make clear that my concern with the program, and my efforts to reform it, were not of recent vintage. Yet my most intense concern and my most energetic (though unsuccessful) efforts at reform go back only seven months, to my January 30 dissenting opinion in *Miller v. Marberry*, discussed at length in Chapter 1.

* * *

I am sole author but heavily indebted to others for help. I received significant help on the staff attorney project (I was largely though not entirely on my own regarding the issue of televising the court's hearings) from Michael Fridkin, the director of the court's staff attorney program, Julie Lyons, one of the program's supervisors, and my team of research assistants at the University of Chicago Law School, where I teach part time (very part time, though this may change with my retirement from judging). I thank Theresa Yuan, the head of the team, and John McAdams, Makar Gevorkian, and Danielle York, the other members, as well as Fridkin and Lyons and the court's circuit executive, Collins Fitzpatrick, for their contributions to my project (Ms. Yuan's prodigious research in the staff attorney programs of the other federal courts of appeals deserves especial notice). I also received helpful comments along the way from, among others, Lisa Nash, a former staff attorney, Ann Jaworski, one of my last law clerks, and Julia Schwartz and

Michael Shakman of the distinguished Chicago law firm of Miller, Shakman, and Beem, who represented me when it seemed that my dispute with the chief judge would escalate to litigation, fortunately averted. I also thank Gary Peeples for helpful critique of an earlier draft of the book and for introducing me to Judge Ronald Lee Gilman's brilliant writing rules (see Appendix Four toward the end of the book), my wife Charlene for careful reading and correction of my manuscript, my tireless secretary Patricia Goldrick for her patience in printing out a long parade of successive drafts of it, and last but certainly not least George W. Rumsey, President of Computer Resource Center, Inc., in Chicago, for connecting me with CreateSpace (see next page) and for the unique technological skills that he deployed in critically scrutinizing successive drafts of the book and by doing so generating revisions that have greatly improved this at-last final copy. I can't thank George enough.

I also want to acknowledge fruitful discussion of the challenges of the staff attorney program with my judicial colleague and good friend of more than 30 years, Judge Joel Flaum, and to thank Marisa Watson, the director of the Third Circuit's staff attorney program, for providing me with the extensive information on that program that I recount at length in Appendix Three to Part One of the book; Chief Judge D. Brooks Smith of the Third Circuit, for generously allowing my research team to draw on Ms. Watson's comprehensive knowledge of his court's program; Michael Schneider, the director of the Fifth Circuit's staff attorney program, for the detailed information about his impressive program that he generously shared with us; federal district judge Virginia Kendall for her insights into the handling of pro se litigation at the district court level; and staff attorneys of my court, but also of other federal courts of appeals, for the valuable insights that they shared with me (often via my research assistants). And finally I wish to thank Thomas Dart, the Sheriff of Cook County, Illinois and director of the Cook County Jail, and the jail's Chief Policy Officer—Sheriff Cara L. Smith—along with other members of the jail staff, for an illuminating tour of the facility, which I discuss later in this book. I also wish to thank the detainees at the jail with whom I talked on my tour, who helped me to understand the problems of incarcerated pro se litigants, who figure prominently in the work of staff attorneys—and in this book.

* * *

I have hopes for the reception of this book (my 66th, though some of the previous ones were jointly authored and some others were successive editions; this book is neither), though it will not make me rich because I am forgoing all royalties; the courts have budgets and I don't want to lose readers because a court is unwilling to shift money from another source to the purchase of my book. Unfortunately I don't know whether any of the courts other than my own have separate book budgets and if so what they might be. But I do know that the Seventh Circuit has a book budget, which is administered by the head of the library of the court of appeals, Gretchen Van Dam—and it is a generous $1.59 million a year. But I am still planning to give copies of my book to the library rather than wait for the library to buy them from Amazon CreateSpace (see the next section of the book), which will be the publisher of the book.

Although there are articles, mainly online, dealing with staff attorney programs, there are as I noted earlier no books on the subject—or rather there were no books until this one. This is surprising when one considers that all 13 federal courts of appeals have staff attorney programs, that there are altogether some 400 staff attorneys in these programs (compared to about 190 in 1980 and 260 in 1994), that many of the programs date back to the 1970s—almost a half century ago—though they have greatly expanded since, and that there are staff attorneys in many federal district courts and state courts as well as in the federal courts of appeal, see, e.g., TexasLaw, "Staff Attorney Positions," https://law.utexas.edu/judicial-clerkships/category/post-clerkship-jobs/staff-attorney-positions/, although I believe that most of them are what are called *pro bono* staff attorneys, meaning lawyers not employed by the district court but on call to represent pro se's appearing in the court. District judges often have assistance in dealing with pro se litigants from what are called pro se law clerks employed by the judges' district court, as well as from the judges' own law clerks, and sometimes from law students, called externs or interns, the main difference being that interns are more likely to be paid. In addition, federal courts, a number of state courts, prisons, and even jails, have libraries—all of which need my book, as it stands alone. I hope to see it become required reading for judges, law clerks, and staff attorneys—and also for law students aspiring to fill any of these positions.

My focus is on staff attorneys employed federal courts of appeals, with particular but by no means exclusive emphasis on the Seventh Circuit. But the cases handled by these staff attorneys are fed to them mainly by federal district courts, and so the judges of these courts are indirect participants in the staff attorney pro-grams of our court and the other federal courts of appeals. This book, the product of more than four months of intensive labor by me and my research assistants, with no support from my judicial colleagues but much from old and new friends throughout the nation, is unique, and it is my hope that you the reader will enjoy and even learn something from it, though I warn you that it is a pretty long book— 300 pages, 100,000 words.

I need to alert the reader, however, to two potentially confusing features of the text. First, I frequently interrupt the flow briefly to indicate the date of a particular statement; I might for example say, as I just did, "as of this writing—July 12, 2017"—or "as of today, August 6, 2017"—in fact both of these dated statements appear in the book. The reason for identifying dates is that I started writing the book on June 9, 2017, just days after the chief judge had elicited from the other judges disagreement with my proposal to be the final reviewer of staff attorney memos and draft orders en route to panels of judges. Today is September 5—more than four months since I began writing the book. The fact that the book covers this entire span persuades me that some readers will be interested to discover the precise point at which a significant statement was made.

Second, though I am now retired, I do occasionally refer in the book to "my court" or "our court," implying that I am still a member of it. But those terms appear only when I am quoting or discussing a portion of the book written before my retirement, a portion thus composed at a time when I was indeed a member of the court.

I want finally to emphasize that although outspokenly critical, the book is also impersonal. I criticize the views of my judicial colleagues on a number of issues but I do not question their good faith. My conflict with the judges is over. Let there be no hard feelings.

September 5, 2017

Enter CreateSpace

I have written many books in my time—in fact, this is my 66th book, though some of have been coauthored and others second or more (in one instance tenth) editions of the same book. All of the preceding 65 were published by a university press, with the exception of one published by Random House. But recently I discovered Amazon's publication program, which is called CreateSpace. At the suggestion of my wife, Charlene Posner, I corresponded with Heather Refetoff, a friend of hers who had published a novel in CreateSpace that Charlene had bought; and through Ms. Refetoff I discovered and became friends with George W. Rumsey, the President of the Computer Resource Center, Inc., whom I mentioned in the preface as contributing notably to the book. Among the Center's many services are publication of books either by means of conventional printing companies or through Amazon CreateSpace, which publishes both online and printed books.

After receiving a note from Ms. Refetoff in which she raved about Mr. Rumsey, I phoned him, and our conversation led to my meeting this very impressive person in his office on August 16 and to my almost instant decision to publish this book, under his guidance, via CreateSpace rather than a university press. That would, thanks to the generosity of Amazon, enable me to obtain from the company a large number of copies of my book at prices within the limits of my resources (I am well off financially, but not wealthy by current standards)—copies that I would aim to distribute free of charge both to federal judges involved in litigation by pro se's ("pro se" is Latin for "for yourself," and in law denotes a litigant who has no lawyer, usually owing to lack of money) and to staff attorneys, who assist judges with regard primarily to pro se litigants. The federal courts are not giving pro se's a fair shake, and I hope that via CreateSpace I will succeed in convincing the judiciary to render greater justice to them. That in fact is the main objective of the book.

My distribution procedure will be initially to mail a copy of the book to every chief federal circuit judge. If any chief judge wants additional copies, whether for the other judges of his or her court or for the court's staff attorneys and/or other staff, I will mail the number of copies requested to that chief judge, again at no charge either to him or to the recipients of the copies—at least until I run out of money. And finally, to the extent my resources permit, I will advertise the book in journals or blogs directed at lawyers, law professors and law students, and staff and inmates at prisons and jails.

Part One

The Staff Attorney Program:
A *Very* Brief Introduction

I was nominated and confirmed as a judge of the U.S. Court of Appeals for the Seventh Circuit, which encompasses the states of Illinois, Indiana, and Wisconsin, in 1981. Between 1993 and 2000 I was the court's chief judge, though purely by reason of seniority, for that is the only (and, I have argued in my just-published book *The Federal Judiciary: Strengths and Weaknesses* (Harvard University Press, 2017)), a mistaken) basis for selecting chief judges of federal courts of appeals. After the expiration of my term, I remained an active member of the court for the next 16 (almost 17) years. But my intellectual activity was never limited to the court; in my lifetime I have authored or coauthored not only many books but also countless articles and blog postings; and though many of the books and articles and blogs preceded my becoming a judge, a large number of them have been written and published since my appointment.

This new book, though it is centrally about the other federal courts of appeals as well, takes me in a new direction, or rather in two new directions. One, the longer and the one I'll begin with, is the critique of staff attorney programs, with particular but not exclusive emphasis on the Seventh Circuit. The other is an evaluation of the refusal of most federal courts of appeals, including the court of appeals for the Seventh Circuit, to allow routine (as distinct from exceptional or no) televising of oral arguments. I argue that the Seventh Circuit's staff attorney program is in need of substantial restructuring, so far resisted by the judges; and I further argue that the court's oral arguments should be televised routinely—another proposal resisted by the judges on grounds that I am convinced, and will endeavor to persuade the readers of this book, are inadequate.

Throughout I'll be guided by Winston Churchill's maxim: "Never give in, never give in, never, never, never, never ... never give in, except to convictions of honour or good sense." (Quoted in William Manchester, *The Last Lion, Winston Spencer Churchill Alone, 1932-1940*, vol. 2, p. 79, 1988.) In this book, I'm a fighter.

Chapter 1

A Fuller Introduction to the
Seventh Circuit's Staff Attorney Program

I imagine that some, maybe many, readers of this book have never heard of "staff attorneys," or if they have heard of them have no clear idea of what they are and do. Yet probably all my readers know what judicial law clerks are, and staff attorneys are a species of judicial law clerk (from here on I shall refer to judicial law clerks simply as law clerks). The primary role of staff attorneys, which is distinct from that of law clerks though there is some overlap, is to advise judges mostly about the court's cases that are not orally argued, often because the appellant has no lawyer. A further important distinction is that while law clerks are hired individually by judges and work exclusively for the judges who hire them, staff attorneys are hired by managerial employees of the court, primarily the senior staff attorney as the director of the court's staff attorney program is called; in the Seventh Circuit today he is a lawyer named Michael Fridkin, and reports, as I'll explain shortly, to the chief judge. He is assisted in the management of the program by supervisory staff attorneys, usually four in number. Below them are about 20 more staff attorneys, usually recent graduates of high-ranking law schools who are hired by the court for just two years, after which they obtain employment primarily in law firms, in government legal agencies such as the U.S. Department of Justice, in law schools (as faculty members), or in law-oriented public-interest organizations.

The Seventh Circuit's staff attorney program, although it has definite strengths, also has definite weaknesses, and can and should be improved significantly, as can in all likelihood the staff attorney programs of some or many of the other federal circuits, of which there are 12 in all besides the Seventh, all discussed to a greater or lesser extent in later chapters of this book. For a serviceable though somewhat dated introduction to the staff attorney programs of the federal courts of appeals, see Elizabeth Armand and Malini Nangia, "Judicial Clerkships: Federal Staff Attorney Positions," 2008, http://luc.edu/media/lucedu/law/career/pdfs/Federal_Staff_Attorney. pdf.

I will be describing in detail, and illustrating at length, the strengths and weaknesses of the Seventh Circuit's staff attorney program, and recommending a number of improvements in it; and on the basis of research into the staff attorney programs of the other circuits I will be pointing out differences between our program and theirs—some to the advantage of those circuits.

I begin, however, by noting that the basic structure of the Seventh Circuit's staff attorney program is not new. A very similar structure was adopted by the Ninth Circuit in 1980, as described in a fine article by Arthur D. Hellman, "Central Staff in Appellate Courts: The Experience of the Ninth Circuit," 68 *California Law Review* 937 (1980). Though that was two years before Congress formally authorized staff attorney programs, they had existed in some circuits since the 1970s. See http://nonpublication.com/stf-fattys.htm. When I was appointed to the Seventh Circuit in 1981, there was already a staff attorney program in force, though it was less well defined, less formal, and less elaborated, than today's program. Indeed the court had had staff attorneys in the 1970s, though very few—just one for every three judges. In Illinois state courts today, often 20 judges share four law clerks; in contrast, every federal appellate judge is entitled to four law clerks and in most of these courts, including the Seventh Circuit, there are more staff attorneys than judges.

* * *

Besides differing from law clerks in being hired not by judges but by administrators (in the Seventh Circuit by the director of the court's staff attorney program, although the court's chief judge has, with the concurrence of a majority of the court's other judges, the final say on the appointment of the supervisory staff attorneys, including the senior staff attorney, which is the official title of the director of the program), staff attorneys are not assigned to a particular judge. Rather each staff attorney is assigned on an ad hoc basis to assist (usually just by submitting a memo or draft order) a judge or a panel of judges in a particular case. As a result, over the course of his or her employment by the court the staff attorney works with many judges rather than, as in the case of a law clerk, just one—the judge who hired the clerk. The court of appeals for the Seventh Circuit has at present, with my departure, 11 judges, 43 law clerks, and, depending on how one counts, 24 or 25 staff attorneys including supervisory personnel. In contrast, as shown in the spreadsheet in Appendix One to Part One of this book, the court of appeals for the Ninth Circuit has 75-80 staff attorneys—more than any other circuit. From the spreadsheet it can also be calculated that the total number of staff attorneys in the federal appellate judiciary is approximately 401.

Law clerks usually are hired for just a year, though some court of appeals judges still have "career clerks," whose time as a judge's law clerk may be coterminous with the judge's time on the court. Staff attorneys, however, in our court are hired for two years (in some other circuits the term is much longer) except that our supervisory staff attorneys are career rather than temporary employees and have an indefinite term of employment. The greater number of law clerks than of staff attorneys (43 versus 24 or 25) reflects the fact that the latter work mostly on less complex cases than the law clerks do—mainly cases in which there is no oral argument and the appellant has no lawyer—and so can take on more cases than the law clerks. The salaries of the two-year staff attorneys and of the judges' law clerks are comparable, however; I don't have complete statistics but I do know that about a third of the law clerks and a fourth of the staff attorneys in the Seventh Circuit court of appeals have annual salaries between $60,000 and $70,000 and some considerably more—including a few in both groups whose annual salaries exceed $100,000 (and sometimes go as high as $150,000) —some because they are long-serving career law clerks and others because they are supervisory staff attorneys.

In the Seventh Circuit as in the other federal courts of appeals. staff attorneys handle a large part of the court's caseload. About half the appellants in our court are pro se's (as noted earlier, the term "pro se," Latin for "on one's own behalf," denotes litigants who do not have lawyers), and appeals by pro se's are referred in the first instance to staff attorneys, who prepare draft orders (suggested orders for disposing of the case) or recommendation memos (similar but usually longer) for submission to one, two, or most commonly three of the court's judges (termed a three-judge panel) for decision, though sometimes staff attorneys answer simple questions by pro se litigants without reporting to a judge. The staff attorneys' work thus broadly resembles that done by law clerks for their judges.

Although judges are not bound by a staff attorney's recommended decision, they tend to rubber stamp it; in that respect staff attorneys have more juridical influence than most law clerks, though it is influence exerted in cases that are on average less important than those handled by law clerks for their judges. Their lesser importance is of course a spur to rubberstamping.

Each staff attorney has a spreadsheet on which to record every case on which he or she works; the spreadsheet is identified by case number, by a brief description of the issues in the case, by the name of the supervisory staff attorney who reviewed the final draft, and by the recommended outcome (usually the denial or grant of the appeal), along with the date of distribution of the recommendation (and usually a draft order) to the judge or judges for decision of the case, the name of the judge or names of the judges if the staff attorney's recommendation is submitted to more than one, and the date on which the final order or opinion was issued by the judicial panel (which sometimes consists of just one judge, sometimes of two, but more commonly, as I noted, of three). These data are used to keep track of how often staff attorneys recommend reversing the decision of the district court (usually a decision to dismiss the pro se's case) rather than affirming it, and how often the judge or judges assigned to the case agree or disagree with the staff attorney's recommendation.

Staff attorneys have a similar spreadsheet for habeas corpus cases, which are cases in which the appellant is seeking to be released from jail or prison, or at least to have his sentence shortened; for merits motions, which are motions to affirm or dismiss an appeal summarily because of an obvious presence or absence of merit; and for motions seeking relief of one kind or another that may be unrelated to the appellant's conviction or sentence, such as better medical care (I'll give examples later) or recognition of religious rights.

Unlike merits filings, which generally are distributed to three judges at once, habeas corpus filings are often presented to just one judge at a time, making the staff attorneys' spreadsheets helpful in keeping track of each judge's vote; for often a motion or other application to the court is decided by just one or two judges rather than by the conventional three. See "Seventh Circuit Operating Procedures 1: Motions," www.ca7.uscourts.gov/rules-procedures/ rules/rules.htm#op-proc.

A complicated set of statutory rules limits the right to appeal the denial of an application for habeas corpus. For example, often the issuance of a certificate of appealability by a federal judge is a prerequisite to seeking habeas corpus in the court of appeals, and often a prerequisite to the issuance of such a certificate is a showing of the denial of a constitutional right of the applicant. See Title 28 of the federal criminal code, ch. 153, especially 28 U.S.C. §§ 2253(c)(1), (c)(2), 2254, and 2255; see also Federal Rule of Appellate Procedure 22(b)(1); *Slack v. McDaniel*, 529 U.S. 473, 484 (2000); and Margaret A. Upshaw, "The Unappealing State of Certificates of Appealability," 82 *University of Chicago Law Review* 1609, 1616 (2015). As a result of these roadblocks many appeals from denials of habeas corpus are dismissed without reference to the possible merit of the appellant's challenge to his incarceration.

There is a considerable literature on pro se litigants, well illustrated by Jona Goldschmidt, "How Are Courts Handling Pro Se Litigants?," 82 *Judicature*, no. 1, July-Aug. 1998, but the focus of the literature is on pro se litigation at the trial level, for it is there that a pro se's lack of legal training and knowledge and the aid of a lawyer places a great strain on judge and jury—indeed the pro se's untutored self-advocacy may border on, or even cross over into, unintelligibility. That is a lesser concern at the appellate level, where the pro se normally will present documents and argumentation that while often not fully lucid usually convey the essence of a legal position that the judges can understand and elucidate; and staff attorneys are able to present to the judicial panel the kinds of argument pro or con the pro se that appellate judges can evaluate without difficulty.

I have extensive though not complete statistics, supplied to me by director Fridkin, relating to the activity of the court's staff attorneys. I know for example that the average number of cases they handle each year is 8,000, of which 5,000 are so routine (such as cases that can be resolved by orders granting uncontested motions for extensions of time) that the staff attorneys dispose of them without consulting a panel of judges; for the operating rules allow "administrative personnel" (mainly staff attorneys) to rule summarily on motions that present nothing out of the ordinary. Of the other, the nonroutine, 3,000 cases, about half are pro se appeals, or other motions or filings by pro se's, that do require judicial consideration.

These non-routine filings fall into several categories. Regarding the handling of pro se motions, which are the most challenging of the submissions to the court that are assessed in the first instance by staff attorneys rather than by judges or law clerks, the following breakdown is informative. The data set is for 2016. The first percentage given is the rate at which staff attorneys recommend granting the type of motion at issue, the second the rate at which the judge(s) grant(s) relief in such a case. Motions by pro se's the denial of which will end a pro se's appeal, average about 300 a year and consist mainly of motions for leave to appeal or for appointment of counsel. Staff attorneys recommend granting relief to the appellant, rather than denying relief, in 13% of those cases; judges the same. As for motions by counseled litigants in original appellate proceedings, the denial of which will end an appeal (about 25 motions a year); petitions under Fed. R. Civ. P. 23(f) (appeals of decisions concerning class certifications); petitions under 28 U.S.C. § 1292(b) (orders that the district court certified for interlocutory review); and petitions under 28 U.S.C. § 1453(c) (removal of class actions from state court), staff attorneys recommend granting relief in 33% of the cases and judges again the same.

Here are some other, though more tentative, statistics concerning the disposition of cases handled by Seventh Circuit staff attorneys en route to the judicial panels that decide the cases. In cases governed by Rule 34 of the Federal Rules of Appellate Procedure, a rule that encourages oral argument at the appellate level if but only if it is likely to contribute to a sound result (see Rule 34(a)(2), quoted below); when that condition is not satisfied there is substituted for oral argument a conference between staff attorneys and a three-judge panel called a "Rule 34 conference" at which one or more judges in a three-judge panel suggest revisions in the staff attorneys' proposed orders (usually between 9 and 12 proposed orders are considered at such a conference) and the orders are then revised and issued.

Currently staff attorneys are recommending affirming the lower court (ordinarily a federal district court in one of the circuit's three states—Illinois, Indiana, and Wisconsin) in 83% of the cases, and the judicial panels are agreeing with the recommendations in 91% of the 83%. Though staff attorneys are recommending reversing in 17% of the cases, panels agreed with those recommendations only 76% of the time, so only 12.9% of the cases are reversed. And in short-argument-day cases ("short-argument days" are days on which simple-seeming cases are argued to panels of three judges, normally by lawyers, but staff attorneys, rather than the judges' law clerks, prepare bench memos—analyses and recommendations—which they submit to the judges before oral argument)) staff attorneys are recommending affirming in 70% of the cases while judges are agreeing with the affirm recommendation 92% of the time, and staff attorneys are recommending reversing in 30% of the cases and judges are agreeing with the recommendation 87% of the time. In past years, agreement with a recommendation to reverse had been in the 65-75% range.

These statistics are somewhat misleading, however. For example, if panels agree with staff attorneys' recommendations 76% of the time and staff attorneys recommend reversing 17% of the time, then as above because 76% of 17% is 12.9%, the judges and the staff attorneys aren't far apart. And as shown in the following table, averaged over the last nine years the difference between panel reversals and staff attorney-recommended reversals is only 1.4% (12% versus 13.4%).

Percentage of cases in which ...

Panels have reversed in pro se (Rule 34) appeals		*Staff attorneys* have recommended reversals in pro se (Rule 34) appeals	
2008	12%	2008	14%
2009	12%	2009	12%
2010	10%	2010	9%
2011	11%	2011	10%
2012	12%	2012	12%
2013	13%	2013	15%
2014	14%	2014	12%
2015	19%	2015	20%
2016	17%	2016	17%
Average	12%	Average	13.4%

Percent Reversed			Circuit
2015	2016	2017	
0.90%	4.30%	2.50%	1st
1.80%	2.80%	2.30%	2d
1.90%	1.80%	2.90%	3d
1.70%	2.60%	2.00%	4th
1.30%	1.70%	1.30%	5th
3.90%	4.20%	4.30%	6th
5.30%	6.90%	5.30%	7th
1.60%	1.50%	1.60%	8th
4.20%	4.30%	3.80%	9th
1.60%	2.60%	4.80%	10th
3.10%	3.10%	3.10%	11th
3.60%	8.00%	2.50%	D.C.
2.80%	3.10%	3.00%	Avge.

Director Fridkin has furnished me with data indicating that the court reverses a higher percentage of pro se cases on the merits than any other federal court of appeals (see tables, page 10).

Notice that in 2015 the Seventh Circuit's percentage was almost twice the average of all the circuits, in 2016 it was *more* than twice the average, and in 2017 (not yet complete) it is again almost twice the average of all the circuits. Nevertheless all the percentages are quite low; none but the D.C. Circuit's surprising 8% in 2016 approaches 10 percent.

I don't have complete statistics for motions or other pleadings unrelated to Rule 34 conferences, or for cases heard on short-argument days. As I've noted, the term "Rule 34 conferences" denotes face-to-face meetings between staff attorneys and judges to discuss the staff attorneys' proposed orders resolving appeals in lieu of oral argument, a substitution permissible as long as the meetings are consistent with subsection 34(a)(2) of the rule, which allows a panel of judges to determine that oral argument is unnecessary if "(A) the appeal is frivolous; (B) the dispositive issue or issues have been authoritatively decided; or (C) the facts and legal arguments are adequately presented in the briefs and record and the decisional process would not be significantly aided by oral argument." Yet in a common variant of (C), found for example in the first footnote of the order deciding *Carter v. JPMorgan Chase Bank, N.A., et al.*, No. 17-1801, 7th Cir. July 26, 2017, and the order deciding *Johnson v. UMG Recordings, Inc., et al.*, No 17-2260, 7th Cir. Aug. 3, 2017), we read that "We [the judges constituting the panel deciding the case] have unanimously agreed to decide the case without argument because the briefs and record adequately present the facts and legal arguments, and argument would not significantly aid the court."

This is awkward wording, however: "unanimously agreed" is superfluous, and the sequence "argument"-"arguments"-"argument" repetitious. All the order had to say was that "we've decided that oral argument is not necessary for the decision of this appeal." A deeper problem with the formula is the failure to explain *why* "argument would not significantly aid the court." A good reason in many cases would be that the appellant or appellee was pro se, and would be completely out of his depth in arguing his case. It is not at all obvious that the fact that "the briefs and record adequately present the facts and legal arguments" is a good reason for denying oral argument, however, for that could be said in most cases in which, both sides being represented by counsel, oral argument is granted as a matter of course without regard to the adequacy of the briefs and the record as substitutes for oral argument.

Awkward wording both similar and dissimilar to that in *Carter* and *Johnson* is found in *United States v. Miranda-Sotolongo*, No. 16-3881, 7th Cir., where we read: "We have unanimously agreed to decide this successive appeal without oral argument because the legal issues have been authoritatively decided." Decided by whom?

I have some statistics, presented in tabular form later, for such motions and pleadings, but here I simply note that in 15 recent submissions the judge who reviewed the staff attorneys' recommended dispositions agreed with all of them, amounting to 14 denials of relief and one reversal of the district court's denial of relief (thus a victory for the pro se appellant). Furthermore, in the period 2013-2016 in which the court received about a thousand requests to certify appeals in habeas corpus cases, 160 (16%) were granted. But permission to file a habeas corpus petition that is successive because the applicant had filed a previous one that had been denied is almost never given, so strict are the statutory criteria for granting such a petition. See, e.g., 28 U.S.C. § 2255(h).

The absence of complete figures for the disposition of the court's cases that are processed in the first instance by staff attorneys may reflect the fact that judges, along with other judicial personnel, including staff attorneys, tend to be much less statistics-oriented than other professionals, including other government officials. How many judges even know how many published opinions they've issued over the course of their judicial career? Few, I suspect. (I am one of the few, however; I have kept a count of all my published opinions since my appointment to the Seventh Circuit on December 4, 1981, a span of 35 and a half years: the current count, probably only slightly inaccurate, is 3,332, an average of 93.9 opinions per year.)

Keeping an accurate workload record is more important for staff attorneys than for judges, because usually the number of staff attorneys substantially exceeds the number of judges—in the Seventh Circuit there are almost twice as many staff attorneys as judges (23 versus 12). And as noted earlier the number of judicial documents written by our staff attorneys for review, critique, and (they hope) approval by the judges is formidable. The judges ought to know how vast, and also to know more than they usually do about the variance in the staff attorneys' cases—in particular, what percentage are cases filed by prison inmates or jail detainees or persons on bail or on supervised release—in other words by persons with criminal records—and what percentage by all pro se's, of whom prisoners are a substantial fraction. Indeed statistics for recent years reveal that for the nation as a whole, slightly more than half of all appeals to federal courts of appeals are by pro se's and that almost half of those pro se's are prisoners.

In 2015, 51 percent of total appeals in all the federal courts of appeals were pro se, and 46 percent of the pro se's were prisoners.

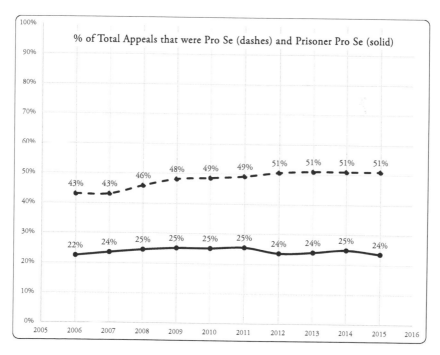

% of Total Appeals that were Pro Se (dashes) and Prisoner Pro Se (solid)

Source: Table 2.4–U.S. Courts of Appeals Judicial Facts and Figures (September 30, 2015).

The corresponding percentages for 2016 were 52 percent and 38 percent—the drop off in the percentage of prisoner pro se's is un-explained. On the special difficulties for the federal judiciary that are posed by prisoner pro se suits, see Robert G. Doumar, "Prisoner Cases: Feeding the Monster in the Judicial Closet," 14 *St. Louis University Public Law Review* 21 (1994)—somewhat dated but still very worthwhile. Fortunately there is growing pressure to reduce the nation's outsized prison population. See, e.g., Holly Harris, "The Prisoner Epidemic," *Foreign Affairs* (March-April 2017).

The burden on the staff attorneys, who handle most pro se cases, is heavy because there are many such cases relative to the number of staff attorneys. In 2016 the Seventh Circuit's staff attorneys in our court, though only 23 in number, were involved in the termination of 1,991 pro se appeals, though a majority (1,199) were terminated for reasons unrelated to the merits of the appeal, such as the appellant's failure to pay required court costs. It should be noted, moreover, that personal contact between staff attorneys and judges, unlike that between law clerks and their judges, is rela-tively infrequent, being limited largely to the Rule 34 conferences; and even there the contact is limited, as the staff attorneys are there to listen to the judges' criticisms of the staff attorneys' proposed orders, rather than to argue in defense of their proposals, which they rarely if ever do.

In the months preceding my retirement I endeavored with some success to have personal contact with staff attorneys, includ-ing supervisory staff attorneys, outside the Rule 34 conference set-ting. I recall one occasion in which Judge Hamilton and I met with a number of law clerks and staff attorneys to discuss at length issues of mutual concern. But my most fruitful discussion with staff at-torneys dates back to a meeting I held with six of them on May 10; here is my write-up of it:

Staff Law Clerk Meeting
May 10, 2017

Attendees:
Judge Posner
Kate Bailey
Grant Gardner
Sarah Wheaton
Sarah Halbach Catalano
Samantha Reed
Andrew Murphy

Notes

Structure of the Office. The Seventh Circuit's staff attorneys' office is divided into three units: merits, motions, and habeas corpus. All staff law clerks (the official title, rarely used, of staff attorneys) spend their first year of the two-year term in the merits unit, where they handle all Rule 34 cases and short argument cases. In the second year of the clerkship, clerks have the option of staying in the merits unit or rotating into either the motions or habeas corpus units. The motions-unit rotations are for a one-year period, while the habeas corpus rotations are for a six-month period. Clerks are invited to express interest in one of the rotations by informing Mike [Fridkin] (for example, a clerk interested in criminal litigation may ask to be placed in the habeas corpus unit), and Mike assigns clerks to units based on the clerks' interest and the needs of the office. Rotation into the habeas corpus and motions units is staggered so that new clerks are always joining a new unit while another clerk, who has already spent several months in the unit, is still completing his or her rotation.

The office is made up of five supervisors including the senior staff attorney, Mike Fridkin. Three supervisors (Mike, Alan Lepp, and Phil Police [the last has resigned, effective in a few months] supervise the lower-level staff attorneys (who work on merits cases), while one supervisor is assigned to habeas corpus (Mia Furlong [also resigned]) and another to motions (Julie Lyons). [As discussed later in the book, Police and Furlong are being replaced by two

newly hired staff attorneys, Kathy Agonis and Matthew Becker.]
The habeas corpus and motions supervisors both handle their own
caseload in addition to supervising the staff attorneys assigned to
their teams.

In addition to the supervisors, there are currently 18 staff attorneys, one permanent clerk (assigned to the motions unit), one
paralegal (also assigned to the motions unit), and an office manager. The office manager handles human resources issues like requests
for leave, new attorney recruitment, training, etc.

The Life Cycle of a Merits Case. When a staff attorney is assigned
a merits case (either a Rule 34 or short argument case), he or she
gathers the parties' briefs, prints the record, and reads the materials.
After analyzing the parties' arguments and conducting further research, the staff attorney presents the case to a supervisor and they
discuss the appropriate outcome of the case. The supervisor may
spot issues that a staff attorney has missed, necessitating further research and analysis, and the two may discuss a case multiple times
to arrive at a recommendation. The staff law clerk then drafts either
a draft order (for Rule 34 cases) or a bench memorandum (for
short argument cases), and hands the draft, briefs, and record off to
another staff attorney for peer review. During the peer review process, another staff attorney will check the citations to case law and
the record and make any stylistic or substantive edits they believe
necessary. The staff attorney assigned to the case will then incorporate those edits and submit the revised draft to a supervisor for
review. The supervisor will also make stylistic and substantive edits
and return the draft to the staff attorney. Sometimes the supervisor
may find an issue that was missed or suggest an entirely different
approach, so the draft may need to be revised several times before
it is ready for distribution to the judges.

When the staff attorneys draft orders for Rule 34 conferences,
their goal is to produce a written product that is both well-reasoned
and understandable for the judges, litigants, and district courts.
While the majority of Rule 34 orders are not published, the orders provide value to the parties and the lower courts by explaining

why the losing party lost, or how the district court's reasoning was flawed.

Comparisons with Other Circuits: Last year, several of the staff attorneys attended the Federal Judicial Conference in Austin, TX. Generally, the conference is attended by permanent staff from each circuit's staff attorney office, and historically the Seventh Circuit has not sent its two-year staff attorneys to the conference. The conference was three days long, and incorporated presentations on topics such as:

- Implicit Bias in the Courtroom
- Appellate Reliance on Independent Factual Research
- A Review of Recent Significant Supreme Court Cases
- Ethical Dilemmas for Federal Appellate Staff Attorneys
- Upcoming Changes to the Sentencing Guidelines
- Gang Violence in Mexico
- The Second Amendment in the Supreme Court and the Circuits
- The Future of the American Death Penalty
- Writing Well and Training Others to Write Well

There were also breakout sessions during which staff attorneys from different circuits could compare the operations of their office with others. These conversations generally focused on habeas corpus cases and how each office was approaching the onslaught of applications to file successive habeas corpus petitions in light of *Johnson v. United States.*

During the three-day conference, the Seventh Circuit's staff attorneys made several observations about how the other circuits' staff attorney programs operate, and noticed significant differences in the following areas: Permanent vs. term clerks, Caseloads, Interaction with judges, and Output.

Permanent vs. Term Clerkships: Most other offices are staffed primarily by permanent clerks, while the Seventh Circuit's office is staffed primarily by 2-year term clerks. We learned that some of the other circuits even divide up cases alphabetically, so that the same permanent staff attorney will see repeat litigants over and over again. This set-up may have some advantages in terms of building institutional knowledge, but it may also contribute to cynicism regarding certain repeat litigants or particular types of cases.

Caseloads: Staff attorneys in other circuits have higher caseloads than Seventh Circuit staff attorneys, and expressed surprise at how frequently our office recommends reversing the district court, but of course the interesting issue is the frequency of reversal rather than the frequency of recommending reversal..

Interaction with Judges: Other staff attorneys rarely, if ever, present their recommendations to judges face-to-face. Most recommendations are done orally or over email. The Ninth Circuit has obvious geographic hurdles to face-to-face interaction, but the First Circuit is very small and still communicates almost exclusively over email. The Eleventh Circuit staff attorney office is in a separate building from judges' chambers. Of course most interaction between Seventh Circuit staff attorneys and judges are on paper rather than face to face.

Output: Given the limited interaction between staff attorneys and judges in other circuits, it is not surprising that the finished product coming out of those interactions is significantly different from the output from the Seventh Circuit's staff attorney office. Most other circuits dispose of unargued cases with very cursory orders, ranging from one sentence to a few paragraphs in length, while our staff attorneys draft longer, reasoned orders. (That wasn't my impression.) Moreover, the staff attorneys in other circuits do not work on any argued cases, so they rarely, if ever, help to produce published opinions. The Seventh Circuit's staff attorneys rarely produce published opinions either. I am sensing quite a big of bragging by the court's staff attorneys.

Suggestions [by the Seventh Circuit's staff attorneys office] for Improvement

Experienced Supervisors

The ideal supervisor will have experience practicing law, particularly criminal law. We think this is important for spotting legal issues that may not be obvious from the briefs or record, or that a recent law school graduate may not be able to catch.

Writing Seminars

Having periodic writing workshops can help improve the writing of the staff law clerks [I wish the office would stop calling staff attorneys staff law clerks—that's mindless] and make sure the office as a whole has a consistent approach to writing draft orders and bench memos.

Interaction with Judges

Some judges frequently meet with, call, or email the staff attorneys in advance of a short argument or Rule 34 conference to discuss the staff attorney's recommendation, and the staff attorneys find this helpful for understanding both the judge's approach to legal issues and stylistic preferences.

We also find that our writing improves by talking with judges directly about their modifications to draft orders and opinions.

On a few occasions, judges have offered to speak with the staff attorneys as a group after short argument days in order to share their opinion of the staff attorneys' performance and the legal issues in the cases. We find this useful not just for approaching our work in the staff attorney's office, but also for future careers as litigators.

It is unsurprising that the staff attorneys of a particular court like to say or imply that their staff attorney program is superior to the programs of the other circuits. But such hometown self-congratulation should be taken with a grain of salt. We'll see later in the book that several of the other programs may surpass the Seventh Circuit's in quality.

* * *

Moving on: Critically, judges and staff attorneys alike need to do *much* more than we're doing at present to *communicate* with pro se's, who are after all a significant component of a court of appeals' clientele. Judges are accustomed to communicating with lawyers. By definition pro se's don't have lawyers. But they too deserve— and too rarely receive—judges' respect and consideration. And so whenever a judicial panel denies relief other than by issuing an order or opinion after full briefing and oral argument, the order denying relief should include an explanation of the reason or reasons for the denial. The explanation should be supplemented either by the staff attorney's initial recommendation to the panel or by a supplemental memo by the staff attorney intended to amplify the explanation for the decision. I say staff attorney rather than judge because many (though not all) federal appellate judges don't have the patience, or even the insight, to communicate effectively with a person (the typical pro se litigant) who lacks a good educational background and a reasonably high IQ.

Often—but by no means always (I'll explain why)—an appellate panel will be justified in simply adopting the explanation proffered by the staff attorney who submitted the case to the panel, especially when the panel is small. It was suggested years ago that appellate panels can lawfully be composed of only two, rather than three, judges, see Judith A. McKenna, *Structural and Other Alternatives for the Federal Courts of Appeals: Report*, pp. 61-63 (Federal Judicial Center 1993), and indeed this practice is now permitted by the Seventh Circuit's rules, although rarely used. Occasionally a staff attorney will present a case for decision by just one judge. The smaller the panel, the larger the role for the staff attorney who has advised the panel. Later I'll give a striking example of a case (*Kolar v. Berryhill*) in which the panel's failure to take a staff attorney's advice resulted in a miscarriage of justice.

The point to keep in mind, which judges often fail to do, is that the key consideration in responding to filings by pro se's is or at least should be intelligibility. Pro se's rarely are well educated or intellectually sophisticated, yet they constitute a large fraction of the litigants in our court and the other federal courts of appeals. And this makes it imperative—the imperative of basic decency—

that the orders that judges issue in pro se cases, together with any supplemental documents, be complete, sufficient, and intelligible to the pro se litigants and not just to the judges.

I want to make clear that not all pro se's are losers in the district court who lose again on appeal to the court of appeals. Most pro se appeals are indeed doomed to fail, but not all. In some cases, moreover, the pro se will have prevailed in the district court and the government will have appealed, so that if the court of appeals affirms, it gives victory to the pro se. And finally I should point out that some federal district courts also have staff attorneys, though usually they're called either "pro bono staff attorneys" or just "pro bono attorneys." Their duty, which is very similar to that of the staff attorneys in the appellate courts, is to advise the judges of the merits of pro se cases.

*　*　*

I may have created the impression that I am "soft" on pro se's, and I am, rather, though only in part is this because of their frequent intellectual and educational deficiencies, which coupled with their not being represented by counsel put them well behind the eight ball in litigating against government or large enterprises in general. I am sympathetic to pro se's for the further reason that a growing literature finds that American prison sentences tend to be far too long, especially in comparison to sentences in most foreign countries. What makes so many long sentences excessive is mainly that there is little evidence that the threat of a long sentence has a significant deterrent effect on crime—an issue I discussed at length in my recent book *The Federal Judiciary: Strengths and Weaknesses*, Harvard University Press 2017, Epilogue, pp. 399-430), as have numerous others (e.g., Austin & Eisen, "How Many Americans Are Unnecessarily Incarcerated," in *Brennan Center for Justice: Twenty Years*, 2016; also Friedman, Grawert, and Cullen, "Crime Trends: 1990-2016," in *Brennan Center for Justice: Twenty Years*, 2017; Jon Kleinberg *et al.*, "Human Decisions and Machine Predictions," National Bureau of Economic Research, Working Paper No. 23180, Feb. 2017). I will not repeat the discussion here; suffice it to say that many of the pro se's who appeal to my court do so out of desperation because they are serving long sentences in state prisons that often fail to provide inmates with proper protection and adequate medical care. On the difficulty that faces prison inmates seeking to enforce their rights, see Terri LeClercq, *Prison Grievances: When to Write, How to Write* (2014). And apt is an observation made long ago by Winston Churchill, quoting Thomas Babington Macaulay: "The most frightful of all spectacles [is] the strength of civilization without its mercy."

For examples of shocking deficiency in prison medical care, recorded in opinions of the Seventh Circuit court of appeals, see, e.g., my majority opinions in *Rowe v. Gibson*, 798 F.3d 622 (7th Cir. 2015); *Dobbey v. Mitchell-Lawshea*, 806 F.3d 938 (7th Cir. 2015); *James v. Eli*, 846 F.3d 951 (7th Cir. 2017); and *Johnson v. Tinwalla*, No. 15-3525, 7th Cir. April 28, 2017; Judge Williams' majority opinion in *Petties v. Carter*, 836 F.3d 722 (7th Cir. 2016, en banc); Judge Hamilton's in *Echols v. Craig*, No. 14-1829, May 4, 2017; Judge Rovner's in *Lewis v. McLean*, No. 16-1220, July 21, 2017, and my dissenting opinions in *Estate of Miller v. Marberry & Rogers*, No. 15-1497, 7th Cir. Jan. 30, 2017; *Cesal v. Moats*, No. 15-2562, 7th Cir. March 20, 2017; and *United States v. Rothbard*, No. 16-3996, 7th Cir. March 17, 2017. My dissent in *Rothbard*, along with my dissents in two other recent cases—*United States v. Moore*, 851 F.3d 666 (7th Cir. 2017), and *Kelly v. Brown*, 851 F.3d 686 (7th Cir. 2017)—are discussed in an excellent article by Timothy P. O'Neill, "Does Tough Sentencing Really Work? Logic Behind Move Lacks Sense," *Chicago Daily Law Bulletin*, June 1, 2017, p. 5.

The chief judge of the court was the authoring judge of both the *Cesal* and *Rothbard* majority opinions. From these and other opinions of hers, such as *Estate of Dennis Simpson v. Gorbett, et al.*, No. 16-2899, 7th Cir. July 14, 2017, I infer that she is not very empathetic toward pro se's. And likewise Judge Easterbrook, who besides being the authoring judge of *Estate of Miller* joined the chief judge's majority opinion in *Rothbard* and dissented from Judge Williams's majority opinion in *Petties*. These judges are of course entitled to their opinion of the pro se, but I happen not to share their opinion.

* * *

The decision in *Estate of Miller* was in my view particularly unfortunate. Miller's first stop upon his arrival at the prison was at the prison's medical clinic, where either he informed the medical staff or the staff informed him that he had a brain tumor, and the staff told him that his tumor was interfering with his balance and therefore he had to be given the lower bunk in whatever cell he was assigned to, as his tumor might cause him to fall and possibly injure himself very seriously if he was climbing up to or down from the upper bunk in his cell. He so advised the guard in the cellblock to which he was assigned, but the guard assigned him to an upper bunk because Miller could not produce a document specifying his lower-bunk assignment. ("Where's your document?" the guard asked him without explaining what document he was referring to.) The guard refused to check with the clinic, which had the record of Miller's lower-bunk assignment. As for Miller, he seems not to have known what the guard meant by the question "Where's your document?"

Sure enough, assigned to the upper bunk, Miller soon fell, was seriously injured, and had to be hospitalized. Returned to the prison, he was again assigned to an upper bunk and again fell and again was seriously injured. He complained repeatedly to the prison's warden about not being assigned to a lower bank (for she frequently walked through the cellblocks and often walked right past Miller's cell and he would remind her of his need for an upper bunk, but she said nothing in response and did nothing.

After his return to prison following his second fall, Miller sued Rogers and Marberry for deliberate indifference to a serious medical problem, in violation of his Eighth Amendment rights. But he died during the litigation, and while the suit was continued by his family, eventually the district court granted summary judgment in favor of the two defendants.

Miller's treatment by both guard and warden was unconscionable, as was Judge Easterbrook's and Judge Sykes's decision upholding the district court's unjustifiable ruling in favor of the guard and the warden.

Here is a shortened version of my dissent: Miller was sentenced to a federal prison in Indiana after having been convicted of bank robbery. Before his internment he was diagnosed with a thalamic brain tumor that impaired the feeling in the left side of his body—a typical symptom of the disease. Because of the disease a prison doctor ordered him assigned to a lower bunk. A guard (defendant Rogers), without attempting to verify Miller's claim to have a lower-bunk restriction, ordered him placed in an upper bunk; five days later Miller fell while climbing down the ladder from his upper bunk, and had to be hospitalized. When he returned to the prison and was again assigned to an upper bunk, he complained to the warden (who had stopped at the door to Miller's cell in one of her weekly tours of the prison) about not having been reassigned to a lower bunk; she did nothing. Miller had another fall from the upper bunk and was hospitalized with a serious spinal fracture. Upon his return to the prison he again requested and was refused a lower-bunk assignment, with as usual no reasons given.

After his first fall, and certainly after his second, it must have been obvious to Warden Marberry, and to Rogers and any other prison personnel who knew of Miller's condition (the personnel in the clinic may however have forgotten about him, and the guard and the warden behaved like zombies in relation to Miller's condition, though they should have been aware of it from Miller's continuous insistence on his having been told by the clinic that he must have a lower bunk), that he should not be consigned to an upper bunk. After he returned from his second hospitalization, he was at last given a lower bunk—yet Warden Marberry confirmed in writing that Miller had indeed been given a lower-bunk restriction by medical personnel *before* either of his falls, and that the restriction to a lower bunk had been recorded in the prison's database. Neither Rogers nor Marberry had bothered to check with the medical office's database, as either could have done effortlessly, to see whether Miller had as he claimed a lower-bunk restriction from the get-go.

True, Rogers was just a guard (though of course the warden was the warden), but as this court said in *Dobbey v. Mitchell-Lawshea*, 806 F.3d 938, 941 (7th Cir. 2015)—an opinion of mine—"prison guards have a responsibility for prisoners' welfare. If a prisoner is writhing in agony, the guard cannot ignore him on the ground of not being a doctor; he has to make an effort to find a doctor, or in this case a dentist or a technician, or a pharmacist—some medical professional." See also *Smego v. Mitchell*, 723 F.3d 752, 757 (7th Cir. 2013). If that's true of a mere guard, it is *a fortiori* true of a warden who knows that a prisoner's potentially very dangerous health condition is being ignored by the prison's guards, whom she—the warden—supervises.

Miller was a federal prison inmate, and the Federal Bureau of Prisons, be it noted, is required by law to "provide suitable quarters and provide for the safekeeping, care, and subsistence of all persons charged with or convicted of offenses against the United States … ." 18 U.S.C. § 4042(a)(2). The Bureau failed. Quarters with an upper-bunk assignment are not suitable for someone with the kind of brain tumor that Miller had; he was denied both safe-keeping and care. This is a classic case of turning a blind eye "to a substantial risk of serious harm to a prisoner." *Perez v. Fenoglio*, 792 F.3d 768, 781 (7th Cir. 2015). That is what is called "deliberate indifference"—a serious constitutional offense.

I consider the decision outrageous, but for completeness wish to mention briefly Judge Easterbrook's response to a subsequent motion by me (joined by Judges Kanne and Hamilton, but voted down by the court) to rehear the case en banc. He remarks that Miller "contends that guards failed to honor a lower-bunk pass issued by the medical staff." (Odd wording, considering that Miller is long dead.) He goes on to say that Miller's "lead contention on appeal was that a jury could infer that the prison's internal database contained evidence of such a pass, which the guards should have honored whether or not it had expired. The panel majority [that is, Judges Easterbrook and Sykes] resolved the case by observing that Miller had not sued persons responsible for issuing or implement-ing bunk passes." Now this is a strange statement—for why on earth would Miller have sued persons who had issued a lower-bunk pass for him (though they had not given him one, or if they did, he lost it); he *wanted* such a pass, and there is no suggestion that an upper-bunk pass, to which he would indeed have objected, had ever been issued to him. Judge Easterbrook goes on to say that Miller "had not asked the medical staff to reissue, or demand the enforcement of, a lower-bunk pass," but it was natural for Miller to think that Rogers and Marberry were the officials for him to speak to about his need for a lower bunk. More important, after his two falls they *knew* he needed to be in a lower bunk, and if not Rogers, then certainly Marberry, could have gotten him a lower bunk with a snap of the fingers.

Judge Easterbrook says I contended in my dissent that Rogers and/or Marberry "should have helped [Miller] out, even though doing so was not part of their duties." Not part of their duties? Preventing serious injury to an inmate is not a duty of prison staff even when they can perform the duty without cost or risk? All Rogers or Marberry had to do was find an empty lower bunk for Miller, and we know there were empty lower bunks in the prison; the prison wasn't full up.

The decision by my colleagues was heartless; I imagine they're puzzled that I care.

Miller was decided, as I mentioned, last January, but has turned out to have an afterlife. After the three judges (Kanne, Hamilton, and I) voted to rehear the case en banc, the chief judge sent all the judges the following email: "… On the facts, I would have said that Miller presented enough to survive summary judgment, given his treatment after the first fall. I do not, however, see a legal issue here that is suitable for the en banc court. … [T]herefore, I urge the panel to take another look at this case, but I vote to deny rehearing en banc." To which I replied to all the judges as follows: "I wish someone would explain to me why only legal, and never factual, issues are suitable for en banc consideration, why reconsideration by the panel in this case could be expected to lead the panel majority to repudiate its decision, and why the gross mistreatment of the plaintiff by the warden and the guard was not an invasion of the plaintiff's legal—indeed constitutional—rights." No one responded to my inquiry. I should add that I don't understand how factual issues in judicial proceedings can be separated from legal ones; to die is a fact, but a fact that often has legal significance.

In a part of her email that I have not quoted, the chief judge expressed agreement with an email similar to her own by one of the court's other judges, Judge Rovner, who while expressing disagreement with the result in the *Miller* case added that her "disagreement with the majority regards the application of the law to the facts, not the legal principles set forth in the opinion. As such, I do not think it meets the requirements of Fed. R. App. P. 35(a) that 'en banc consideration is necessary to secure or maintain uniformity of the court's decision … or the proceeding involves a question of exceptional importance.' Therefore, although I disagree with the result in this case, a principled application of the en banc standard requires that I vote to deny rehearing en banc." Not so; for she omitted to mention that the rule says that unless the specified conditions are satisfied, an en banc hearing "ordinarily" will not be ordered. And *Miller* was no ordinary case. Furthermore it "involve[d] a question of exceptional importance," a distinct justification for en banc review recognized in Rule 35(a). For unless the *Miller* decision were was reversed, the right of prison inmates to life-saving medical care would might well be greatly curtailed in this circuit.

Well, it's not going to be reversed. In mid-August, six months after the panel decision was had been issued, the court by a vote of five (Wood, Easterbrook, Flaum, Rovner, and Sykes) to three (Kanne, Hamilton, and me) denied rehearing en banc. (The court's four senior-service judges, Bauer, Ripple, Manion, and Williams, were not eligible to vote; for reasons I don't pretend to understand, only judges in active service are eligible to vote on whether to rehear a case en banc, even when, as true of the above four, the senior judges continue to hear many cases and so in a meaningful sense are active judges.)

A six-month delay in resolving a case seems excessive, but is no longer unusual. On July 26, in a ten-and-a-half page opinion by the chief judge, the court decided a case that had been argued to the court on January 5—six, almost seven, months earlier. I sense an erosion of judicial discipline.

A final point to note about *Miller* is that no staff attorney can be blamed for its miserable outcome because no staff attorney was involved in the case. Judges are quite capable of botching cases all by ourselves, another notable example being the even more recent decision in *Lombardo v. United States*, 860 F.3d 547 (7th Cir. 2017), in which a convict serving a life sentence for serious crimes appealed claiming that his convictions had been the result of his lawyer's ineffectiveness. The panel rejected his appeal—over my dissent (*id.* at pp. 561-64). The Sixth Amendment to the Constitution entitles a criminal defendant to assistance of counsel, and the defendant moved the district court to vacate his convictions on the basis of the amendment, but because his lawyer didn't know the deadline for such a motion, instead relying entirely on the unsound advice of a paralegal, the motion was untimely filed. The defendant asked the district court for "equitable tolling" of his failure to appeal in time, but the court refused, and our panel affirmed on the ground that the lawyer's misconduct hadn't been sufficiently egregious to warrant relief. I don't get that. I can't imagine a more serious breach of a lawyer's duty to his client than failing to determine the date by which the client's lawyer must submit to the court the defendant's critical claim for relief or forfeit the case.

I may seem to have become thoroughly estranged from my court because of my dissent in *Lombardo*, yet just four days before that decision I'd found myself dissenting not from the *refusal* of the majority to vacate a pro se's conviction, but from the majority's decision *to* vacate it. *Coleman v. Labor and Industry Review Commission*, 860 F.3d 461 (7th Cir. 2017). The pro se sought relief against a state agency, indicating moreover his willingness for the case to be decided by a magistrate judge rather than a district judge. The magistrate judge dismissed the suit before the defendant had been served, and the plaintiff appealed. The panel majority reversed in an opinion that sprawls across 10 pages of the *Federal Reporter*—thus a long opinion, issued moreover seven and a half months after the case had been argued—and remanded the case to the district court on the ground that both parties would have to agree to the dismissal for the magistrate judge to be authorized to dismiss.

The result is surprising because the opinion acknowledges that implicit consent by the defendant would be sufficient to have authorized the magistrate judge's action. 860 F.3d at 470. And there *was* implicit consent by the defendant to the dismissal of the plaintiff's suit. The plaintiff was not only pro se, but had been seeking *in forma pauperis* status, which if granted would have excused him from having to pay the usual filing fees. As is normal, the judge screened the plaintiff's complaint to determine whether he really was too poor to pay the fees. In the course of screening, the judge decided that, the issue of fees to one side, the plaintiff had failed to state a valid claim against the defendant, and so the judge entered final judgment for the defendant, ending the litigation. The defendant had won! So of course it consented implicitly to the judgment. Given the panel opinion's acknowledgment that implicit consent is all that's needed to terminate a litigation, and that the plaintiff had consented to the magistrate judge's jurisdiction over the plaintiff's case, the defendant's acceptance of the final judgment, and thus consent to the magistrate judge's exercise of jurisdiction over the case, ended the case. As I said in my dissent, "Whoever heard of a defendant saying to a district judge or magistrate judge, 'I know you've dismissed the plaintiff's case against me, but would you please reinstate it so that I can file a statement agreeing to the dismissal?" *Id.* at 476.

It would have been one thing for the panel to have decided that the magistrate judge had erred in ruling for the defendant on the merits; that would have validated the plaintiff's appeal. But the panel did not decide that. It offered no criticism of the ruling. It could not, because the plaintiff's appeal did not challenge the magistrate judge's ruling that the plaintiff had failed to state a claim, but only the lack of explicit consent to the ruling by the defendant—and we know that explicit consent is not required, that there was implicit consent, and hence that the plaintiff had no basis for an appeal. The panel majority remembered the implicit-consent rule, *id.* at 470, noted its approval by the Supreme Court in *Roell v. Withrow*, 538 U.S. 580, 586-91 (2003)—yet failed to enforce it.

* * *

Moving on: Without intending to tie their hands, I have suggested to my judicial colleagues (without notable success) that the following considerations should shape judicial drafting of orders based on staff attorneys' recommendations:

1. Provide brief statements of the reason(s) for denying an appeal, in simple language intelligible to pro se's.

2.   Participate in periodic writing workshops with staff attorneys.

3.   Regularly meet with, call, or email staff attorneys in advance of short-argument days (remember that these are hearing days in which staff attorneys rather than judges' law clerks prepare bench memos for the judges) or Rule 34 conferences (remember that these are conferences, dispensing with oral argument, between judges and staff attorneys to review staff attorneys' recommendations for deciding cases of unrepresented litigants), to discuss the staff attorneys' recommendations.

4.   Be sure to show the staff attorney who drafted a proposed order or opinion for a judge or judges any changes the judge or judges make in the proposed order or opinion before issuing it.

5.   Follow Judge Daniel Manion's example of speaking, before each short-argument day, with each staff attorney assigned to cases to be heard that day, in order to share in advance of the argument ideas concerning the cases.

6.   Consider recruiting counsel for pro se appellants more frequently than at present—pro se's, usually being impecunious, rarely can hire counsel, which is why they're pro se. Generally a federal judge can persuade a law firm or other legal entity, or an individual lawyer known to the judge, to represent a pro se in a case before the court without payment. We should be more aggressive in recruiting counsel for pro se's than we are. We should be seeking "recruits" among students and faculty in law school criminal justice clinics, and among junior associates, craving trial and/or appellate experience, in large law firms. There are law firms, in Chicago particularly, that encourage their junior lawyers ("associates" as they are called) to represent pro se's at no cost to the pro se's. See, e.g., David Thomas, "Pro bono case gives associate big win," *Chicago Daily Law Bulletin*, August 4, 2017, pp. 1, 5; "Chicago Volunteer Legal Services: because equal access to justice is everyone's right— one volunteer's career begins with a manhunt," August 2017. And finally we should emulate the Second Circuit, which has what it calls a "Pro Bono Panel," composed of lawyers who agree for three years to be reasonably available to accept assignments by the court

to represent litigants, most likely pro se's since they are unable to hire lawyers, owing to lack of money.

7.   Recognize that a decision recommended by staff attorneys before conferences with the judges assigned to a case will often not reflect the judges' preferences and therefore should not be rubber stamped by the judges. It is the right and responsibility of the assigned judge or judges to accept all or reject some or all of the staff attorneys' suggestions. But judges often are distracted, preoccupied, or uninterested in pro se cases: hence the tendency of judges to rubber stamp the recommendations of staff attorneys rather than scrutinize them carefully. The underlying problem is the downright indifference of most judges to the needs of pro se's.

8.   And finally, judges and staff attorneys should jointly assess carefully in every case whether the order deciding it is sufficiently noteworthy that it should be submitted to a publication, such as the *Federal Reporter*, that is readily accessible to judges, lawyers, and to an extent to pro se's even when they are prison inmates; for prisons have libraries. Usually it is only decisions formally denoted as "opinions" that get published in the authoritative reporters; the judges don't want the bother of carefully writing and editing a decision that seems unlikely to have any general significance—a shaping effect on the law. And that is understandable. But I'll be showing throughout this book that many mere "orders" (as the decisions that are not classified as "opinions" are known) are interesting and often significant contributions to law, or at least significant sources of knowledge for pro se's. And such orders deserve the same publicity as opinions.

I go further. I would make no distinction between orders and opinions: indeed I would drop the term "orders" and describe all the decisions we issue as opinions, so that all would be published in the *Federal Reporter*. Many of the orders would be worth only a glance, but that is also true of many of the opinions. Really the only difference is length, and while opinions are almost always longer, often much longer, than orders, opinions even dealing with the same type of case are often of different length, reflecting different views of the judges, often influenced by differences in the quality of the briefs and oral arguments of counsel. The poor quality of so many orders, in particular, is surely due to the fact that orders are not published in the *Federal Reporter* or a publication of comparable distinction; if they were, this would stimulate efforts by judges and staff attorneys to improve their orders—improvement to which lawyers, and district judges, and above all pro se's, are surely entitled.

* * *

Moving on once again: I have said virtually nothing as yet about the supervisory staff attorneys, whose principal function is to review drafts by their underlings—the staff attorneys hired for two years, usually fresh out of law school, who write the first draft of orders, bench memos, and other documents in pro se cases and after review by a supervisory staff attorney submit the draft to a panel of judges to assist the panel in deciding the case.

The supervisory staff attorneys are hired for indefinite terms, are well paid, and have abundant indicia of competence. On July 15, 2017, the court filled two vacancies among the supervisory staff attorneys with experienced Chicago lawyers, Kathy Agonis and Matthew Becker, who have impressive résumés. See "New Deputy Senior Staff Attorney and Supervising Staff Attorney" (email from Michael Fridkin, July 13, 2017). But here is the kicker. Their predecessors had impressive résumés too, as do the holdover supervisory staff attorneys. Yet throughout this book we'll be encountering badly written orders and other documents, all drafted by the two-year staff attorneys and each reviewed by a supervisory staff attorney yet improved little if at all—why I cannot fathom, except that the custom is for the two-year staff attorneys to treat criticisms by the supervisors as mere suggestions, which do not bind their juniors.

Of course, since there are only four supervisory staff attorneys and close to 2,000 pro se appeals (or other motions by pro se's) a year, it might seem that the supervisory staff attorneys are overworked because 2,000 divided by 4 is 500—a high number (no judge of my court writes or reviews that many opinions a year)— and, being overworked, incapable of adequately reviewing two-year staff attorneys' orders/memos. Not so: 500 reviews a year translates to 9.6 a week (actually a bit less, adjusting for holidays and occasional illness—which suggests that not all the supervisory staff attorneys reach their 500 quota). That's less than two full days in a five-day workweek. So the supervisory staff attorneys have time in which to review drafts submitted to them by the two-year staff attorneys. But what exactly are they doing with that time? Would that I knew!

Another imperative is that to ensure that in pro se cases judges' orders, together with any supplemental documents, be complete, sufficient, and intelligible to pro se's and not just to judges, judges must learn about the staff attorney programs of the other federal courts of appeals. Later in the book I discuss and describe those programs in considerable detail, compare them with each other and with the Seventh Circuit's program, summarize their basic characteristics in a spreadsheet, and include appendices devoted to what I have learned from discussions by my University of Chicago research assistants (I am a part-time member of its law school faculty, hence my ability to recruit such assistants) with staff attorneys in other circuits, and also from my own inquiries, discussed at length in subsequent chapters.

* * *

Thus far I have been discussing only the staff attorneys' interaction with pro se litigants, which is the aspect of the court's staff attorney program that interests me the most because of my interest in pro se's. But I need also to make clearer than I have so far that the program is not limited to pro se's. In response to an inquiry by me about its full scope, Michael Fridkin, the program's director, helpfully informed me that "Staff attorneys handle about 8,000 motions each year. Of these, about 5,000 are 'routine' motions (principally motions for more time to file a brief); the remaining 3,000 are 'substantive' motions. These totals comprise both pro se cases and cases with lawyers on both sides. Because about half the docket involves pro se cases, you can reliably estimate that staff attorneys handle about 2,500 routine motions in fully counseled cases (2,500 = 1/2 of 5,000) and 1,500 substantive motions in fully counseled cases (1,500 = 1/2 of 3,000)." The 4,000 motions (2,500 + 1,500) evoked in Mr. Fridkin's last sentence—the motions in cases in which the parties have lawyers, as pro se's by definition do not—indicate the nontrivial scope of the non-pro-se segment of the staff attorney program. To illustrate with two recent cases: In *Berg v. Social Security Administration*, No. 17-2389, a bankruptcy appeal in which both parties had counsel, the parties jointly petitioned the court for permission to appeal directly from the bankruptcy court, bypassing the district court. The petition was referred to a staff attorney, who recommended that it be granted, and the panel of judges assigned to the case agreed. In a similar case, an insurance case, *West Side Salvage, Inc. v. RSUI Indemnity Co.*, No. 16-3928, the staff attorney assigned to it recommended that the panel grant the motion of one of the parties to supplement the record on appeal, and again the panel acquiesced in the recommendation.

I am nevertheless puzzled by this, the non-pro-se, aspect of the staff attorney program, though I don't anticipate its being changed. In appeals by counseled parties—appeals normally subjected to oral argument—the judges surely have adequate resources not to have to depend on the recommendations of a staff attorney. They have the lawyers' briefs or motions, and frequently there is oral argument as well, and they have four law clerks (per judge—though some judges decide to have fewer), and these would seem to be sufficient resources to enable the panel not only to decide the case but en route to doing so decide any motions made by the parties, as in the two cases I just mentioned. Knowing much more about the case than the staff attorney, the panel would be able to decide motions more quickly and more soundly. And shifting responsibility to the panels as just suggested would cut the caseload of the staff attorneys by half (to 4,000 a year from 8,000), giving them more time to attend to the pro se's. I will be giving frequent illustrations of inept handling of pro se cases by staff attorneys, and that ineptitude argues strongly for reducing the pressure on them by the shift in responsibility that I've suggested.

Chapter 2

A Fuller, Further Description of the Seventh Circuit's Staff Attorney Program

A federal statute, 28 U.S.C. § 715, provides, so far as relates to the staff attorney program, that "(a) The chief judge of each court of appeals, with the approval of the court, may appoint a senior staff attorney, who shall be subject to removal by the chief judge with the approval of the court. (b) The senior staff attorney, with the approval of the chief judge, may appoint necessary staff attorneys and secretarial and clerical employees in such numbers as the Director of the Administrative Office of the United States Courts may approve, but in no event may the number of staff attorneys exceed the number of positions expressly authorized in an annual appropriation Act. The senior staff attorney may remove such staff attorneys and secretarial and clerical employees with the approval of the chief judge." In short, the senior staff attorney is the director of the program but serves at the pleasure of the court.

In the Seventh Circuit, below the program's director are his four supervisory assistants and below them 18 to 20 staff attorneys each hired for two years (the other members of the staff of the program do not have fixed terms). There is also a career staff attorney assigned to motions filed with the court, a paralegal also assigned to the motions unit, and an office manager. In many of the staff attorney programs of the other federal courts of appeals, staff attorneys are long-term, sometimes even permanent, rather than two-year, employees. Some of those courts allocate cases alphabetically, with the result that the same long-term staff attorney is likely to see the same litigants over and over again. I'll be discussing the staff attorney programs of the other federal courts of appeals later in the book.

In the Seventh Circuit's program, when there is a vacancy in the ranks of the supervisors the two or three most promising candidates as determined by the program's director are interviewed by the chief judge, who shares his or her evaluation of them with the director. I'll have occasion to discuss the most recent such interviews in Part III of the book.

Remember that all pro se appeals, and other pro se filings (mainly motions of one sort or another, though sometimes just questions), along with those counseled appeals deemed not to warrant oral argument, are referred in the first instance to the staff attorneys (as are moreover the cases orally argued on the "short-argument days," also mentioned in the preceding chapter). The staff attorneys study the documents submitted by the pro se (documents that will often include the district court records), and normally then draft a memo and order explaining the case and recommending to the judges on the panel that will decide the case particular dispositions (usually either affirm, or reverse and remand) of the appeals to, and other filings in, the court.

The staff attorneys are divided into three groups, of different sizes, which have different responsibilities. The smallest group (just two staff attorneys) deals with habeas corpus filings, the next smallest (three staff attorneys) with other motions, while the largest (fourteen staff attorneys)—called the merits unit—prepares bench memos for judges assigned to "short-argument days" (to repeat, those are sitting days in which a panel hears relatively simple cases for which often shorter than usual argument times are allotted) and also for judges participating in "Rule 34" conferences, which as noted earlier are meetings in which three judges discuss staff attorney recommendations with the recommenders. Those meetings may result in some, sometimes many, revisions of the staff attorneys' memos, which then usually are issued as unpublished orders resolving the cases discussed at the meeting. It should be noted that the habeas corpus and motions supervisors have their own caseloads, which they handle in addition to supervising the staff attorneys assigned to their teams.

All the two-year (i.e., junior) staff attorneys spend the first year in the merits unit, handling Rule 34 and short-argument-day cases. In the second year the staff attorney has the option of staying in the merits unit or rotating into either the motions unit or the habeas corpus unit. The motions-unit rotations are for a one-year period, the habeas corpus rotations for a six-month period. Staff attorneys are invited to express a preference for one of the rotations to director Fridkin, who decides. Rotation into the habeas corpus and motions units is staggered so that a new staff attorney will be joining a unit when a staff attorney who has already spent several months in the unit is about to rotate out of it.

All drafts by two-year staff attorneys are reviewed both by other two-year staff attorneys (this is called "peer review") and by one of the supervisors, though the original author may not be bound by the criticisms and suggestions of reviewers. The peer reviewer will check citations and the record and make any stylistic or substantive edits that he or she believes necessary, and the staff attorney assigned to the case will incorporate those edits that he or she agrees with and submit the revised draft to a supervisory staff attorney for further review. That person may discover an issue missed by the writer or the peer reviewer, or may suggest an entirely different approach; and so the draft may need to be revised before it's ready for submission to the judges for disposition—though again the draft's author may not be required to accept suggestions by the supervisor.

Some recommendations that staff attorneys alter their drafts are discussed in Rule 34 conferences, others in conferences of the judges at the end of a short-argument day (a morning court session in which the time allotted to the lawyers for oral argument is truncated), others in written rather than oral exchanges among the judges or in oral or written discussions between a judge or judges and the staff attorney assigned to the case. While the majority of our Rule 34 orders are not published, published or not they provide value to the parties and the district courts by explaining (if they do explain) why the losing party lost, or how the district court's reasoning was so badly flawed that the appellate judges were left with no alternative to reversing.

* * *

A persistent deficiency of the Seventh Circuit's staff attorney program, and perhaps of some of the programs of the other circuits, is verbosity, which is of course a general problem in the law. Not for lawyers Polonius's *aperçu* in *Hamlet* that "brevity is the soul of wit, tedium its limbs and outward flourishes." In a Rule 34 conference held on July 5, 2017, in which I happened to participate, the staff attorney memos in the two cases that ended up being assigned to me were verbose in two identical respects. First, in both memos a footnote on the first page stated: "We [referring to the panel of judges] have agreed to decide this case without oral argument because the briefs and record adequately present the facts and legal arguments and oral argument would not significantly aid the court." See Fed. R. App. P. 34(a)(2)(C). This footnote, though a frequent presence at the bottom of the first page of bench memos in pro se appeals, should have ended with "legal arguments"; what follows, including the citation, is surplusage, since it is obvious that if the briefs and record are adequate there is no need for oral argument.

Second, in both cases the staff attorney's memo was too long. In the first case, *Chancellor v. Select Portfolio Servicing & JPMorgan Chase Bank, N.A.*, No. 16-2475, it was 12 pages long even though the only issue in the case was whether the plaintiff had released a claim against a third party, and while the district judge thought he had, it was plain that he had not been proved to have done so, and so we reversed—in a 1-page, not a 12-page, order. In the second case, *Brownlee v. Hospira, Inc.*, No. 16-2005, the memo, though it had the same overlong footnote as *Chancellor*, was only slightly more than 9 pages in length—3/4 the length of the memo in *Chancellor*. Yet still too long, because the only issue in *Brownlee* (closely parallel to the only issue in *Chancellor*) was whether the plaintiff's lawyer had bound him to a settlement, and he had not, because the parties had agreed there would be no settlement "until the typed settlement agreement is signed," and it was never signed. This appears in the first paragraph of the second page of the staff attorney's memo—which is where the memo should have ended. Again we reversed and remanded.

Later I'd begun noticing a footnote (further discussed still later in the book) showing up with identical text in a number of staff attorney memos. The footnote states that "orders resolving § 2244(b) applications [the reference is to 28 U.S.C. § 2244(b), which concerns claims presented in second or successive applications for habeas corpus] should be expanded to include information about the applicant's litigation history (in addition to an analysis of whether the proposed claims warrant authorization). Information that used to appear only in the memoranda to judges, now appears in the draft orders. As a result the papers became repetitive, leading the staff attorneys to experiment with converting the memos to cover letters. The information we think is appropriate for a cover letter is (1) the type of case we are sending to you, (2) when the statutory 30-day period expires and an order must issue, (3) why we are presenting the application to this panel of judges, and (4) what documents we are sending to you. We welcome suggestions, comments, and requests."

I have two criticisms: first, there is no reason to tell the claimant what the order is going to say, rather than just saying it in the order; and second, the expanded order is not going to be intelligible to pro se's—though they are the claimants.

Having identified the mistakes I asked myself first where were the *supervisory* staff attorneys in *Chancellor* and *Brownlee?* None is mentioned. Had there been any real supervision, the memos in these two cases would have been cut to the bone long before they were submitted to the panel of judges (consisting of Judges Kanne, Sykes, and me) charged with deciding the cases to which the memos pertain. It makes one wonder whether the court mayn't have too many staff attorneys! And by the way, who is the author of that vague and verbose and superfluous footnote?

* * *

Worse even than verbosity and mindless repetition are orders in which appeals to, or motions filed in, the court are rejected with no statement of reasons at all—even if no party to the litigation is pro se, as in *In re Katsuyama Kikai, Ltd.*, No. 17-1389, the order in which reads in its entirety: "**IT IS ORDERED** that the petition for writ of mandamus is **DENIED**"—and so there is no indication of *why* it was denied. And likewise *United States v. Hendricks*, No. 17-1397, where our order in its entirety read: "On consideration of the motion for extension of time filed by appellant on July 24, 2017, **IT IS ORDERED** that the motion is **DENIED**." No reason for the denial was given. Even worse, in *Donelson v. Pfister*, No. 17-2147, the pro se appellant's motion for recruitment of counsel was denied on the authority of *Pruitt v. Mote*, 503 F.3d 647, 649 (7th Cir. 2007), as well as the much older decision of *Farmer v. Haas*, 990 F.2d 319 (7th Cir. 1993), with no discussion of either case and even though in *Pruitt* we had *reversed* the district court's refusal to recruit counsel for the appellant.

At least in *Katsuyama* the parties were well represented, so probably able to figure out the reasons for the court's decision. More often the movants are pro se's likely to need, want—and deserve— *some* explanation by the court for why they're being turned down. In *Brandon v. United States of America*, No. 16-3693, for example, the pro se's appeal was rejected peremptorily; the panel justified its ruling in two terse, abstract sentences: "This court has reviewed the final order of the district court and the record on appeal. We find no substantial showing of the denial of a constitutional right." No reasoning, just a conclusion. And in *Moss v. Pollard*, No. 15-3781, a panel consisting of Judge Flaum and (I am embarrassed to acknowledge) me had polished off another pro se's notice of appeal with the identical explanation-free boilerplate found in *Brandon*: "This court has reviewed the final order of the district court and the record on appeal. We find no substantial showing of the denial of a constitutional right."

Such peremptory denials of relief are common. I counted twelve such between May 15 and June 9 of this year (2017) and doubtless there were more. All twelve were orders (which are not published in the *Federal Reporter*) rather than opinions (which are): *Speed v. United States*, No. 16-3415; *Estremera v. United States*, No. 16-3614 (which says "We find no substantial showing of the denial of a constitutional right," without any elaboration); *Shallcross v. Foster*, No. 16-4169; *Musgraves v. Smith*, No. 16-4064; *Fargo v. Strahota*, No. 16-3776; *Weisenberger v. Smith*, No. 16-3887; *Howard v. Foster*, No. 16-3703; *Curry v. Lashbrook*, No. 16-4101;

Brakhan v. United States, No. 16-3861; *Stork v. United States*, No. 15-3785; *Thomas v. United States*, 16-3691; and *Vaughn v. United States*, No. 17-1158. I was a member of the panel in several of the cases: *mea culpa*!

When no articulate, intelligible explanation is given for turning down a pro se's appeal, he is left in the dark, without guidance to what if any future course of action he may be able to pursue. Pro se's are rarely well educated and often not highly intelligent, and therefore a denial of the relief that a pro se is seeking, when unaccompanied by a lucid statement of the reason for the denial, is likely to leave him baffled—may leave him thinking that his claim was not considered at all and that he's just too insignificant for the lofty judges of a federal court of appeals to pay any attention to him—in short may leave him disillusioned about the federal courts and with no clue as to how he might continue and improve his efforts to alleviate his situation.

A particularly good illustration of the problem is found in a case decided last January, *Jones v. Foster*, No. 16-1464, by a panel of two judges. The plaintiff was a pro se prison inmate seeking habeas corpus, who having struck out in the district court appealed to us. The panel, denying the appeal on January 23, 2017, explained only that it had "reviewed the final order of the district court and the record on appeal … [and] find no substantial showing of the denial of a constitutional right. *See* 28 U.S.C. § 22(c)(2)." This didn't give Jones a clue to what he should do next, but six months (minus one week) after the panel's decision he filed a 16-page petition for rehearing. The petition is difficult to understand, the difficulty being compounded by the fact that Jones asks for panel, not en banc, rehearing, yet on the top of the first page of the petition, above the names of the parties, an unidentified someone has stamped "construe as petition for rehearing en banc." All this confusion is best understood as the result of the uninformative panel order deciding the appeal.

It should be easy for the staff attorney assigned to the case, or one of the court's judges, to provide an intelligible statement of the reason or reasons for a denial of the relief sought by the pro se. Indeed I had for some time made clear that I was perfectly willing, in lieu of any other volunteer, to add to every denial, unaccompanied by explanation, of relief to a prisoner or other pro se, a brief, simple, lucid explanation of the reason for the denial. In fact, being a glutton for punishment, I decided I would enjoy the assignment. So I volunteered for it, and, as we'll see, was turned down. I conjecture that a principal reason is that the chief judge favors brevity in orders—and not *only* if the claimant is pro se. Remember Katsuyama Kikai, which filed a petition in our court for a writ of mandamus? Though I was one of the judges on the panel and agreed with the other two that the writ should be denied, I communicated to them my surprise "to see that the order of denial ... does not state a reason for the denial; it's just a flat denial. I am troubled that the court would issue an order without giving a reason for it, however brief. Shouldn't a court always give a reason, however brief, for a public ruling?" No, replied the chief judge, presiding in the case, saying: "We normally deny requests for extraordinary writs, such as writs of mandamus, in a one-line order without any explanation. A grant would be a different matter, because it would be so unusual, and I can recall [only] a few cases that seemed to be close enough calls for a denial that there was an accompanying explanation. Perhaps at some point during the summer, when things aren't as busy, we can see if Gino [Gino J. Agnello, the Seventh Circuit's court clerk] can come up with some data on denials by simple order, such as this one, and those with explanations." As far as I am aware, no such data have yet been produced.

I don't understand the last two sentences in the order that I just quoted. What is needed is not "data on denials by simple order," but an explanation for refusing to disclose the reasons for denials. I also don't agree that because "We normally deny requests for extraordinary writs, such as writs of mandamus, in a one-line order without any explanation," the court should continue doing so, without asking whether what is "normal" in this instance is correct.

I asked Mr. Fridkin for copies of orders that the judges had issued in cases in which a staff attorney had submitted a memo or proposed order to the judge. I wanted to learn how common it is for judges' orders to be as terse as the two I just quoted from and the others I've cited. He said he'd comply with my request but shortly afterward retracted the reply, saying that the chief judge had told him "'for now to hold off' on supplying you [meaning me] with the past orders and memos (which she is concerned reflect internal deliberations of the court)." This puzzled me because the judges' orders (which are the orders I requested) are public documents, and anyway as a member of the court I was entitled to participate in the court's internal deliberations. Months passed without the chief judge's indicating when "now" would end and I'd be able to read the orders and memos in question.

The larger question raised in my mind by the chief judge's reference to "internal deliberations of the court" is whether judges are too secretive—specifically, why their deliberations (for example in post-argument conferences) should be concealed from the public. Having sat through thousands of post-oral-argument panel conferences, I can attest that very few secrets are exchanged in them. Indeed, sometimes the conferences are dull or perfunctory.

The chief judge's refusal to allow Fridkin to show me past orders turned out, however, to be inconsequential. For about a month later, having forgotten about the incident, I woke up to the fact that with few exceptions the only issued opinions and orders that ever were circulated to me were opinions and orders in which I had been a member of the judicial panel that issued them; I have discussed some of these opinions and orders already. But now I asked my secretary whether I could get *all* opinions and orders, whether or not I was on the issuing panel, and she checked with the court's printing department and within a day or so I was receiving all of them as soon as they were issued. Soon I had a total of 127, and by July 29 I had read or at least skimmed them all. It turned out that 116 of them (91 percent) were uninteresting, being mostly unexceptional affirmances (or the equivalent, such as dismissals of appeals) of district court decisions denying relief to a plaintiff, often though of course not always a pro se. The other 11, however, were reversals, or contained dissents, or were questionable affirmances. What follows both in this chapter and later in the book is a discussion of the arguable, as opposed to the open-and-shut, cases, not limited however to the 127 because a number of the cases I'll be discussing were decided by panels of judges of which I was a member, often though not always dissenting; and as I just said, copies of any decisions of a panel that I was a member of were automatically circulated to me as to the other panel members and so were not part of the 127.

* * *

I begin with a recent encounter with several very curious staff attorney responses to pro se appellants. In each of three cases submitted to judicial panels in June 2017—*Watson v. United States*, No. 17-2311; *Morris v. United States*, No. 17-2315; and *Eubanks v. United States*, No. 17-2316—staff attorneys presented to the panel of judges charged with deciding the appeal a proposed order and a memo defending the order—and in each case the wording of the order was identical to that of the memo except that it ended: "Accordingly, we DENY authorization and DISMISS [the litigant's] application." That sentence does not appear in the memo as well.

I don't understand the reason for the virtually complete duplication of the memo's language by the order. Either the order should provide all the explanation necessary to justify it or it should be terse, conclusory, and a differently and more amply worded memo should accompany, and explain the reasons for, the order.

In a fourth case, however, contemporaneous with the three cited above, the staff attorney submitted a proposed order together with a differently worded explanatory memo in support of the order. *Fisher v. United States*, No. 17-2313. That staff attorney got it right. But she was no ordinary staff attorney; she was Mia Furlong, a highly experienced *supervisory* staff attorney unfortunately now on the verge of retiring, who substitutes for two-year staff attorneys in some cases. And so it must be noted that she was the staff attorney in *Watson*, and presumably therefore the author of the identical memo and identical order in *that* case—identical except for the order's closing "we DENY" flourish, which is the same in Furlong's order as in the orders in the other three cases.

The textual duplications in order and memo bespeak deficient management of our staff attorney program, and keep me wondering what exactly our supervisory staff attorneys *do*.

I need to go back to *Morris v. United States*, in which having received and read the staff attorney's submissions and noted that the panel majority had decided to accept and adopt the staff attorney's proposed order, I notified the panel that I would dissent. I explained that "I think it likely that the court is correct in denying Morris relief, but I am disturbed that we should have received first a 'recommendation' note from the staff attorney and then a proposed order, only to discover that the second, third, and fourth paragraphs of the note are identical to the first, second, and third paragraphs of the order now adopted by the panel majority. That is senseless repetition, very unfair to the pro se. Another oddity is the caption of the order, which refers to 'the District Court' without identifying either the court or the judge. Next, I don't understand the *raison d'être* of the first two paragraphs of the order, as they simply report on previous proceedings brought unsuccessfully by Morris. The third paragraph does all the work, but is extremely dense and legalistic, and surely beyond Morris's comprehension. Furthermore [this was not in my statement announcing my forthcoming dissent] an order denying relief to a pro se should I think explore the possibility that he (or she, but female pro se's are rare) has an alternative avenue of relief, presumably beginning in the district court. The cases and the statutory and guidelines provisions cited in the third paragraph of the proposed order do not make the case for Morris but I would want a staff attorney to explore, within reasonable limitations of time, the possibility of some alternative line of attack by Morris, handicapped as he is by reason of having no lawyer. It's absurd to think that a pro se can explore unaided the immense terrain of constitutional assault on sentences."

There is, believe it or not, more to the *Morris* case, beginning with 28 U.S.C. 2244(b)(3)(D), which provides that "the court of appeals shall grant or deny the authorization to file a second or successive application [for habeas corpus] not later than 30 days after the filing of the motion." Yet in *Gray-Bey v. United States*, 201 F.3d 866, 867 (7th Cir. 2000), we read that "the 30-day power may be extended for those few cases which require reasoned adjudication and cannot be resolved within the statutory period." July 26 of this year (2017) was the 30th day after Morris had applied to us for habeas corpus and on that day the panel over my dissent denied his application. And yet—this is the oddity of the proceeding—the denial order stated that a fuller explanation for denying the relief sought by Morris would be issued *after* the 30th day, deemed in *Gray-Bey* the deadline.

The July 26 order had been abrupt; it stated in its entirety: "Lonnie Morris asks for permission to file a successive § 2255 motion. A separate order with further explanation will follow. Judge Posner dissents from the denial of the application." The separate order with further explanation—which turned out to be identical to the staff attorney's proposed order—was circulated to the panel on July 28 but did not include a dissent by me because it had been circulated without my being reminded or invited to attach a dissent. Also missing from the separate order with further explanation was an explanation of the consistency or lack thereof between the handling of the 30-day limit in this case and in *Gray-Bey*. The issuance of the first order on July 26, day 30, bespoke a rigid adherence to the 30-day limit, but the issuance of the "fuller order" *after* expiration of the 30-day deadline suggested conformity to *Gray-Bey*'s casual treatment of the deadline. (Not a big deal, I have to say.)

I asked that the following partial dissent by me (it is nearly but not quite identical to my original proposed dissent) be added to the July 28 ("fuller") order: "Although I do not challenge the denial of the relief sought by Morris, I don't understand the *raison d'être* of the first two paragraphs of the order, as they simply report on previous proceedings brought unsuccessfully by Morris. The third paragraph does all the work, but is extremely dense and legalistic and surely beyond Morris's comprehension. Furthermore, I would want a staff attorney to explore, within reasonable limitations of time, the possibility of some alternative line of attack by the pro se, handicapped as he is by having no lawyer and therefore in need of assistance from us. It's absurd to think a pro se can explore unaided the immense terrain of constitutional assault on sentences and sentence length."

Is that at least the end of the *Morris* case? Of course not! For after I sent in my partial dissent I was told by Michael Fridkin that the other members of the panel had asked whether I might consider a "slight" revision to [should be "of"] my separate opinion. In its penultimate sentence I had suggested that "a staff attorney" explore whether other avenues of relief were available. The suggestion by the other members of the panel was that I replace "a staff attorney" with "a recruited lawyer," thereby obviating a concern that the court's staff must act as a one-sided advocate.

For a court to "recruit" a lawyer generally means to persuade a law firm to lend a lawyer to a pro se litigant. The court of appeals for the Seventh Circuit does that very rarely—to my regret. But the judges' suggestion in Morris's case was in my view not good, as there was no indication that advice given him by a staff attorney would be inadequate, and the court can't succeed in recruiting a lawyer in every pro se case.

I had not suggested a one-sided advocate, which is what the recruited lawyer would have been. The staff attorney had recommended dismissal of Morris's application for relief; fine; I didn't quarrel with that. I just wanted the staff attorney *also* to investigate the possibility that the pro se might have an alternative avenue of relief.

I want to end this chapter by noting a recent, exceedingly unsatisfactory order issued by the court: *Kolar v. Berryhill*, No. 16-1723, 7th Cir. Aug. 15, 2017. The plaintiff-appellant was seeking social security disability benefits to help her deal with her fibromyalgia—"a common and chronic disorder characterized by widespread pain, diffuse tenderness, and a number of other symptoms. The word 'fibromyalgia' comes from the Latin term for fibrous tissue (*fibro*) and the Greek [terms] for muscle (*myo*) and pain (*algia*). … [F]ibromyalgia can cause significant pain and fatigue, and it can interfere with a person's ability to carry on daily activities. … Scientists estimate that fibromyalgia affects 5 million Americans age 18 or older." *Kennedy v. The Lilly Extended Disability Plan*, 856 F.3d 1136 (7th Cir. 2017)." Kennedy won her case, but Kolar lost in an order that occupies two pages but would fit comfortably in one. Without bothering to consider any of her arguments, such as that one physician had "erred in discrediting the opinion" (concerning the gravity of her fibromyalgia) of another physician, the panel remarked that "we do not review the decision of an ALJ [administrative law judge] as if it were the opinion of a district court on summary judgment," but ask merely "whether substantial evidence supports the ALJ's ultimate decision." I don't know what sense that can make; the average quality of the Social Security Administration's administrative law judges is below that of federal district and court of appeals judges, and anyway the panel discussed none of the evidence, let alone assessed its substantiality, but merely noted the ALJ's "ultimate decision [was] that Kolar's pain is mild."

This was lazy judging—made worse by the fact that the panel failed even to mention the superb staff attorney memo that recommended reversal of the order of the district court upholding the Social Security Administration's denial of benefits, and makes clear that Kolar's pain is not mild, for if it were her physicians would not have prescribed narcotic drugs to treat it. Here is a brief paraphrase of the staff attorney's memo:

Before applying for benefits Kolar had been diagnosed with multiple disorders of the neck and upper spine and was taking a staggering number of drugs daily. She had seen at least seven medical professionals since 2003 but had obtained only limited relief from their treatment. Despite a mass of medical evidence supporting her testimony of disabling pain caused by her fibromyalgia, the administrative law judge rejected her testimony as non-credible, remarking that she (i.e., the administrative law judge) would "explain…her conclusion that Kolar's account of her pain is "unsupported and even contradicted by the medical evidence in the record." Yet as explained in the staff attorney's memo, the administrative law judge never got around to "[pinpointing medical evidence contradicting Kolar's statements" nor "clearly say which of Kolar's allegations she [the administrative law judge] deem[ed] unsupported." Instead the administrative law judge emphasized findings that Kolar has a "normal gait," ignoring evidence that her gait is slow, but more important ignoring the fact that a normal gait did not refute her complaints of severe pain, which resulted in her being prescribed dangerous drugs, such as OxyContin, a powerful narcotic. The administrative law judge also exaggerated Kolar's ability to work full time—she had to switch to part-time work years ago.

Enough! The staff attorney's memo is 26 pages long. It is devastating. It was not referred to by the panel, which rubberstamped an incompetent administrative ruling. The result was a miscarriage of justice.

Chapter 3

An Introduction to the Staff Attorney Programs of the Other Twelve Federal Circuits

I mustn't confine my analysis of staff attorney programs to my court's program. There are 13 federal courts of appeals (which I list next with their geographical coverage)—and all of them have such programs:

- D.C. Circuit (District of Columbia)
- Federal Circuit (also in D.C.; handles appeals from several specialized federal courts and administrative agencies)
- First Circuit (Maine, Mass., New Hampshire, Puerto Rico, Rhode Island)
- Second Circuit (Conn., New York, Vermont)
- Third Circuit (Delaware, New Jersey, Pennsylvania, Virgin Islands)
- Fourth Circuit (Maryland, North Carolina, Virginia, West Virginia)
- Fifth Circuit (Louisiana, Mississippi, Texas)
- Sixth Circuit (Kentucky, Michigan, Ohio, Tennessee)
- Seventh Circuit (Illinois, Indiana, Wisconsin)
- Eighth Circuit (Arkansas, Iowa, Missouri, Nebraska, North Dakota, South Dakota)
- Ninth Circuit (Alaska, Arizona, California, Guam, Hawaii, Idaho, Montana, Nevada, Northern Mariana Islands, Oregon, Washington (state))
- Tenth Circuit (Colorado, Kansas, New Mexico, Oklahoma, Utah, Wyoming)
- Eleventh Circuit (Alabama, Florida, Georgia).

Often the programs differ from that of the Seventh Circuit in interesting ways. For example, staff attorneys in many of the other federal circuits rarely present their recommendations to judges face-to-face—indeed may rarely have any personal contact with a judge. Most recommendations by those staff attorneys are communicated to the judges by phone or email, and judges then issue orders without consulting the staff attorneys who presented the cases to the judges with recommendations. In both the First and Second Circuits, for example, staff attorneys have little face-to-face contact with the judges, though this is also true in the Seventh Circuit, as most of the personal contact between judges and staff attorneys is limited to Rule 34 conferences, which are intermittent and decide only a fraction of the pro se appeals. It's unclear to me that phone or video contact is inferior to person-to-person contact.

The First Circuit's staff attorney's office screens pro se cases, bail appeals, recalcitrant witness matters, Social Security appeals, *Anders* brief cases, and cases in which parties have waived oral argument, to see whether any of the cases should be recommended for the oral argument calendar. All cases that do not require oral argument are then assigned to a staff attorney. The staff attorney's office is too small (approximately 20 staff attorneys) for specialization, so the staff attorneys get a mix of all case types.

Senior staff attorneys, who have been in the office longer, screen the cases and will "batch" and "weight" cases. "Batching" means that cases with similar issues, as identified by the Clerk's Office or a senior staff attorney, get assigned to the same panel for faster processing. "Weighting" (not weighing) means determining the relative complexity of the case. Line staff attorneys then read case briefs, write memos, and draft short opinions for each panel. The judges do not meet in person but instead vote in a round-robin (serial) fashion whether to accept the drafted disposition or return the case to the staff attorney's office for a different disposition or minor edits. Cases can also be moved to the oral argument calendar if a judge on the panel wants to hear it. First Circuit staff attorneys tend to stay in the job for long terms, though the office hires part-time staff attorneys when the caseload becomes heavier. The salary for a line staff attorney ranges from $73,940 to $88,283. Sometimes, although rarely, staff attorneys work on argued cases. They will also occasionally draft local rules or work on policy matters.

The Second Circuit's staff attorney program and practices are similar to those of the First Circuit, but the Second Circuit has a heavier caseload and in consequence its staff attorney program is much larger—35 to 36 staff attorneys, versus 18 to 22 in the First Circuit—and much more specialized, than the First Circuit's. The program is divided between immigration staff attorneys and staff attorneys that handle other non-argued cases (habeas cases, *Anders* motions, and pro se appeals). The second group is further divided, into three teams: pro se appeals, counseled motions, and pro se motions, with staff attorneys moving through all three teams during their five-year terms. But procedures in the Second Circuit's staff attorney's office mirror those in the First Circuit. Staff attorneys screen cases, rating them as easy, medium, or difficult. They also assign a case-type designation to avoid any panel getting too many time-consuming cases. But the Second Circuit does not "batch" cases to speed up processing. Line staff attorneys prepare a bench memo and a draft summary order for each case. The judges vote serially. Judges can refer petitions to the regular argument calendar, deny it, grant it, remand it, or specify some other action. Judges have one week to send on the voting sheet. There is no face-to-face conferencing over these cases.

Breaking the order of discussion for a moment, I note that in contrast to the circuits I've been discussing, judges in panels of the Tenth Circuit have for many years been meeting face to face with each other and also with staff attorneys to discuss the decision of cases not slated for oral argument (and thus consisting primarily of pro se cases); about a third of the court's cases are decided at these conferences. Interestingly, currently all the staff attorneys are career staff, unlike the Seventh Circuit's staff attorneys, of whom all but four (five including the program's director) are hired for just two years.) (More on the Tenth Circuit later in this chapter.)

In the Third Circuit's Staff Attorney's Office, supervisory staff attorneys work closely with a different batch of 4-5 staff attorneys every six months, and they have the final say on proposed dispositions. The staff attorneys insisted to my research team that interviewed them that the supervisory staff attorneys' edits and contributions to proposed orders prevented any badly written or badly argued memos from being sent out of the office.

Time-sensitive cases involving emergency motions have deadlines but other cases have due dates, with the older cases being given priority for completion. Staff attorneys write memos for unknown panels of judges (both standing motions panels and standing merits panels). They also draft proposed orders and per curiam opinions; the text of a per curiam opinion, however, is mainly for the benefit of the pro se litigant. In close cases, the staff attorneys provide alternative orders to the panel and argue in a cover memo for which order they prefer. Additionally, "unlist" memos are written for supervisory staff attorneys.

Finished work product is sent to panels with levels of urgency based on the case type. Emergency motions are sent when they are ready, substantive motions that are not time-sensitive are sent once a week, usually on Thursdays, in batches of 5 to10, to each panel, and fully-briefed pro se cases are sent once they are ready (usually at a rate of two cases sent to each panel per week). The staff attorneys get the most feedback on their work from supervisory staff attorneys, rather than judges.

Finally, none of the responding staff attorneys had gone directly from law school to the office. Many noted that they became staff attorneys either because they had enjoyed clerking and the work in the staff attorneys' office was the closest match to that kind of work, or because they didn't much like practice.

I discuss the Third Circuit's very interesting program at greater length in Appendix Three to Part One.

The Fourth Circuit has the third largest federal Staff Attorney's Office (called the Office of Staff Counsel), composed of 40-50 staff attorneys headed by a senior staff attorney and four supervisory staff attorneys. The staff attorneys do not screen cases—attorneys in the Clerk's Office do. All immigration, employment discrimination, direct criminal, prisoner, habeas, Social Security, FTCA (Federal Tort Claims Act), ERISA (Employment Retirement Income Security Act), and pro se appeals are automatically referred to staff attorneys.

Interestingly the court provides informal briefs on its website to help pro se litigants clarify their appeals. These forms ask litigants to identify issues and write supporting facts or arguments pertaining to each issue. Case citations are optional. The forms help determine whether a case should be shifted to the argument track. For non-argument cases staff attorneys prepare a memorandum and a draft disposition (there is some de facto specialization within the office for different types of case, particularly tax, bankruptcy, immigration, and Social Security appeals.) The judges on each panel then decide the case via email rather than face-to-face. The final product is often an unpublished per curiam opinion—indeed the Fourth Circuit has the highest percentage of unpublished opinions of all the circuits. Many of these opinions dispose of cases in four sentences, often boilerplate language unchanged in the past two decades.

Former Chief Judge William Wilkins praised the staff attorney's office, saying that staff attorneys allow judges and their clerks to "minimize the time spent on the large number of pro se and counseled cases that do not present factual or legal issues that require oral argument for appropriate resolution. This enables us to allocate additional time to those more complex cases that are set for oral argument."[1] And a senior staff attorney has said that the staff attorney's office serves indigents "because cases are decided far more quickly."

I omit discussion of the Fifth Circuit's Staff Attorney's Office because it, along with the Third Circuit, which I have already discussed in this chapter, is the subject of a very long, detailed, and exact description, supplied to my research team by the director of that court's staff attorney program, in Appendix Three to Part One.

The Sixth Circuit's approximately 32 staff attorneys handle pro se cases, immigration cases, employment discrimination cases, direct criminal appeals, cases about prisoner rights and non-prisoner rights, habeas cases, and Social Security cases. The staff attorneys first screen cases for jurisdiction, with the screening being complet-

---

[1] "Staff Attorney Offices Help Manage Rising Caseloads," Nonpublication.com, at http://www.nonpublication.com/stffattys.htm.

ed by a jurisdictional specialist and afterwards by a judicial panel. The staff attorneys assign a number for the time anticipated to be spent on the case and for the level of difficulty (easy, moderate, or difficult), and group together cases with similar issues for a panel to decide. Motions panels, not staff attorneys, handle substantive motions. The staff attorneys can assign a pro bono lawyer to pro se litigants in particularly salient cases. All nonargued pro se cases are routed to the line staff attorneys.

As in the other staff attorney's offices, the staff attorneys "work up" cases. Pro se cases are assigned randomly, although some attorneys specialize in some areas, such as immigration law, Black Lung cases, or Social Security cases. Thirty days before panels meet, staff attorneys' memoranda are forwarded to all three judges. The panels convene at the end of argument days and discuss both the argued and the unargued cases. This format is unique to the Sixth Circuit. Also unique is its practice of routinely explain[ing] its decisions on stays. Its orders generally explain the type of relief the petitioner is seeking, summarizes the arguments the petitioner made in support of the stay, and provides a brief analysis of those arguments. None of the other circuits comes close to this level of detail. The staff attorneys also review Criminal Justice Act vouchers to reimburse pro bono lawyers defending indigents. They prepare an index of published opinions for the court to serve as a resource until opinions are published in the Federal Reporter.

In the Eighth Circuit, each line staff attorney reports to a Supervisory Staff Attorney, who is assigned to edit and oversee the work of four line staff attorneys and whose primary task is to oversee the substantive and technical accuracy of memoranda and proposed orders and opinions prepared by the line staff attorneys for submission to three-judge panels. Duties include setting priorities and schedules for staff attorney work; monitoring work performance; providing advice and assistance on work in progress; editing, reviewing, revising, and approving the line staff attorneys' work products; and training and recruitment. Supervisory Staff Attorneys also provide support to the Senior Staff Attorney [the head of the program, corresponding to Michael Fridkin in the Seventh

Circuit] as needed, including assisting in administrative functions and performance reviews of the line attorneys. The line attorneys are appointed for two years and are responsible for researching procedural and substantive legal issues in the appeals pending before the court and summarizing their work in memoranda for the three-judge panels that decide the cases appealed to the court. The memoranda include recommendations on how the judges should rule. In addition the line staff attorneys review the records of lower courts and agencies for cases on appeal and sometimes write draft opinions and orders for the judges.

Regarding the Ninth Circuit, its very distinguished, long-service Judge Alex Kozinski succinctly and candidly explains that "the circuit shares approximately 70 staff attorneys, who process roughly 40 percent of the cases in which we issue a merits ruling. When I say process, I mean that they read the briefs, review the record, research the law, and prepare a proposed disposition, which they then present to a panel of three judges during a practice we call "oral screening"—oral because the judges don't see the briefs in advance and because they generally rely on the staff attorney's oral description of the case in deciding whether to sign on to the proposed disposition. After you decide a few dozen such cases on a screening calendar, your eyes glaze over, your mind wanders, and the urge to say O.K. to whatever is put in front of you becomes almost irresistible."[2] His vivid description of judicial rubber stamping underscores the high stakes of staff attorneys' getting dispositions right in the face of the circuit's substantial geographic hurdles to face-to-face interaction between judges and also between judges and staff attorneys.

The office's 75 to 80 staff attorneys (making it the largest federal appellate staff attorney's office) work on memorandum dispositions (affectionately dubbed "memdispos") for pro se cases, immigration cases, employment discrimination cases, direct criminal appeals, prisoner rights cases, non-prisoner rights cases, habeas cases, Federal Tort Claims Act cases, and pro se contract and intellectual prop-

---

[2] Alex Kozinski, "The Appearance of Propriety," *Legal Affairs*, at http://www.legalaffairs.org/issues/January-February-2005/argument_kozinski_janfeb05.msp (2005).

erty cases. Board of Immigration Appeals cases feature particularly largely in the Ninth Circuit's caseload.

The office is divided into a motions/pro se unit and a research unit. Staff attorneys in the motions/pro se unit inventory cases by their weight (1 for well-settled law, 3, 5, 7, 10 for most complex law, and 24 for death penalty), type, involved issues, and probable difficulty after briefing. Inventoried cases are then calendared. Cases with similar issues are entered into a database that allows text searches and these related cases are heard by judges in a single sitting. Pro se appeals with particularly novel or unresolved issues are appointed attorneys. The rest of the pro se cases, though, are automatically assigned a weight of 1 and passed on to the staff attorney's office.

The staff attorneys in the research unit then take over, writing proposed "memdispos" that are then presented in person before each panel. One former supervising staff attorney at the Ninth Circuit writes that he "saw no evidence that the judges took staff memoranda on faith; on the contrary, even in cases in which the court relied heavily upon the staff, the judges routinely read the precedents or the portions of the record that were crucial to the decision." Interestingly, the court allows publication of unpublished dispositions if individuals write letters to the clerk's office "stating concisely the reasons supporting publication. If the request is granted, the unpublished disposition will be redesignated an opinion and published." The specter of a "hidden judiciary," enabled by staff attorney's offices and the decisions issued by them, is that much lessened by this mechanism.

In the Tenth Circuit, judges perform all screening of cases. Non-argument cases are then moved to the staff attorney's office, whose director assigns line staff attorneys a mix of cases. Cases include social security issues, diversity, discrimination, civil rights, federal agencies, criminal issues, taxes, bankruptcy issues, and pro se issues. Pro se appellants can submit almost anything as a brief, so long as they show a good faith effort to present the issues. The Clerk's Office maintains a database of frequent filers and sends this list to the circuit judges to enforce the Prison Litigation Reform

Act's "Three Strikes" provision. It is unclear how often judges request this—it most likely depends on judges' remembering individual litigants' names.

A recent job posting suggests that, as noted earlier in the chapter, the Tenth Circuit still has face-to-face conferences (one of the job responsibilities of a staff attorney remains "conferring" with judges). Staff attorneys also draft and update legal reference works used by judges and their clerks. For example, in 2011, the staff attorney's office hired temporary staff attorneys to update a Deskbook and Immigration Manual.

The Eleventh Circuit trains new staff attorneys ("line staff attorneys") by assigning each one to a supervisory staff attorney in one of six areas for one month: sentencing, direct criminal appeals, habeas, employment, immigration, civil rights. At the beginning of the month the line staff attorney receives easier cases, progressing to harder ones by the end of the month. Throughout this training period and at the start of every two months, they receive in their mailboxes a stack of cases. Line attorneys must complete a quota of cases by the end of every two months. Whether or not they succeed, however, depends on the complexity of each case. If a line staff attorney is coming close to the end of her two months and is not close to completing her quota, he or she may return to the pool to be randomly assigned additional cases in the hope of getting simple cases to boost his or her number of completed cases.

For research, line staff attorneys refer to two resources in addition to Westlaw: six physical spiral-bound case-law books specific to each of six areas of research and an online database of every staff attorney decision ever made in the Eleventh Circuit. Staff attorneys interviewed by my staff at the circuit primarily understood their task to be translating the irrelevant, unverified, and often physically illegible facts presented by pro se appellants into legal arguments that could be understood and accepted by judges.

Their primary audience was and is not the litigants but the judges on each panel (though the staff attorneys do not know which judges will be assigned to a case). Memos are reviewed by an "editing buddy" of the staff attorney's choice and a supervising staff attorney, who has the final say on proposed decisions. Once the memos leave the staff attorneys' office, staff attorneys receive no feedback on their case unless they take it upon themselves to track the outcome.

The staff attorneys interviewed at the Eleventh Circuit seem disposed to remain in government work, although it is too early in their respective careers to know whether they've ruled out private practice altogether. They were not under the impression that firms hire staff attorneys just to enable the firms' other lawyers to skip grunt work.

Curiously, one staff attorney's prime interest in becoming a staff attorney had come from her law school internships in Tanzania and Bangladesh, where she saw stacks and stacks of pending cases, some twenty years old, languishing in the closets of the courthouses. She wanted to see how the American court system managed its heavy caseload so relatively quickly.

The caseload of the D.C. Circuit reaches virtually every area of federal law, and is unique in the number of cases it handles that are brought against the executive branch. The staff attorneys are located in the Legal Division of the Office of the Clerk of the court of appeals; the division's principal responsibility is to recommend to the court the disposition of substantive and procedural motions, appeals decided without oral argument, and emergency matters. Staff attorneys conduct legal research, prepare legal memoranda, draft proposed orders, respond to judges' inquiries, and make oral presentations. They meet with three-judge panels in formal conferences about twice a month to present their recommendations, but they also present their recommendations orally to the judges in chambers when handling time-sensitive emergency motions.

Last is the Federal Circuit, which has nationwide jurisdiction focused on patent cases and cases originating in a variety of federal administrative agencies. Surprisingly (and I have found no explanation) its Staff Attorneys' office is by far the smallest of any of the federal courts of appeals. There are only 4 attorneys in the office, of whom 2 are hired initially for a term but can become permanent.

Any vacancy is advertised on the Federal Circuit website and usa-jobs.opm.gov. The office primarily focuses on motions work prior to a case being put on the calendar. The office will consider both 3Ls and law graduates for staff attorney positions.

* * *

I have still more points to make about some of staff attorney programs other than that of the Seventh Circuit. Last year a number of our court's staff attorneys attended a national conference of staff attorneys, which introduced our staff attorneys to the staff attorney programs of the other circuits. Consistently with a point noted earlier in this chapter, our staff attorneys who attended the conference reported back that the staff attorneys they met from other circuits have on average less face-to-face contact with judges than our staff attorneys. Our staff attorneys also learned that many of the staff attorneys in the other circuits are reluctant to recommend reversal of a district judge and are never involved in orally argued cases. Later in this book, in Appendix One to Part One, readers will encounter spreadsheet that provides a national perspective on staff attorney programs, followed by summary results of research conducted by my team of law school research assistants on the staff attorney programs of the other circuits. The reader will learn that although our program has certain advantages, as yet there is no confirmed basis for deeming the Seventh Circuit's program the very best of all the federal staff attorney programs.

A statement by Chief Judge Katzmann of the Second Circuit, although it omits mention of the supervisory structure of his court's staff attorney program, eloquently describes a program similar to ours except (as just noted) with regard to face-to-face contact between judges and staff attorneys: "The lawyers in the Staff Attorney's Office of the Second Circuit Court of Appeals provide objective legal advice to the judges of the court on all immigration cases, substantive motions (both pro se and counseled), and pro se appeals. These matters compose nearly one-third of the court's docket, and are consequential to litigants, their families, and the development of the law. In a given case the assigned staff attorney drafts a single, neutral bench memo for all three members of the panel. Their work product thus ensures that the judges are, quite literally, on the same page. By long tradition the Second Circuit has hired recent law graduates to serve in the Staff Attorney's Office. Modeled on a clerkship, the post gives junior lawyers the unparalleled opportunity to write for all 22 judges of the court. Like our chambers law clerks, our staff attorneys handle a wide variety of civil, criminal and agency cases, but they may also become experts in federal appellate procedure, habeas corpus, and immigration. The judges of the Second Circuit appreciate the diligence and expertise of our staff attorneys, whose professional work is essential to the adjudicatory process of the court. "It's worth noting that the Second Circuit has almost twice as many judges as the Seventh: 22 versus 12.

The lesson to be kept in mind: the federal courts of appeals are not homogeneous!

* * *

The Eleventh Circuit's staff attorney program is interestingly different from both the Seventh's and the Second's in respects going beyond my earlier description of the Eleventh Circuit's program: "The office has approximately seventy attorneys, including career supervisory staff attorneys and staff attorneys who serve on staggered two-year terms. The principal task of the office is to assist in the disposition of appeals through the preparation of legal memoranda. The types of cases the office presently handles include (1) direct criminal appeals involving sentencing guidelines and guilt/innocence issues, (2) all pro se appeals, including collateral attacks on criminal convictions by state and federal prisoners, and civil rights suits under 42 U.S.C. § 1983, (3) employment discrimination cases, (4) immigration cases, and (5) social security appeals. There are also three specialized units within the office. The Jurisdiction Unit assists the court in the initial review of all appeals filed for the purpose of determining appellate jurisdiction. The Issue Tracking Unit serves to track and catalog relevant legal issues. The Motions Unit processes certain substantive motions, including those for *in forma pauperis* status, certificates of appealability for 28 U.S.C. §§ 2254 and 2255 appeals, transcripts at government expense, and motions to appoint, withdraw, and/or substitute counsel. www.uscourts.gov /careers/current-job-openings/83709.

For completeness I note that many law firms employ staff attorneys, regarded as junior to the firm's associates and traditionally (though less so at present) assigned mainly to document review. I discuss only judicial staff attorneys in this book.

And briefly to wind up, I note that while the First Circuit is small, communications between its staff attorneys and judges are mainly by email, while the Eleventh Circuit's staff attorney office is in a separate building from the judges' office suite (I avoid the jejune term "chambers"). Furthermore, circuits other than the Seventh tend to dispose of cases presented by staff attorneys in more cursory orders. And as staff attorneys in the other circuits rarely work on argued cases, they, unlike the Seventh Circuit's staff attorneys, rarely help to produce published opinions, as the Seventh's do in short-argument-day cases. That said, however, we'll see that at least two other federal circuit courts, the Third and the Fifth, appear to have a better-organized staff attorney program than the Seventh and others may as well. So stay tuned!

Chapter 4

Improving the Court's Staff Attorney Program:
Introduction

An informal discussion before my retirement between six of the Seventh Circuits current staff attorneys and me produced the following suggestions for "best practices" of our (indeed of any) staff attorney program:

Experienced Supervisors: The ideal supervisory staff attorney will have had experience practicing law, particularly criminal law. This is important for spotting legal issues that may not be obvious from the briefs or the record, or that a recent law school graduate may be unable to catch. But as far as I know the court has never actually had an "ideal" supervisor.

Writing Seminars: Periodic writing workshops can help improve the writing of staff attorneys and ensure that the office as a whole has a consistent approach to writing draft orders and bench memos.

Interaction with Judges: A few judges frequently meet with, call, or email staff attorneys in advance of a short-argument day or Rule 34 conference, to discuss their recommendations; the staff attorneys find that such interactions help them understand both the judge's approach to legal issues and his or her stylistic preferences. Staff attorneys also find their writing improved by discussing with judges any changes in the staff attorneys' draft orders and opinions that the judges make or suggest. (The need for such improvement is a focus of this book, as the reader will soon discover.) Yet such discussions are rare. On a few occasions, however (routinely in the case of Judge Manion), after short-argument days the judges discuss with the staff attorneys the cases they have heard, in order to share their opinions of counsels' performance and the legal issues in the cases.

* * *

A description of the court's staff attorney program would be incomplete without introducing the reader to Donald J. Wall—technically not a member of the program though a former director of it and thus a predecessor of Michael Fridkin. Wall is currently Counsel to the court's Circuit Executive (Collins Fitzpatrick), and one of his duties that overlaps with the duties of the staff attorneys is to screen all appeal filings to make sure they're within the court's appellate jurisdiction, and if not to order the appellant either to abandon the appeal or refile it in a form that invokes our jurisdiction, if that is possible. Staff attorneys who encounter problems of appellate jurisdiction in the cases they work on often seek Wall's advice. Although he has frequent interaction with staff he also brings pre-argument jurisdictional issues directly to judges with recommendations for resolving them.

Another area of his expertise is the recruitment of counsel. Pro se appellants—and such appellants are by far the most frequent in cases that get referred to staff attorneys—are by definition not represented by a lawyer, usually owing to lack of money and/or lack of familiarity with the legal profession. If therefore a pro se appeal has apparent merit, there may well be a compelling case for the court's attempting to recruit counsel (on a volunteer basis—the court cannot draft a lawyer to represent a party in litigation in the court), and Wall is the court's expert in that domain, as he is in issues of appellate jurisdiction. His connections, however, are almost entirely to Chicago law firms; as a result recruitment of lawyers for pro se's appealing from decisions in other parts of the circuit has lagged.

Another point of interest is that the types of duties that Wall handles are handled in other circuits by staff attorneys; his role in Seventh Circuit appears to be unique.

I need to say more about recruitment of lawyers for pro se's, and I might as well say it here.

* * *

Irregularity in the workload of a staff attorney program requires attention if the program is to be understood. Until two years ago, when the Supreme Court in *Johnson v. United States*, 135 S. Ct. 2551 (1915), invalidated part of the Armed Career Criminal Act and made the invalidation retroactive, out of about two thousand applications for habeas corpus received since 1996 our staff attorneys had recommended granting the application only three times and the court had granted it only once. But after the decision in *Johnson* we received more than 500 requests for permission to file a successive habeas corpus petition, and staff attorneys recommended and the court granted permission in roughly half. That increase in requests was illustrative of the significant complication in the administration of staff attorney programs that is brought about by the occasional unexpected surge in filings when thousands of inmates file renewed petitions seeking immediate release on the basis of recent changes in the law.

The most recent surge arose from the Supreme Court's holding in *Johnson* that the clause of the Armed Career Criminal Act that defines a violent felony to include a crime that "involves conduct that presents a serious potential risk of physical injury to another," 18 U.S.C. § 924(e)(2)(B), is unconstitutionally vague. To cope with the surge, two staff attorneys were added to our habeas corpus unit by loan from the Rule 34 and short-argument-day units, respectively. The two staff attorneys were able to handle the habeas corpus applications without losing ground. But when a surge is unexpected a court may have a lot of difficulty altering staff assignments to cope with it.

Chapter 5

The Principal Problems with the Seventh Circuit's Staff Attorney Program at Present, and My Suggested Solutions

So far this book has been mainly concerned with sketching the basics of the staff attorney program concept. Let the drums now roll and the trumpets sound and the excitement begin.

Since the beginning of April 2017 I have devoted a great deal of my time to trying to solve a problem that bedevils our staff attorney program and the parallel programs in other circuits, I am sure. The problem, already alluded to, is a frequent failure of judges and staff attorneys to communicate intelligibly with the pro se's (many of them prison or jail inmates) who file appeals, petitions, or motions with our court. ("Pro se" is, as mentioned earlier, Latin for "on one's own behalf." A pro se litigant is a litigant who has no lawyer.) These applicants for relief by our court are very often poorly educated and/or of limited intelligence; yet they are Americans (with some exceptions) entitled to know the reasons for our deciding their cases, whether by reversal of an adverse district court decision or, more commonly, by affirmance of such a decision. Although our staff attorneys are carefully picked, able, and hard working, many of them lack critical writing skills, a lack I blame not on them but on the current American culture, which in part because of the influence of the electronic revolution on communication fails to train even able students to write clearly, which is to say communicate intelligibly to the intended audience. And weak writing skills at the staff attorney level spell weak understanding at the pro se level. A very fine law clerk recently completed her year with me, leaving behind a slogan of her invention that ought to be etched in all the offices of my court's staff attorney office complex:

"legal writing should always be simple and sensible, and conventions and assumptions should always be interrogated."

A complication worth noting is that some of the federal court of appeals judges, including some on my court, are what are termed "senior judges," a form of semi-retirement. A federal judge must be at least 65 years of age and have served in federal courts for 15 years to qualify, with one less year of service required for each additional year of age. Senior judges are eligible to take smaller caseloads than the other (called "active") judges; on average their caseloads are about half as large as those of the judges in active service. Stephen B. Burbank, *et al.*, "Leaving the Bench," 161 *U. Pa. Law Rev.* 1 (2012). Yet in my court at least, in which four of the eleven judges are senior, their caseloads do include cases prepared for and submitted to them by the staff attorneys.

* * *

Moving on: Together with my law clerks and two of my University of Chicago research assistants, I recently visited the Cook County, Illinois, jail (Cook County is the county in which the City of Chicago is located). It is the third-largest jail in the United States, currently housing on average about 9000 detainees (as the jail's prisoners are termed). See Cook County Department of Corrections, www.cookcountysheriff.com; Patricia Manson, "Cook County Jail out from U.S. Oversight," *Chicago Daily Law Bulletin*, June 13, 2017, p. 1.

The jail is managed by Thomas Dart, the Sheriff of Cook County, an *outstanding* public servant—indeed the jail's saviour (see Manson article, *supra*). He talked to us visitors at length, emphasizing the difficulties he faces because of staff problems resulting from unionization, budgetary control by the county government, the FMLA (Family Medical Leave Act, sometimes manipulated to enable employees to go AWOL by claiming to have a sick family member who requires their presence at home), and above all the reluctance of state judges to hold trials for the jail's detainees (arrested but not convicted) promptly. Detainees may languish for years in the jail because no state judge will schedule a prompt trial for them, hoping the jail will get tired of holding them and release them and they'll vanish and their trials be cancelled.

To his great credit Sheriff Dart is a pioneer in allowing detainees not believed to be dangerous to be bailed out of jail and allowed to live at home while awaiting trial, each wearing an electronic ankle monitor that enables the jail to keep track of his whereabouts and thus make sure he doesn't leave home without the permission of jail staff. But because not all detainees are eligible for bail (or so obviously harmless that they can be released with no restrictions at all), Sheriff Dart and his staff can't overcome the scandalous sluggishness of the state trial courts, as a result of which detainees frequently spend more time in the jail awaiting trial than they spend in prison after eventually being tried and sentenced.

Thus, as shown in the following table compiled by the jail's Chief Policy Officer, Sheriff Cara Smith, in January 2017, 107 detainees spent a total of 10,479 "dead days" in the jail, defined as days spent in pre-trial custody that exceeded the length of time required to satisfy their sentences of imprisonment. The average number of dead days per detainee was thus 98, which equals 3.26

Sentence	# of people	# of dead days
1 yr	56	2919
14 mo.	1	148
1.5 yrs	8	746
22 mo	1	6
2 yrs	20	1651
30 mo	2	3
33 mo	1	28
3 yrs	13	1817
42 mo	2	51
4 yrs	1	33
6 yrs	1	219
9 yrs	1	2858
Total	107	**10479**

months—a nontrivial time to languish in jail awaiting trial: effectively a bonus sentence. Notice for example that the 56 detainees sentenced to a year's imprisonment each had 52 dead days, which extended their period of incarceration from a year to almost 14 months. And notice finally how the dead days increased by almost five months ($148/30 = 4.9$) the length of incarceration of a person who had been sentenced to 14 months in prison.

Some of the jail's detainees—about 300 a year, we were told on our tour—file suits in federal district court; often they are complaining about the living conditions in the jail. They are among the pro se's who are likely to appeal to my court if they lose in the district court.

There is more to the jail's problems. From page 7 of a 2013 article by C.E. Olsen in the *Cook County Sheriff's Reentry Council Research Bulletin*, entitled "An Examination of Admissions, Discharges, and the Population of the Cook County Jail, 2012," we learn that between 2007 and 2012 the average length of stay in the jail increased 19% (from 47.9 days to 57.0 days) while the median time increased from 11 days to 12 days (a 9.1% increase)—and this despite the fact that jail admissions fell during that period. The article describes various reasons for the increased length of the jail stay, including "longer court processing times because of more complex cases, fewer resources available in the courtrooms to process cases, more people staying in jail before they are convicted and sentenced to prison because they could not post bond, or all of these factors" (p. 8).) I haven't found more recent reports.

I wanted to talk to some of the jail's detainees because I had never visited a jail before (and only once a prison); I wanted to get a better feel for what after all are major "customers" of my court. Because it was getting late I had time to speak to only five of them; I believe they were randomly selected to meet me. What I found interesting was that all of them were pleasant, articulate, unthreatening, and really seemed quite normal. One of them was especially articulate and clearly *very* intelligent, and afterwards I asked one of the prison staff what a person like that was doing in jail—and he'd been in the jail for 24 months, and had told us he'd been in jail *many* times in the course of his life (he appeared to be in late middle age). The staff person didn't know, but conjectured, based on experience with other detainees, that this one was addicted to illegal drugs, because while well behaved in jail, where he had no access to such drugs, in the past as soon as was released he would resume his addiction and as a result soon find himself back in jail to await a trial, though if the delay in the start of the trial were long enough he'd probably be released from jail before then—only to return, however, when he relapsed into addiction.

My principal research assistant, Theresa Yuan, recently sent me this moving note about our visit to the jail:

> And while you have spoken and written about the five men you spoke to that day, I found that the most memorable part of the experience was the line of men behind those five, all holding their pink complaint forms. They were lining up without being entirely sure if they would be heard or not, and in the end, they weren't. I think there's a big need in law to hear these individuals out, and I also think it would be a colossal waste of my resources and experiences to not work on that, and I am also very grateful that working for you this past year has allowed that me to see these individuals and think about this.

I am very sorry to say that I had failed to notice the men holding pink complaint forms.

I consider my tour of the jail to have been an eye-opening experience, and talking to the five detainees I also was reminded of the two criminal offenders whom I had talked to in the federal prison (Buttner, in North Carolina) that I'd visited—one a bank robber, the other a murderer, both very pleasant and appearing to be entirely normal and not denying they'd committed the crimes for which they'd been convicted and sentenced and evincing no bitterness at their fates.

From my two encounters, limited as they have been, with the incarcerated I take away a sense that most jail detainees and prison inmates are basically fairly normal people who because of bad luck, psychological problems, poor judgment, lack of family support, or other internal or environmental misfortunes, simply have great difficulty living a law-abiding life. There are some monsters in the mix, but I suspect they're a small minority. The murderer for example explained to me that if you're in the illegal-drug trade, as he had been, you're not infrequently in a position where to survive you have to kill—that or be killed yourself. The obvious solution is not prison; it is to decriminalize the illegal trade in drugs, except Fentanyl, the most dangerous.

These people are in a sense our (the federal judges') clients, and we need to understand them better than most of us judges do, and we need our staff attorneys to understand them, which they have *great* difficulty doing because their lives are so remote from those of the pro se's who provide the grist for the staff attorneys' mills. In my experience approximately half of our staff attorneys do not, and I fear cannot, explain to a pro se—in part for the reasons I've just offered, but in equal part because they can't keep their sentences short, because they can't avoid legalisms, because they can't eschew quoting judicial opinions, because they do not understand sentence structure—why the pro se's claim is being accepted or rejected.

Rejection is the more common result, yet rejection need not mean the end of the road to freedom for the pro se. He may have alternative avenues of relief, of which he may well be and remain unaware if we reject his appeal or other motion without an explanation *intelligible to him.* And that will often require a staff attorney memo (for the judges aren't going to bother with it) that is written very simply, in short sentences, without citations to or quotations from judicial decisions, and that subjects the written arguments of the pro se to the Flesch-Kinkaid Reading Test, which is a simple algorithm (downloadable from the Internet free of charge) for determining the educational level necessary to understand a given text. In a recent case of mine (*Davis v. Moroney*, discussed at length shortly), in which a prison guard beat up a prisoner without justification and was sued by him, the guard served the plaintiff with a set of interrogatories that the prisoner refused to answer. He refused because he *couldn't* answer them. They required, I discovered by application of the Flesch test, an 8th or possibly 9th grade education to understand, and the plaintiff had only a 6th grade education (and, he claimed, without contradiction, to have an IQ of only 66, which makes me doubt that he could actually read at a 6th-grade level).

And when our decision, in the most common type of pro se case—a decision affirming dismissal of his suit by a district court—leaves the pro se with a possible alternative remedy of which he is unaware, we should sketch that alternative in our order or opinion rejecting his current appeal in order to give him a fighting chance of future success.

I don't believe that any judge of my court other than myself has ever used the Flesch test, and I am doubtful whether, in any but the rarest of circumstances, a judge other than myself has ever sought to recruit a lawyer to represent a pro se either in our court or in a district court of our circuit, has ever insisted that our order resolving a pro se appeal be intelligible to the pro se, or has ever rewritten (as opposed to lightly editing) a staff attorney memo. In these respects we have been negligent on a massive scale. We have failed and are failing to do justice to our pro se's. We fail to listen and we fail to communicate. Our staff attorney program is at best a partial, incomplete success.

As for myself, I date from an era long prior to the current culture of indolent reading and writing and mindless tapping on a cellphone. I entered college (Yale) at age 16 in 1955, having skipped my senior year of high school. I had written a book-length essay in high school on the decline of the British Empire. Indeed I'd been a voracious reader and writer since first grade. I majored in English at Yale, wrote extensively, culminating in a book-length study of William Butler Yeats's late poetry, and graduated summa cum laude despite having annoyed several of my professors, being rebellious by nature. I then went to Harvard Law School, was president of the law review, graduated first in my class despite having again been a rather obnoxious student (which I am told on good authority precluded my receiving a teaching offer from Harvard—for which I remain grateful), and wrote extensively throughout my three years. I then wrote opinions for Justice Brennan, for whom I clerked the year after graduating from law school. I worked next for the Federal Trade Commission (more writing), then was an assistant to the Solicitor General of the United States (and wrote many briefs as well as arguing cases in the Supreme Court), then was general counsel of a federal task force on communications policy (a good deal of writing), then entered academia (continuous writing), became a full professor at the age of 30, and went on to edit what quickly became an influential journal, to write many books and countless articles and blog posts, and to create (with a distinguished fellow academic and a brilliant law student) a consulting firm (Lexecon) that I am told currently has an income of some $300 million a year (I sold my entire interest in the firm when I was appointed to the court in 1981); and since my appointment I have, as mentioned in the Preface, written 3,332 judicial opinions.

I recite all this not (I hope) to brag, but to establish my credentials as an experienced writer. Beginning in late March or early April of this year (2017), wanting to do something for the pro se's, within a few weeks I reviewed 39 staff attorney memos in pro se cases, roughly half of which were adequately written, though many could be improved, the other half not adequately written; and I edited that half to be intelligible to pro se litigants, that is, to poor readers. On the basis of that experience I proposed to the chief judge early in June 2017 a plan that had the support of Michael Fridkin, the director of the staff attorney program. The plan was that I would review all staff attorney memos and draft orders before their submission to panels of judges to decide the cases. *I* would not decide the cases unless I happened to be on the panel and had the support of its other members. Otherwise I would simply pass on the edited staff attorney memo or order to the judges who were on the panel *and they would do with it what they pleased.* In dealing with the staff attorneys I thus would be operating as Fridkin's assistant, mentoring to the staff attorneys, rather than as a judge.

Did I receive any credit for wanting to help out the pro se's in this way without enlarging my judicial authority at the expense of my judicial colleagues—in fact diminishing my authority? Of course not! The pro se's are not a popular segment of our clientele; I like them but I don't think any of the other judges do. In Chapter 5 the readers of this book will learn that my proposal (to review the staff attorneys' memos and draft orders), though supported by Fridkin, was rejected by the chief judge and the other judges of the court. Plus I received an angry anonymous note purporting to be from 17 of our court's staff attorneys accusing me of unfairly criticizing the staff attorneys. That was a misunderstanding. As I said earlier, our staff attorneys are carefully picked, able, and hard working, but many of them are deficient in the writing skills necessary to communicate with pro se's, who in my opinion are or should be the particular learner-beneficiaries of orders or opinions communicated to them by the court. Being deficient they need help; they are not receiving the requisite help from each other, from the supervisory staff attorneys, or from the other judges; they would have gotten it from me had I been permitted to review staff attorney memos and draft orders before their submission to the judicial panels.

However I need to qualify my criticism of the staff attorneys' work in the following respect. The bench memos they write to prepare the judges for "short-argument days"—those oral-argument days on which staff attorneys take the place of the judges' law clerks—tend to be quite well written; this is mainly I think because the parties to the cases argued on those days are almost always represented by lawyers, which makes it easier for judges and staff to understand the cases and decide them intelligently. Yet mistakes do creep into the bench memos even in such cases. I'll give examples drawn from bench memos in a short-argument day, July 6, 2017, on which I happened to be the presiding judge of the panel. In a case argued that day called *Vanprooyen v. Berryhill*, No. 16-3653, the staff attorney's bench memo states that the plaintiff, who had medical problems, "at her next appointment [with her psychiatrist] reported that her mother had thrown out her Xanax, which had helped, so [the psychiatrist] refilled the prescription." The clause beginning "so" at the end of the sentence makes clear to the reader that it was the Xanax that had helped, but until then the reader doesn't know whether what had helped the plaintiff was the Xanax or mom's throwing it out.

That glitch was the only significant defect in the staff attorney's bench memo, and I therefore asked her to convert the memo into an opinion that I'd circulate to the other two judges on the panel (and have now done so)—but only after tightening the memo; for while staff attorney memos are often too short, sometimes (the verbosity problem) they're too long. The bench memo in the *Vanprooyen* case was not verbose, but still I was able to shorten it, from 4295 to 2877 words, though oddly the shorter version took up more pages—12 versus 10.

In the next case, *United States v. Lopez*, No. 16-4172, involving an appeal by a convicted drug offender, the bench memo states that "the charging documents underlying two of [the defendant's] convictions specified that he caused bodily harm to another, implicating the use of physical force ... ." I don't know what "implicating the use of physical force" means, though I imagine it's a clumsy substitute for "which implies that he used physical force"–as how else is bodily harm caused? (Actually of course, bodily harm is frequently caused, sometimes deliberately, without use of physical force, as in deliberately failing to treat a sick person with the correct medicine.) Elsewhere there is a mysterious reference to "the two arms of the battery statute," and a mysterious denial "that Illinois's enhanced domestic battery statute [citation] did not qualify as a crime of violence." How can a statute be a crime?

And in my last example from the July 6 short-argument day, *Davis v. Cross*, No. 15-3681, the bench memo oddly states that the appellant, who had participated in a bank robbery, may not have "intended the bank robbery to be armed." (Presumably what is meant is that the robbers did not intend to be armed.) On the same page there are references to 28 U.S.C. §§ 2241 and 2255 but no explanation of what these statutes say, except that the reader is told that to obtain relief under the second of the two statutes a defendant is required to show that his trial involved an error "grave enough to be deemed a miscarriage of justice" and on the next page that the requirement "is tied with the merits of his claim that erroneous instructions led the jury to convict him despite his innocence." I don't know what the second statement means. I note that no effort is made in the bench memo to define "miscarriage of justice," though it's a technical legal term unlikely to be intelligible to most pro se litigants. Indeed I'm not sure it has a precise meaning to judges. To some judges, me for example, it just means an error by the trial judge or jury serious enough to have produced a mistaken verdict.

*　*　*

Returning for a moment to the anonymous letter to me purporting to be from 17 staff attorneys, I don't think it had anything to do with the rejection of my plan to screen staff attorney memos en route to the panels of judges. The rejection (discussed at greater length in the next chapter, and in Part Three of the book) had rather to do, I believe, with a desire of the court's judges for uniformity, and a related fear that I am getting too big for my britches, and the disagreement, of which more later, between the chief judge of the court and me concerning the administration of the staff attorney program.

Here I focus on the first ground, rejection by other judges. Judge A doesn't want to see Judge B given responsibilities and opportunities denied to A. I think some at least of my colleagues feared that I was bidding to "take over" the staff attorney program. Now in fact few if any of my judicial colleagues had or have any but the most passing interest in the program. Still, it is an established program, resolving several thousand cases a year, and there was I think fear that I was wanting to annex it—that I was already a well-known judge and now would be even better-known while they would be thrust into the shade. If that was their fear it rested on a misunderstanding of my projected role in the program. As I've tried to explain, I was not going to manage the program; Fridkin was; he is the program's director and would remain so; I would be his assistant. The staff attorney memos and draft orders would continue to undergo peer review followed by review by supervisory staff attorneys, but now there would be a further tier of review: Posner review. I would be in effect the fifth supervisory staff attorney. Had the modesty of my projected role been understood by my judicial colleagues, I don't think they would have balked. And I can't imagine their thinking me unqualified for the task I wished to undertake.

The failure of understanding was in part at least my fault. I did not discuss with any of the other judges my plan, except the chief judge, with consequences discussed later. I don't know whether she understood the plan fully or conveyed it accurately to the other judges, but I doubt whether they understood or understand it, for I was the only judge actually interested in the staff attorney program, though much later we'll see the chief judge having become interested in it. I told her about my plan for the program at a lunch that I had with her on June 5. I failed to foresee any opposition, and received none from her on that occasion. I did not foresee that the next day my plan would be scotched in separate communications to all the other judges, leaving me out of the loop, unable to respond cogently because I knew neither what she had said to them or they to her.

Let me try to summarize my concerns with the court's current staff attorney program, which are multiple, and explain how I would have resolved them without stepping on the toes of the other judges.

Some staff attorneys write very well—where by "very well" I mean not elegantly or brilliantly or engrossingly but merely clearly in the sense of conveying meaning intelligibly to the intended audience. But others don't write very well; and some don't *consistently* write well. The intended audience for staff attorneys' writings is in the first instance judges whom the staff attorneys are advising, but in the second instance it is or should be the litigants who will be affected by the judges' rulings, rulings influenced by and not infrequently drafted by staff attorneys. I'll be arguing that the court is failing to communicate effectively with the litigants whose cases are evaluated in the first and often final instance by our staff attorneys.

I blame the communicative inadequacies of staff attorneys' memos and draft orders and other writings in part on the writing programs of the law schools. Those programs are taught principally by adjuncts who unduly emphasize punctuation (with emphasis for example on not accidentally italicizing periods, even though italicized periods are indistinguishable to the naked eye from roman ones) and command compliance with the citation rules set forth in the *Bluebook* (a 600-page horror: see my recent book *The Federal Judiciary: Strengths and Weaknesses* 46-48, 61-64 (2017)). And no doubt in part—probably larger part—the inadequacies of legal writing by staff attorneys as by other lawyers are a cultural phenomenon rather than anything special to law—an aspect of a general decline in the emphasis that schools and colleges, including law schools, place on writing skills, a cultural decline, reaching deeply into the school system (see, e.g., Dana Goldstein, "Why Kids Can't Write," *New York Times, Education Life*, p. 8, Aug. 6, 2017), that appears to be related to the growth of fast, low-cost consumer electronic communication. We're rapidly becoming—the young particularly—a nation of semi-literates. See, e.g., "7 Charts That Show How Americans Spend Their Time," https://www.vox.com/2014/4/11/5553006/how-americans-spend-their-time-in-6-charts.

Moreover, the staff attorneys' caseloads often are too heavy—and so the courts need more staff attorneys, though budgetary limitations may preclude obtaining more (though I doubt it—for we'll see that some of the federal courts of appeals have more, sometimes many more, staff attorneys than we do), and so for now the need is to provide guidance on writing well to the staff attorneys we have, where "well" means not elegantly but merely clearly and promptly and accurately and fast. Some effort is I grant being made to provide our new staff attorneys with instruction in writing well—every year both our supervisory staff attorneys and some of our judges try to teach newly hired staff attorneys how to write well. But the effectiveness of the instruction wanes quickly; it rarely lasts for the entire two-year terms of the staff attorneys, and therefore the instruction should be repeated, or amplified, during their terms, perhaps every six months—but probably more frequently.

But what *form* should the instruction take? There are reasons to doubt the efficacy of verbal instruction in writing, lectures on good writing, and instructional books directed at lawyers, such as Stephen V. Armstrong and Timothy P. Terrell, *Thinking Like a Writer: A Lawyer's Guide to Effective Writing and Editing* (Kindle Edition 2009); George D. Gopen, *The Sense of Structure: Writing from the Reader's Perspective* (2004); Ross Guberman, *Point Taken: How to Write Like the World's Best Judges* (2015); and Antonin Scalia and Bryan A. Garner, *Making Your Case: The Art of Persuading Judges* (2008). The problem is not that these books are inaccurate or badly written; they're not; it's that their length and detail are likely to muddle the reader. And the evidence for this is that of the literally thousands of briefs that I've read or skimmed in my 35 years as a judge, I have found few to be well written; most have been verbose, repetitive, and inarticulate. Intelligent people—and most of the lawyers who appear in our court are intelligent—can learn to write well by writing, and criticizing their and others' writing and being criticized by readers for their writing. But I don't think many of them can be *taught* to write well by reading books that claim to be able to teach lawyers to write well.

A useful experiment therefore might be to instruct new staff attorneys in *self*-instruction—explain to them that after drafting a memorandum or order they should read it through very slowly, looking for and striking, when found, the following deficiencies: words that are too long, or are ambiguous because of multiple meanings, or that are simply obscure; long sentences; interrupters such as unnecessary citations and quotations; repetition; superfluity; unnecessary jargon; leaning too heavily on citations to judicial opinions that do not apply the law to facts sufficiently similar to the facts of the cases that are the subject of the memos and draft orders; and succumbing to grammatical errors and poor organization.

A possible motto for my suggested approach to improving the staff attorneys' writing skills is a *bon mot* by the distinguished Anglo-American editor Harold Evans, quoted in a review of his recent book *Do I Make Myself Clear? Why Writing Well Matters*: "What really matters is making your meaning clear beyond a doubt." (The review is by Jim Holt and is entitled "The Man With the Red Pencil: Harold Evans, editor par excellence, explains why good writing is a moral issue," *New York Times*, Book Review section, May 21, 2017, p. 24.) Properly trained, properly motivated staff attorneys should be able to make the meaning of their orders and memos clear to those pro se appellants and petitioners and movants who should be the ultimate readers of what staff attorneys write.

Granted, some people simply can't learn to write well. But few staff attorneys fall into that category. The reason is that serving as a federal staff attorney has become a coveted job, which done well imparts a career boost. The two-year stint that is typical in our court (not in every federal court of appeals, however—it is substantially longer in many of those courts) provides experience highly valued by many law firms and government legal agencies, and as a result many staff attorneys can look forward to lucrative future employment in the private or public (less lucrative, but often more prestigious and satisfying) sector. And while the salaries of two-year staff attorneys are modest (I give some figures shortly), career staff attorneys, who often occupy supervisory positions, are usually paid at least $100,000 a year and often significantly more.

Rarely are the writing deficiencies of staff attorneys attributable to intellectual deficiency, laziness, or boredom, or even to overwork, but rather to lack of adequate practice, or experience, in writing well—in particular lack of experience or feel for communicating clearly with unsophisticated readers, as most pro se's are. And that lack can be rectified by careful instruction within the staff attorney program—including self-instruction. (Small suggestion: careful placement, which has become rare, of the word "only." Suppose I say I only eat fruits. Read literally this could mean that eating fruits is my only activity, which is hardly plausible. But if instead I say I eat only fruits, I make clear that eating fruits is not the only thing I do, though it may be the only thing I eat.)

Lately my friend Gary Peeples has introduced me to "Judge G's Writing Rules." Judge G is Judge Ronald Lee Gilman of the Sixth Circuit Court of Appeals, who has ingeniously decomposed writing instruction into a multitude of short, sensible, readily comprehensible rules, which I strongly recommend to law clerks, staff attorneys, lawyers, and judges as superior to the books I cited earlier. For a brilliant summary of the rules, see "Effective Brief Writing," in U.S. Court of Appeals Judge Ronald Lee Gilman, "How to Magically Win on Appeal," Federal Bar Association Seminar, Oct. 28, 2016, www.fedbar.org/Image-Library/Memphis-Mid-South-Chapter/Judge-Gilman--How-to-Magically-Win-on-Appeal.aspx-?FT=.pdf. Unfortunately, because of the number of his rules and their cumulative length I have had to group them in an appendix that directly precedes the index to this book.

In the spring of 2017 I carefully examined 39 staff attorney memos that had been submitted to me (as to other members of the court—for most of the court's decisions are by panels of judges rather than by individual judges) within the space of a few weeks for a vote on the staff attorneys' recommendations. Of these memos 21 were competently written and their recommended disposition was persuasive. The other 18, however—almost half—were badly written (though the recommended *disposition*—the bottom line so to speak—was often persuasive notwithstanding the inferior prose, for analysis and articulation are separate skills). They needed to be, but hadn't been, rewritten before they would be ready to be shown either to judges asked to approve them or to the litigants. Besides discussing several of the badly written memos with their authors I wrote extensive comments on all those memos, amounting to editing them. A few pages on I reproduce my comments on several of them—one very badly written, the others not very badly written but very definitely improvable.

Staff attorney memos, draft orders, etc. are as I've said submitted to and reviewed by judges. But it is rare for a judge of this court to concern himself or herself with the writing style of such documents; and that is unfortunate because the staff attorneys need to write better for the sake of the litigants, so many of whom have limited education; and one way in which they can learn to write better is for the documents they submit to judges to be reviewed *for style* by the judges. A great deal of judicial writing is by law clerks rather than by judges, and there is no doubt that some law clerks are better writers than their judges, and some who are not do the writing anyway because the judges don't want to bother to write. Few judges, however, have the time or inclination for editing staff attorneys' memos, or sparing their law clerks to do so. Which is why my undertaking to review and improve staff attorneys' memos and draft orders would not have stepped on the toes of any of my judicial colleagues—I only wish I'd made that clearer and managed to persuade the chief judge to allow me try out my plan.

Complications in rectifying the writing difficulties of staff attorneys include not only differences among judges in stylistic sensitivity but also differences in their drafting preferences—differences that impair uniformity among the ultimately issued orders. Some judges of our court (not I, though) want the order as issued to include an introductory footnote which states: "We have agreed to decide this case without oral argument because the briefs and record adequately present the facts and legal arguments, and oral argument would not significantly aid the court." That language is derived from, and indeed is materially identical to, language in Rule 34(a)(2)(C) of the Federal Rules of Appellate Procedure, *which in its entirety states that* "oral argument must be allowed in every case unless a panel of three judges who have examined the briefs and record unanimously agrees that oral argument is unnecessary for any of the following reasons: (A) the appeal is frivolous; (B) the dispositive issue or issues have been authoritatively decided; or (C) the facts and legal arguments are adequately presented in the briefs and record, and the decisional process would not be significantly aided by oral argument." Oral argument is in any event rare in pro se cases, since by definition the pro se has no lawyer, though very occasionally the court will recruit a lawyer for him.

Some judges want an opening orientation paragraph in the order issued by them in a pro se case that has been processed (as most pro se cases are) by a staff attorney. Some think staff attorneys should be citing legal authority and the district court record more often than they do. Some want a more robust or frequent use of a separate cover memo, prepared by a staff attorney, that precedes the actual draft order and usually is addressed just to the judge and not to the parties to the case.

I don't criticize judges for having variant tastes regarding staff attorneys' recommendations. Judges even of the same court tend to differ significantly from each other regarding their approaches to their jobs, in part because of different backgrounds and experiences, differences in age, policy, values, intelligence, patience, and so forth. One response to variance in judges' preferences regarding the structure or wording of staff attorney orders is to encourage the panels of judges to assign one of the judges to take primary responsibility for the case, in recognition that the decision recommended to the panel by a staff attorney before a conference with the panel will not reflect the preferences of all the judges but instead will be a default approach that may omit for example a Rule 34 footnote, citations to the record, or an opening orientation paragraph; it will then be up to the assigned judge to accept or reject some or all of the staff attorney's suggested alterations.

But that is not a realistic, let alone a complete, solution to the problem of communication from the court to the pro se litigants whose submissions are evaluated in the first instance by staff attorneys. For even after peer review and review by supervisory staff attorneys, the memos and draft orders that our staff attorneys prepare and submit to us judges for decision are often in need of further editing—editing that the submissions are unlikely to receive from the judges, however. For the judges, wanting to economize on time and rarely much interested in pro se's, especially when they are prison or jail inmates as they so often are, rarely bother to forward a staff attorney's memo or draft order to the pro se litigant rather than simply issuing a simple order granting or denying, with or without a sentence or two explaining why, the relief the litigant is seeking.

And that is the most serious problem with the current program. I have already suggested that the staff attorney's memo or draft order or other written submission to the judge or panel of judges assigned to a pro se's case should be sent to the pro se along with the judge's or panel's decision to grant or deny the relief sought by the pro se, and often it is not. But here I add that mine is not just a good idea; it's essential. The court's order is unlikely to tell the pro se why he lost or won his appeal—indeed it may dispose of his case in two words (I have often seen this), such as **PETITION DENIED**. And that tells him nothing. He needs to know *why* the court ruled as it did, for without that information he won't know what to do next—abandon his attempt to obtain relief from his present predicament, which might for example be a very long prison term, very unpleasant and even likely to involve dangerous conditions of confinement, an excessively long period of supervised release, or inadequate health care (very common in the prisons in the Seventh Circuit)—or explore some alternative avenue of relief, for often there is one or more alternative routes to the alleviation of the miseries of incarceration. The necessary information can easily be included in a staff attorney's memo. But not only must the memo be sent to the pro se with the court's decision order; it must be written at a level and with the care that will make the memo informative to the recipient. And it is in the production of such documents that many staff attorneys need practice and instruction.

To ensure that the staff attorney's document is accurate and intelligible to the pro se, a further level of review of such documents is required. And it should be uniform review, not left to the particular judge or panel that is responsible for deciding the case—and uniform review means as a practical matter review by one person. But could one person—I for example—review all the documents that our staff attorneys submit to judges? Yes, if review is limited to cases presented by staff attorneys to judges for decision. Roughly half the Seventh Circuit's decisions fall in that category. In 2016 the total number of cases decided by our court was 2,309 (source: *U.S. Courts of Appeals—Judicial Business* 2016, Table B-3A, www.uscourts.gov/statistics-reports/us-courts-appeals-judicial-business-2016). Half of that would be 1,154 or 1,155, which divided by the number of weeks (52) in a normal year amounts to a shade over 22 a week.

I informed the chief judge that I'd consider it a privilege, an honor, and a treat to be assigned to review, to edit, 22 staff attorney memos or other drafts every week; and as I am a *very* experienced writer and was when I suggested to the chief judge that I undertake such a project, I was and am confident that I'd do a good job. I wouldn't be stepping on the toes of the other judges, because I would not be performing the review function as a judge, but serving rather as a part-time member of the staff attorney program. I would be, as noted earlier, the third tier of review: peer review, supervisory staff attorney review, Posner review. I would be in effect another Fridkin assistant. I would not be the decider of *anything*, any more than he is; I would not be voting on whether to grant or deny relief to the pro se applicant but merely advising on how to make sure that the pro se was well informed of the court's reasons for affirming or reversing the district judge's decision. The judge or panel assigned to decide the case would be free to reject my advice, my edits, and make their own revisions—or no revisions—of the staff attorney's submission—though I would hope that my revision of the staff attorney's memo would satisfy the deciding judge or panel *and be included in any order sent to the pro se*. That is *very* important because, as I keep repeating, I am convinced that we owe it to the pro se's to explain, in language they can understand, the reason or reasons for our decision, whether the decision is to affirm or reverse the district court's order.

I emphasize that I was just proposing an experiment—surely worth trying, but, if it failed, easily discarded. I don't understand why the chief judge rejected it, but as a result has made me pessimistic that staff attorney draft orders and memos, and judicial memos based on staff attorneys' draft orders and memos, will attain adequate writing quality in the Seventh Circuit.

It is notable that as shown in the table (next page) there is a high rate of agreement between the judges and the staff attorneys regarding the proper disposition of pro se cases (though the chart is incomplete because I don't have accurate statistics for all the categories of cases handled by our staff attorneys). The significance of such agreement is that it indicates that judges generally agree with staff attorneys' memos, and I would expect them (which is to say us, for I am one of them) to be all the more willing to do so the higher the quality of those memos.

Further on the subject of interaction between judges and staff attorneys, I point out that in Rule 34 conferences—which remember are conferences between staff attorneys and judges in which the judges go over the staff attorneys' memos—the memos as amended by the judges are usually the foundation for the orders issued to the pro se applicants, and so the applicants receive much more feedback than when the order is merely a bare conclusion (e.g., **PETITION DENIED**—I would call that zero feedback), or a conclusion with no more than one or two sentences of explanation.

On a separate front, the staff attorneys would benefit from hearing directly from judges what the judges think about the bench memos prepared by staff attorneys for short-argument days. Judge Manion's practice of meeting with staff individually before a short-argument day is time-consuming for him but helpful for

---

Percentages of motions in which staff attorneys request that relief be granted (first figure) versus percentages granted by the judges (second figure):

Counseled petitions for permission to appeal under Fed. R. Civ. P. 23(f) from an order of a district court granting or denying class action certification:

25.64%	26.50%

Counseled petitions for permission to appeal under 28 U.S.C. § 1292(b):

53.85%	56.41%

Counseled petitions for permission to appeal under 28 U.S.C. § 1453(c)

40%	40%

In forma pauperis motions in PLRA (Prison Litigation Reform Act) cases

20.16%	20.56%

In forma pauperis motions in non-PLRA (Prison Litigation Reform Act) cases

10.76%	10.76%

Motions to appoint or recruit counsel

8.77%	9.36%

---

staff, and I would hope the other judges would emulate his practice.

Let me close this discussion by recapitulating, but also adding, a few suggestions for the staff attorneys:

1. Delete the conventional first footnote (on oral argument, Rule 34(a)(2)) in cases in which the appellant does not request oral argument; in cases in which he or she does request it but there are compelling reasons to deny the request, explain the reasons, fitted to the case rather than boilerplate.

2. Limit review of a staff attorney's draft order to one person.

3. The order should not begin with the announcement of the result. That creates the impression that the judges decided first, then thought of reasons for the decision.

4. The order should be in simple English, not legal jargon. Citations should be kept to a minimum.

5. There should not be a separate memorandum expressing doubts or uncertainty about the draft order. Any significant points made in such a memorandum should instead be incorporated in the draft order.

6. The Flesch test, the test of readability mentioned earlier, should be applied to every draft order in a pro se's appeal to make sure the order is intelligible to a pro se. On the nature and use of the test see, e.g., www.readability./flesch-reading-ease-readability-formula.php; or else Google Flesch. Downloading and use of the test are free of charge.

Chapter 6

Improving Output

Illustrative of the staff attorney writing problem in my court are several recent staff attorney memos that I have spent a good deal of time going over with the aim of improving each one to the point of making it fully accessible, meaningful, and intelligible to the pro se who was appealing, and that I print below. I leave it to the reader to decide whether I succeeded in the endeavor. Passages in the first memo that I've italicized are passages that I believe should have been deleted (the italicization is intended simply to make the passages clearer to the reader) as mere surplusage or clearly unsound. Passages in black are either passages added by me to the memo in an effort to improve it, or comments on the memo; context will show which are which. Finally the names of the staff attorneys are omitted, as they are throughout the book, to spare them embarrassment; for their errors, their deficiencies, are not willful. Here is the first memo:

TO: Judge Posner, Judge Kanne, Judge Hamilton
FROM: [Omitted]
RE: Short Argument Day, April 25, 2017
DATE: April 18, 2017
RECOMMENDATION: AFFIRM

No. 16-2471

MICHAEL DAVIS, *Plaintiff-Appellant,*	Appeal from the United States District Court for the Central District of Illinois.
v.	No. 13-1462
DONALD MORONEY, *et al., Defendants-Appellees.*	Sara Darrow, *Judge.*

BENCH MEMORANDUM

Michael Davis, an inmate at Illinois Pontiac Correctional Center, sued a guard, Donald Moroney, for *allegedly* using excessive force against him, but the district court dismissed the suit for failure to prosecute. Davis now challenges the denial of *a subsequent* motion for relief from judgment under Federal Rule of Civil Procedure 60(b). *He* argues that exceptional circumstances warrant relief from the judgment, principally because his alleged mental impairment prevented him from prosecuting the case without counsel. *Because I [i.e., the staff attorney] conclude that the district court did not abuse its discretion in denying the motion, I recommend affirming.*

Background
    Davis filed this suit under 42 U.S.C. § 1983 in 2013 against **guard Moroney along with the prison's warden and other prison officials** responsible for the prison's grievance process. In his complaint Davis alleged that **while** speaking with another inmate **he** accidentally bumped into Moroney, apologized *to Moroney, but Moroney hit him in the jaw, throat, and chest. (Id. at 5.)* Moroney then twisted his arm behind his back, slammed his head into a wall, and *placed him in* [sic] handcuffed him. *(Id. at 5–6.)* The other defendants, in an effort to cover up Moroney's assault, conspired to deny him access to the prison's grievance procedure by failing to process and return his grievances. *(Id. at 9–13.)* Davis *then* asked the district court to recruit counsel **for him**, stating that he "had to

obtain complete assistance" to prepare his complaint. *(Appellant's Br. App. at 3.)* He **had** tried to secure counsel on his own, he added, and referred to a letter from a law firm corroborating his attempt to obtain representation, **but no** letter was attached to his motion. *(Id.)*

The district court screened Davis's complaint, see 28 U.S.C. § 1915A, and allowed **him** to proceed on his excessive-force claim *against Moroney. (Appellant's Br. App. at 6–7.)* But the court dismissed **the** conspiracy claim against the other defendants **on the ground that** Davis **had no** federal constitutional right to a grievance procedure and **therefore** could not "present a meritorious claim." *(Id. at 7.)* The court also denied Davis's motion for counsel because he had not demonstrated that he **had** made a reasonable attempt to obtain counsel. *(Id.)*

Discovery ensued, but Davis failed to respond to interrogatories concerning his attempts to exhaust his administrative remedies. Moroney moved to compel discovery.*(Doc. 9, Motion to Compel.)* Two months later Davis responded by again requesting counsel, stating that he had a mental illness and was unable to aid the inmate who was preparing his court filings. *(Appellant's Br. App. at 10–12.)* Davis attached *to his motion* an affidavit from the assisting inmate, Claude McGee, who asserted that "[i]t is almost common knowledge that Mr. Davis has a mental illness" and that Davis's "judgment is substantially impaired, along with his perceptions of reality, all of which rendered it essentially impractical to effectively communicate with Mr. Davis to meet deadlines, [or to] fully and fairly participate in the discovery process." *(Appellant's Br. App. at 13–14.) Another* two months later, the district court denied Davis's request for counsel because he had not demonstrated that he'd tried to secure counsel on his own and because his claim was "not unduly complex and relies largely on information of his personal knowledge." *(Appellant's Br. App. at 17.)* The court allowed Davis 21 more days to respond to the interrogatories. *(Id.)*

On the twenty-first day, Davis renewed his motion for counsel, *(Appellant's Br. App. at 18–21),* asserting that the case was difficult for him because he **reads at** a 6th-grade *reading* level, lacks communication skills, and has a "paranoid delusional disorder." *(Id.*

at 19.) He also attached his "legal mail card," which cataloged his incoming and outgoing mail to a number of law firms. *(Id. at 21.)* And he asked the court to order the prison to turn over his medical records. *(Id. at 19.)* **Meanwhile,** having received still no response to his interrogatories, **Moroney** filed another motion to compel discovery. *(Doc. 13, 2nd Mot. to Compel.)*

The district **judge** took no action for nine months, **then** issued a scheduling order stating that "there are no pending issues requiring discussion." *(Doc. 14, Scheduling Order, at 1.)* **The order directed** Moroney to provide Davis with, among other things, Davis's "relevant medical records" and "relevant grievances and all responses to those grievances." *(Id. at 3.)*

One month later Moroney filed a motion to dismiss **Davis's suit** under FED. R. CIV. P. 41(b) for lack of prosecution *(Doc. 17, Mot. to Dismiss)*, because Davis still had not answered the interrogatories. The district **judge promptly** issued **two** orders: the first denied Davis's renewed motion for counsel on the ground that his "claim is not unduly complex and relies largely on information within his personal knowledge," and instructed Davis to request his medical records through his institution *(Appellant's Br. App. at 22)*—**whatever that means**—and the second warned Davis that the case would be dismissed unless he filed answers to Moroney's interrogatories within 14 days. *(Appellant's Br. App. at 23.)*

Twenty days later Davis filed a motion to reconsider the denial of his motion for appointment of counsel *(Appellant's Br. App. at 24–31)*, but did not respond to the interrogatories. The district court **then** granted Moroney's motion to dismiss **Davis's suit,** explaining that he'd failed to comply with **the judge's** orders directing him to respond to the interrogatories. *(Appellant's Br. App. at 32.)* The **judge** also denied Davis's motion to reconsider [**what exactly?**] as moot. *(Id.)*

Twenty-eight days later, on October 29, 2015, Davis filed a "Motion to Reconsider/Reinstate Cause" and argued that the court had disregarded his "possible mental impairments" that prevented him from effectively litigating his case. *(Appellant's Br. App. at 34.)* He also asked the court for more time to find an attorney. *(Id. at*

34–35.) The court did not find Davis's arguments "persuasive" and **so** denied the motion. *(Appellant's Br. App. at 37.)*

Nine days later Davis filed a Rule 59(e) motion to alter or amend the judgment, stating that he was "extremely slow mentally," that he lacked the ability "to produce any form of effort to pursue this cause," and that the circumstances were exceptional because he had "insufficient knowledge of any complexity of the case" and could not represent himself. *(Appellant's Br. App. at 38–41.)* The court denied this motion the next day as untimely, pointing out that Davis had missed the 28-day deadline for making a "genuine" motion under FED. R. CIV. P. 59(e). *(Appellant's Br. App. at 42.)*

Five months later, Davis filed another motion for counsel (his fourth) based on his mental deficiencies. *(Doc. 24, Mot[ion]. for Counsel.)* He mentioned that his I.Q. score was under 73 and that he could not understand Moroney's pleadings. *(Id. at 1–2.)* The court denied the motion, presumably because the case had been dismissed, but noted that it was not clear whether Davis intended to request counsel for an appeal. *(Text Order, 4/1/2016.)*

Two months later Davis again moved for relief from judgment, under FED. R. CIV. P. 60(b)(1) and (b)(6), **again mentioning his mental shortcomings.** He stated that he has an I.Q. of 66 and the "mind of a child" *(Id. at 43–44)*, is barely literate, and could not meet the court's deadlines without aid or supervision. *(Id.)* In light of these difficulties (as well as his inability to understand Moroney's interrogatories), he added, the court should have appointed counsel *(Id. at 44–45)* **for him.**

In May 2016 the district court denied his motion for relief from the judgment, **noting that Davis had not responded** to Moroney's interrogatories despite two orders directing him to do so, and **Moroney's defense** had been prejudiced by Davis's failure to respond. *(Id.)*

Analysis

The only issue in this appeal, as agreed by the parties, concerns the denial of Davis's Rule 60(b) motion. Assisted by counsel that this court recruited *(No. 16-2471, Order of July 7, 2016)*, Davis argues that the district **judge** wrongly decided that motion because

she didn't account for his exceptional circumstances—specifically, his mental impairments. *(Appellant's Br. at 14–.)* Davis also contends that **like the plaintiff in** *Donald v. Cook County Sheriff's Department*, 95 F.3d 548 (7th Cir. 1996), his difficulty litigating this case **has stemmed** from the district court's handling of **it**—specifically the judge's direction in **her** scheduling order that Moroney provide Davis with his medical records and grievance forms and **the judge's** delay in responding both to Moroney's second motion to compel and Davis's renewed motion for counsel. *(Id. at 15, 18–21.)*

The controlling issue is whether Davis has established a basis for relief under Fed. R. Civ. P. 60(b), **which so far as relates to this case allows a court to relieve a party from a final judgment on grounds of "excusable neglect" (Rule 60(b)(1), or "any other reason that justifies relief" (60(b)(6). While relief under Rule 60(b) has been described as "an extraordinary remedy ... granted only in exceptional circumstances,"** *Bakery Machine & Fabrication, Inc. v. Traditional Baking, Inc.*, **570 F.3d 845, 848 (7th Cir. 2009), the circumstances of this case are extraordinary, notably Davis's intellectual limitations.**

Davis also argues that the district court did not properly consider his impairments and lack of resources in its denials of his motions for counsel. (Appellant's Br. at 17–18.) His argument may have been compelling if it had been made in a direct appeal from the judgment but, as Moroney points out, Davis may not use Rule 60(b) to circumvent the time limit for filing appeals. See Mendez v. Republic Bank, 725 F.3d 651, 660 (7th Cir. 2013). He could have presented his arguments in a timely appeal of the underlying dismissal, see, e.g., Henderson v. Ghosh, 755 F.3d 559 (7th Cir. 2014), but the time for filing such an appeal expired in November 2015, and he didn't file his Rule 60(b) motion until May 2016.

Davis next argues that the district court erred by not considering his October 19, 2015, motion to reconsider—filed 28 days after the entry of judgment—as a motion under Rule 59(e). (Appellant's Br. at 21–24.) He contends that the district court did not evaluate that motion under the proper standard and as a result he may not have understood that he should have filed an appeal. (Id.

at 24.) But as Moroney points out, this court lacks jurisdiction to consider the district court's denial of the motion because Davis did not file a timely notice of appeal. (Appellee's Br. at 27–31.) The district court denied the motion on October 20, 2015, and Davis did not file a notice of appeal until June 13, 2016, well beyond the permitted 30 days. See FED. R. APP. P. 4(a)(1)(A). That limit is jurisdictional with no equitable exceptions, see *Bowles v. Russell*, 551 U.S. 205, 214 (2007); *Bell v. McAdory*, 820 F.3d 880, 882–83 (7th Cir. 2016).

The staff attorney recommends affirming the district court's denial of the motion, but while he makes **plausible points they are outweighed by the equities in favor of Davis stemming from his severe intellectual limitations, coupled with his lack of legal assistance; and while review of a district court's denial of a Rule 60(b) motion is deferential, if the judge is "very far off base ... or omitted to consider some important relevant factor," the denial cannot stand. *Tolliver v. Northrop Co.*, 786 F.2d 316, 319 (7th Cir. 1986). And that is this case. Notably the district judge accorded undue weight to Davis's failure to respond to Moroney's interrogatories—given that the interrogatories were little better than a ploy aimed at a person incapable of responding intelligently. The information sought included "the number of grievances you wrote related to the issues in your complaint; ... the date on which you wrote each grievance[;] the date(s) of submission of each grievance to your counselor; the date(s) of submission of each grievance to the Grievance Officer; the date(s) of submission of each grievance to the Administrative Review Board; whether you submitted the grievance(s) to anyone else; the manner in which you submitted the grievance(s) at each level; The name of any person to whom you gave the grievance(s) at each level of the process; the date(s) of response(s) at any level; the date(s) of final determination(s) by the Administrative Review Board; and whether you are in possession of any grievance(s) or grievance response(s) related to this lawsuit. If you are not, state why you are not."

Not only did most of these questions exceed Davis's intellectual capacity to answer, but *all* the information requested** from Davis resided in the files of the prison and were thus immediately accessible by Moroney. Davis was unlikely to have retained the dates demanded by Moroney, copies of the grievances he had submitted, or the names of most of the persons to whom he had submitted his grievances, or to understand "each level of the process." But as a member of the prison's staff and in cahoots with the other defendants, Moroney had access to *everything* Davis had filed with the prison administration and so had no need to seek information from Davis, a quest that amounted to harassment of a mental defective.

To test whether Davis, given his mental handicaps, could have understood all or at least most of the orders he received both from the district judge and from Moroney, one of my law clerks conducted an experiment using the Flesch Reading Ease Readability Formula. Downloadable free of charge from the Internet (see, e.g., Readability Formulas, "The Flesch Reading Ease Readability Formula," www.readabilityformulas.com/flesch-reading-ease-readability-formula.php (visited May 1, 2017)) and included in the commonly used word-processing program Microsoft Word, the Flesch test is used to estimate the difficulty of understanding a given text. The formula is simple: it measures the ratio of syllables to words, and words to sentences, in the text; the higher those ratios the more difficult the text is to understand. Of course other characteristics of a text contribute to how difficult it is to understand; in complex, sophisticated texts—James Joyce's novel *Finnegans Wake,* for example—two syllables, or two words, of the same length may differ greatly in difficulty of comprehension. (To illustrate quite at random, four lines below "pectoral" on one of the pages of Joyce's novels appears the word "alebrill," but knowing what pectoral means won't help you to understand alebrill, or the sentence in which it appears.)

But legal texts are rarely that difficult, and when they are not the Flesch formula is a helpful heuristic that correlates with difficulty. For example, the average ratios of random samples of the *Harvard Law Review* are higher than the average ratios of random samples of *Time* magazine; thus, *Harvard Law Review* is more difficult to read. See Rudolf Flesch, *How to Write Plain English* 26 (1979). Having determined how difficult the text is, the Flesch formula translates that score into a prediction of what educational level a reader would have to have attained in order to be able to understand the text.

The Flesch test applied to Moroney's interrogatories reveals that comprehension of the interrogatories requires reading ability consistent with having completed 8th, maybe 9th, grade in school. The most optimistic assessment of Davis's reading ability is that he can read at a 6th-grade level, and the Flesch test suggests that a 6th-grade level is too low to enable a person to understand the interrogatories.

Davis in short needs help—he needs a lawyer badly. He did not have a fair opportunity to prosecute his case. As in *Donald v. Cook County Sheriff's Dept.*, 95 F.3d 548, 554 (1996), "the plaintiff's difficulties are traceable in considerable part to the way the matter was handled by the district court." The district judge, although purporting to apply the standard for deciding whether to recruit pro bono counsel set out in *Pruitt v. Mote*, 503 F.3d 647 (7th Cir. 2007) (en banc), ignored *Pruitt's* emphasis on the need to consider whether the *particular* plaintiff is competent to litigate his own claims, including whether he is competent to "prepar[e] and respond[] to motions and other court filings" himself. *Id.* at 655.

In combination, the plaintiff's severe intellectual handicaps, his apparently diligent efforts to pursue his case despite those handicaps, his potentially meritorious claim, and the irregularities of the district court's handling of the case, amount to "extraordinary circumstances" justifying relief from the final judgment under Rule 60(b)(6) of the Federal Rules of Civil Procedure. See *Ramirez v. United States*, 799 F.3d 845, 851 (7th Cir. 2015); *Donald v. Cook County Sheriff's Dept.*, 95 F.3d at 554. The denial of Davis's motion for relief from final judgment is therefore reversed and the case remanded for further proceedings consistent with the analysis in this opinion.

REVERSED AND REMANDED.

Before leaving *Davis v. Moroney*, I want to point out how the staff attorney's memorandum evolved in the course of preparation. The first version of the memo, the version that immediately preceded peer review by a fellow staff attorney, was two pages longer than the two later versions; its introductory paragraph differed substantially from the introductory paragraph of the two later versions; and it emphasized the procedural posture of the case—an appeal from a denial of a Rule 60(b) motion to reopen the case—and withheld from the reader any description of the underlying nature of the case or the issue on appeal. The second version incorporated the peer-review edits and immediately preceded supervisory review by a supervisory staff attorney. The third version is the one that was sent to me after the staff attorney adopted edits from both his peer and his supervisor. In all three versions the substantive analysis of the issue presented by the case—whether the plaintiff's mental impairments warrant reopening the case—occupies less than a third of the memo. The issue is never even precisely identified in the first version; the other memos restate facts from the briefs, the parties' positions, or general propositions of law.

Although the memo in the next case, as originally received by me from the staff attorney (a different staff attorney from the author of the memo in the *Davis* case), was shorter and better written than the first, it still needed work in order to be fully intelligible to the pro se petitioner. Here is that memo before I altered it (much less than I altered the first one):

MOTIONS MEMORANDUM

Petition for writ of mandamus
TO:	Judge Posner
FROM:	Name omitted
RE:	*In re Kenneth Lewis*, No. 17-1843
DATE:	May 19, 2017
PANEL:	Judges Bauer, Posner, Flaum
RECOMMENDATION:	DENY petition

I present this petition to you [those are the staff attorney's words in his memo] because it was filed when you [meaning me—Judge Posner] were on the motions panel. This mandamus petition relates to *United States v. Lewis*, nos. 14-2442, 14-2597 (7th Cir. April 20, 2016), in which this court affirmed Kenneth Lewis's conviction for wire fraud, vacated his conviction for money laundering upon the concession of the government that it had insufficient evidence to sustain the conviction, and remanded the case for resentencing on only the wire fraud conviction. The district judge (Judge Shadid] resentenced Lewis on August 17, 2016, to 125 months' imprisonment, 3 years' supervised release, and restitution of approximately $5.5 million. The district court entered an amended judgment on August 22, 2016. Lewis never filed a direct appeal from the resentencing; the appeal would have been due September 5, 2016.

Lewis later filed a petition for mandamus in this court, challenging both the resentencing and the conviction. This court denied the petition. *In re Kenneth Lewis,* No. 16-3229 (7th Cir. Sept. 29, 2016).

Lewis now files another petition for writ of mandamus. Most of his contentions relate to matters that predate his first appeal, however. For example, he complains that Judge Shadid relied on an inaccurate presentence report in 2014 at Lewis's initial sentencing, which was vacated by this court. He also complains that his arrest in 2012 was actually a kidnapping by the police. As relief, he asks this court to vacate his convictions. He had an opportunity to raise those challenges in his appeal. This court's decision to affirm his convictions forecloses further relief except through a properly filed petition for habeas corpus—see 28 U.S.C. § 2255.

Lewis also challenges Judge Shadid's calculation of the loss amount. But Lewis should have raised those contentions in a direct appeal from the resentencing, and he offers no reason why he did not—or was unable to—file a direct appeal from his resentence. These challenges also are not the proper subject of a mandamus petition. He could raise them in a timely filed habeas corpus petition.

Thus I [the staff attorney] recommend[s] denying his petition. I propose that the order state that most of Lewis's contentions were addressed in his first appeal, see *United States v. Lewis*, nos. 14-

2442, 14-2597, (7th Cir. April 20, 2016), and he did not file a timely direct appeal from his resentencing. He may, as noted above, raise challenges to his convictions and resentencing through a timely filed petition for habeas corpus.

Please let me know if I may provide further information or analysis. Judge Bauer and Judge Flaum have voted to deny the petition.

And here is the staff attorney's memo with my criticisms and suggested substitutions again in boldface, and bracketed, for clarity:

I **[the staff attorney]** present this petition to you **[the judge]** because it was filed when you were on the motions panel. This mandamus petition **[filed by a pro se]** relates to *United States v. Lewis*, nos. 14-2442, 14-2597, (7th Cir. April 20, 2016), in which this court affirmed Kenneth Lewis's conviction for wire fraud, vacated his conviction for money laundering upon the concession of the government that it had insufficient evidence to sustain the conviction, and remanded the case for resentencing on only the wire fraud conviction **[why resentence him?]**. The district court resentenced Lewis on August 17, 2016, to 125 months' imprisonment, 3 years' supervised release, and restitution of approximately $5.5 million. The district court entered an amended judgment on August 22, 2016. Lewis never filed a direct **[no need for "direct"]** appeal from the resentencing; the appeal would have **[had to be filed by]** September 5, 2016.

Lewis later filed a petition for mandamus in this court, challenging both the resentencing **[no, he challenged the new sentence, and the memo should explain what the new sentence was]** and the conviction. This court denied the petition. *In re Kenneth Lewis*, No. 16-3229 (7th Cir. Sept. 29, 2016).

Lewis now files **[no, has now filed]** another petition for writ of mandamus. Most of his contentions relate to matters that predate **[not pre-date]** his first appeal, however. For example, he complains that Judge Shadid relied on an inaccurate presentence report in 2014 at Lewis's initial sentencing, which was vacated by this court. **Lewis** also complains that his arrest in 2012 was actually a kidnapping by the police. As relief, he asks this court to vacate his convictions [**which convictions? Only one conviction, a conviction for wire fraud, has been mentioned**]. He had an opportunity to raise those challenges [**challenge, not challenges**] in his appeal [**but did not**]. This court's decision to affirm his convictions [**again, just one conviction**] forecloses further relief except through a properly filed petition for habeas corpus, **see** [**should be roman not italic**] 28 U.S.C. § 2255.

Lewis also challenges Judge Shadid's calculation of the [**alleged**] loss amount. But Lewis should have raised those contentions [**it's one contention, not several, so should not be plural**] in a direct [no need for **direct**] appeal from the resentencing [**not from the re-sentencing, but from the sentence imposed in the resentencing**], and Lewis does not offer any [**better would be offers no**] reason why he did not–or was unable to—file a direct appeal from his resentence [**no, from his second sentence**]. These challenges [**no, just one challenge**] also are [**is**] not the proper subject of a manda-mus petition, though he can raise them [**it**] in a timely filed habeas **corpus** petition.

Thus I recommend denying his petition. I propose that the or-der [**to be issued by the court in this case**] state that most of Lew-is's contentions were addressed in his first appeal, *United States v. Lewis*, nos. 14-2442, 14-2597 (7th Cir. April 20, 2016), and he did not file a timely **direct** [**should be omitted**] appeal from his resen-tencing [**again, from his second sentence, not from the process of resentencing**]. He may raise challenges to his convictions and resentencing through a timely filed petition for habeas corpus, *see* 28 U.S.C. § 2255.

Please let me know **if** [**should be whether**] I may provide fur-ther information or analysis. Judge[**s**] Bauer and Flaum [**not Judge Bauer and Judge Flaum**] have voted to deny the petition.

* * *

Another recent case that presents issues similar to those in *Da-vis* and *Lewis* is *Hoban v. Anderson, et al.*, 7th Cir No. 16-1246, an order (not an opinion, that is, not published, at least in the usual places, such as the *Federal Reporter*), issued on May 5, 2017, by a panel of three judges the day after the appeal had been filed. The order states (with some stylistic changes by me intended to make the order more readable):

Joseph Hoban, an Illinois prisoner, sued prison officials under 42 U.S.C. § 1983 on three claims: first, they subjected him to unlawful conditions of confinement while he was in segregation; second, they ignored his medical needs, also when he was in segregation; and third, they failed to protect him from a serious threat to his safety after he left segregation. We have agreed to decide the case without oral argument because the briefs and record adequately present the facts and legal arguments, and oral argument would not significantly aid the court. FED. R. APP. P. 34(a)(2) (C). The district court granted summary judgment in favor of the defendants. It ruled that some claims were time-barred, others were administratively unexhausted, and on another claim, he presented insufficient evidence from which a jury reasonably could find liability. We affirm the judgment in all respects.

Before Hoban arrived at Pontiac Correctional Center in September 2010, he had been injured and threatened by members of the Latin Kings gang at other prisons. At Pontiac he briefly received protective custody. About nine months after he arrived there, though, Hoban was found guilty of assaulting another inmate named Echols, who Hoban believed was a member of the Latin Kings. Hoban was punished with disciplinary segregation for six months, which took him out of protective custody.

During his first twelve days in segregation, Hoban experienced problems. He reports that his cell had feces and blood on the walls and mattress, was "stiflingly" hot, and had no running water, necessitating that he drink water from the toilet. As a result of these conditions, he says, he "broke out with some rashes" and experienced nausea, vomiting, and dehydration. Hoban suffers from bipolar disorder and depression; although he received medications for these conditions, he did not receive several of his other medications—antacids, painkillers, and medicated shampoo.

Hoban responded with his first of two grievances in this case. In this grievance he complained about his conditions of confinement, his inability to receive his medicines, and his conviction for

assaulting Echols. After twelve days in this cell, Hoban was transferred to a different segregation cell, where, he said, "[e]verything
worked and it was very clean." About three weeks later, Pontiac's
warden, Randy Pfister, denied the grievance. Hoban appealed, but
the Administrative Review Board rejected the appeal. With this
decision on September 13, 2011, Hoban exhausted his conditions-
of-confinement and medical-indifference claims.

While Hoban was still in segregation, he filed a second grievance. In it he sought to return to protective custody upon his release from segregation. The request was supported by his counselor,
but the prison lieutenant who reviewed the grievance, Edward Vilt,
recommended to Pfister that it be denied. Vilt reasoned that Hoban's "paranoia" created "a security concern for the other inmates
housed in the [protective custody unit]" and his [i.e., Hoban's]
fight with Echols was "not indicative of an inmate in need of protection." Pfister accepted the recommendation and denied Hoban
protective custody.

Hoban did not wait for the review process for his second grievance to conclude before filing a complaint in this suit, which principally raised failure-to-protect claims. He alleged that by denying
him protective custody Pfister and other named prison administrators had been deliberately indifferent to his safety. The district
court screened the complaint under 28 U.S.C. § 1915A(b)(1) and
dismissed it.

Hoban appealed, and we vacated the judgment because he had
pleaded plausible claims, overlooked by the district court, against
unnamed correctional officers. See *Hoban v. Godinez*, No. 12-1763,
2012 WL 5395186, at *2–3 (7th Cir. Nov. 6, 2012). We also ruled
that, since he alleged that Latin King members attacked him after
he gave a named defendant (Terri Anderson) a list of their names,
his claim against her could go forward.

Hoban meanwhile finished pursuing at the prison the exhaustion of his second grievance, the one that had raised his failure-to-
protect assertions. At his hearing before the Administrative Review
Board, he gave the Board's chairperson, Sherry Benton, a list of
names of Latin King inmates who, he said, "tried to murder" him
and photos of his "bloody" body after he had been attacked by Lat-

in King members at Cook County Jail. Benton nonetheless recommended to Anderson that she uphold the denial of Hoban's grievance requesting protective custody. As Benton explained, Hoban had no declared enemies on file; no other prisoners had declared him an enemy; Pfister had not found "sufficient verifiable information to warrant Protective Custody placement"; and Hoban was found guilty of attacking Echols, a Latin Kings member. Anderson accepted the recommendation and repeated these reasons for denying Hoban protective custody on February 8, 2012.

After his second grievance was denied, Hoban returned to the general population. He shared a cell with Michael Pinon, a Hells Angel member and self-proclaimed hit man for the Latin Kings. Before Pinon became Hoban's cellmate, Hoban warned the gallery officer not to put them in the same cell, but she disregarded the warning. According to Hoban, during the first night in their cell, Pinon "lunged" at him, starting a fight that resulted in "[s]ome scratches" to Hoban, but "nothing serious." The next morning Hoban reported the fight to a prison guard and was moved to a different cell.

Hoban amended his complaint on December 11, 2013. He restated failure-to-protect claims against Anderson and Pfister and added a failure-to-protect claim against Vilt who recall had recommended, before Hoban had filed his original complaint, against putting him in protective custody. Hoban also sued Vilt for exhibiting deliberate indifference to his medical needs while he was in disciplinary segregation. In addition he brought a failure-to-protect claim against Benton, who had recommended against protective custody after Hoban filed his original complaint. Finally Hoban added new claims against Pfister and Vilt, who, Hoban said, had rebuffed his complaints about the disciplinary segregation cell's "inhumane conditions."

The district court granted summary judgment in favor of all the defendants. Regarding the conditions-of-confinement and medical-indifference claims in the amended complaint, the court ruled them untimely under the applicable two-year statute of limitations. The court also ruled that Hoban had not exhausted his administrative remedies for his failure-to-protect claims against the defendants, other than Benton, because he had filed his original complaint against them before the Administrative Review Board had completed its grievance proceedings. The court further ruled that Hoban had not established a triable question on the merits against Benton.

On appeal Hoban first raises two arguments about the timeliness of the conditions-of-confinement and medical-indifference claims that he maintains on appeal. These claims first appeared in his complaint filed on December 11, 2013. According to him, the accrual date for these claims should have been in February 2012 (when his second grievance was exhausted). He is wrong. The district court correctly used September 13, 2011, the date that he exhausted his first grievance. That is the grievance that raises his complaints about the conditions of his cell in segregation and his inability to receive some of his medicines. The exhaustion of those claims ended the tolling of the statute of limitations that occurred during the administrative grievance process and triggered the two-year time limit to sue. *See Gomez v. Randle*, 680 F.3d 859, 864 (7th Cir. 2012).

By contrast his second grievance focused on his request for protective custody. Because Hoban filed these newly stated claims on December 11, 2013, and the filing deadline for these claims was September 13, 2013, the district court correctly found the claims time-barred.

Second, Hoban contends that the district court erred by not granting him equitable tolling for his conditions-of-confinement and medical-indifference claims. He asserts that his recruited lawyer "abandon[ed]" him for about eight months after these claims accrued. But his attorney's alleged neglect does not warrant tolling the statute of limitations because complying with the filing deadline was not attributable to an "extraordinary circumstance" outside of Hoban's "control." *Menominee Indian Tribe of Wis. v. United States*, 136 S. Ct. 750, 756 (2016). Tolling the statute of limitations based on his attorney's alleged negligence would render the limitation meaningless. See *Williams v. Sims*, 390 F.3d 958, 963 (7th Cir. 2004).

Hoban next challenges the grant of summary judgment to Benton on his claim that she was deliberately indifferent to the threat from Latin King members. He points to his affidavit stating that he gave her a list of Latin King inmates who "tried to murder" him and showed her pictures of his "bloody" body after attacks by the gang at Cook County Jail. Based on this evidence, he asserts that a jury reasonably could find that Benton knew that he faced a substantial risk of serious harm. He is incorrect because he declared in his affidavit that the Latin King inmates on his list were not at Pontiac Correctional Center (where he is incarcerated); they are all housed at Stateville and Menard Correctional Centers. Hoban's list of hostile inmates at other prisons is too vague a threat to his safety at Pontiac for a reasonable factfinder to conclude that Benton had "actual knowledge of impending harm" to him. *Dale v. Poston*, 548 F.3d 563, 569 (7th Cir. 2008) (internal quotation marks omitted). See also *Davis v. Scott*, 94 F.3d 444, 446–47 (8th Cir. 1996) (jury could not reasonably conclude that prison officials exhibited deliberate indifference by returning prisoner to "the general population" when "the inmates on [his] enemies list were no longer incarcerated" at the prison).

Hoban finally argues that he exhausted his administrative remedies for his failure-to-protect claims against other defendants, relying on *Barnes v. Briley*, 420 F.3d 673 (7th Cir. 2005). He understands *Barnes* to say that, even if a prisoner does not exhaust claims in his original complaint, the court may properly consider them in an amended complaint as long as the amended complaint contains an exhausted claim. The district court correctly concluded that 42 U.S.C. § 1997e(a) barred Hoban's failure-to-protect claims against Anderson and Pfister because those claims were not administratively exhausted when he first brought them in his original complaint. Hoban misreads *Barnes*, which held only that when filing an amended complaint, a prisoner may bring a claim newly *discovered* after filing the original complaint and administratively exhausted by the time of the amended complaint's filing. See *Barnes*, 420 F.3d at 678. All of the facts regarding Hoban's claim that Pfister failed to provide him with protective custody were known to him when he filed his original complaint. Moreover Hoban did not exhaust his claims against Pfister and Anderson before filing his original complaint. Because he is "time-barred by the prison's grievance policy from further pursuing administrative remedies for these events, he could do nothing to cure the failure to exhaust." *Hill v. Snyder*, 817 F.3d 1037, 1040 (7th Cir. 2016).

But this creates a problem: the district court granted summary judgment in favor Vilt on exhaustion grounds for the failure-to-protect claim even though he hadn't asked for that relief. Ordinarily before a district court enters summary judgment against a plaintiff, the plaintiff is entitled to a chance to present his evidence and arguments for why a trial is needed. See *Celotex Corp. v. Catrett*, 477 U.S. 317, 326 (1986); *Hotel 71 Mezz Lender LLC v. Nat'l Ret. Fund*, 778 F.3d 593, 603 (7th Cir. 2015). But the fatal flaw in Hoban's failure-to-protect claim against Vilt is the same as applies to the failure-to protect claim against Pfister: Hoban knew of these claims when he first sued for not receiving protective custody, but he had not yet exhausted his administrative remedies. He gives us no reason on appeal to believe that he did not know of his failure-to-protect claim against Vilt before filing his original complaint or that the exhaustion analysis for Vilt is any different from the unexhausted claim against Pfister. So the district court did not commit reversible error in granting summary judgment for Vilt.

Affirmed.

Haste makes waste, all right; the court's order was issued the day after the appeal was filed, an interval too short for thoughtful consideration of a complex case. A further curiosity to note about this order, besides how protracted (1986 words) and tedious it is, is the extreme improbability that the plaintiff could understand it; indeed I have difficulty understanding it myself, with its twists and turns and changes of identity of *dramatis personae*.

I have omitted the only footnote in the order, which appears on the first page and states: "We [i.e., the three judges on the appellate panel: Kanne, Sykes, and Hamilton] have agreed to decide the case without oral argument because the briefs and record adequately present the facts and legal arguments and oral argument would not significantly aid the court. Fed. R. App. P. 34(a)(2)(C)." That is rarely true, and certainly was not true in the *Hoban* case, where oral argument might have cut through the confusion and repetition evident in the court's order.

Upon reading the order I emailed the judges of my court the following message: "I vote to grant rehearing en banc. The fact that a five and a half page order was issued one day after submission of the case to this court is only the first of several dubious actions or inactions asserted in the order. On the second page of the order, second full paragraph, Hoban seems to me to have stated a valid grievance concerning conditions in segregation. Third paragraph too: the complaint, not denied in the order, that he hadn't been given his medicines. And the last paragraph on this page says that Hoban is paranoiac, but the author seems unaware that paranoia is a serious mental condition. On page 3 the order states in the second paragraph that Hoban provided photos of his 'bloody' body after he had been attacked by Latin King members. The order does not address that issue. In the following paragraph he alleges that he was forced to share a cell with a Hells Angel who was also a self-proclaimed hit man for the Latin Kings, and that the Angel lunged at him. The order does not comment on the incident. The remainder of the order is convincing--but only if one assumes that Hoban is as sophisticated a defender of his rights as his lawyer would be, if he had a lawyer, which he did not until the filing of the petition for panel rehearing and rehearing en banc, which precipitated the panel's order though it is not discussed in the order, though the petition is an impressive legal document."

To my pleased surprise, one of the judges on the panel—Judge Hamilton—responded constructively (and without being contradicted by either of the other two members of the panel) as follows: "The panel has not yet finished voting on the petition for panel rehearing. Dick [Posner] makes some points that I would like to study before the entire court needs to vote on this. (Note that the PFR [petition for rehearing] was filed by counsel and is stronger than the plaintiff's pro se submissions.) I suggest that we hold off on the en banc voting, perhaps for a week or so, until the panel can report on its final vote on the PFR."

A victory for me, though only a preliminary one—and, it seems, a pyrrhic one. For no judge, not even Judge Hamilton, voted to rehear the case; instead on July 28 he circulated a message explaining why he thought the panel decision was correct after all—yet answered none of the points I had made in my call for rehearing.

* * *

Here is another case in which a staff attorney's memo submitted to me required considerable revision:

TO: The Honorable Richard A. Posner
FROM: Name deleted
IN RE: *Lehn v. Scott and Rauner*, 16-2916
Motion by Party-In-Interest Attorney General Lisa Madigan for Summary Reversal and Remand to the District Court
DATE: June 16, 2017
PANEL: Judges Posner, Flaum, Sykes
RECOMMENDATION: GRANT summary reversal and remand
ATTACHMENTS: Motion
Lehn's appellate brief
District Court Order
Lehn's complaint

I present to you party-in-interest Attorney General's petition for summary reversal because one of the judges on the motions panel when it was filed on June 12, 2017 has a conflict and you are next on the motions rotation. I also will present the motion to Judge Flaum and Judge Sykes. I recommend granting the motion.

Plaintiff-appellant Donald Lehn, acting pro se, sued Governor Bruce Rauner and Greg Scott, director of Illinois's Rushville Treatment and Detention Center, under 42 U.S.C. § 1983. Lehn, who is civilly committed under Illinois's Sexually Violent Persons Commitment Act, 725 ILCS 207/1–99, alleges the defendants violated his due process rights under the Fourteenth Amendment by not "providing treatment of sufficient quality and quantity to facilitate his release." Specifically, he alleges that several of his treatment providers have opined that he no longer presents a sufficient risk of sexual violence to subject to commitment and/or that he should be transferred to either a halfway house or some other community-based treatment facility in order to build an adequate support network before release. But, Lehn says, the defendants refused to allow him to be treated in a community-based facility, telling him that the Act does not allow such facilities. Lehn further alleges that his treatment providers called for him to acquire necessary vocational or educational skills before release but that Rushville offers no vocational or educational training. Finally, Lehn says that the defendants would not allow him to obtain his own vocational and educational books and asserts that this violates the First Amendment.

The district court dismissed Lehn's amended complaint for failure to state a claim, see 28 U.S.C. § 1915A. The court concluded that Lehn had no enforceable right to less restrictive housing. Moreover, the court went on, Lehn's allegations that certain mental health professionals had recommended his release implicate the federal habeas corpus statute and are not cognizable under § 1983.

Lehn appealed. This court recruited counsel for Lehn and invited the Office of the Illinois Attorney General to file a response brief as party-in-interest. Instead, however, the Attorney General's office moves for summary reversal and remand to the district court.

I recommend that the panel grant the motion for summary reversal. The two cases cited by the Attorney General are on point and dispositive. In *Hughes v. Dimas*, this court held that allegations that a civilly-detained person is not being provided treatment designed to lead to his eventual release states a claim under the Fourteenth Amendment. 837 F.3d 807 (7th Cir. 2016). And in *Hughes v. Farris*, this court held that the denial of vocational training recommended by treatment providers can violate the due process clause if the denial is not based on the professional judgment of a mental-health expert. 809 F.3d 330, 334 (7th Cir. 2015). Lehn's allegation that the defendants are refusing to comply with the treatment plan provided by mental-health professionals states a claim under § 1983 and the Fourteenth Amendment. I do not think further briefing is necessary.

I note that the Attorney General does not address the dismissal of Lehn's First Amendment claim, but I think it is appropriate to summarily reverse the decision on that claim too. The district court dismissed this claim on the ground that it is precluded by a previous suit of Lehn's in state court, *Lehn v. Scott*, No. 4-14-0415, 2015 WL 9590327 (Ill. App. Ct., December 30, 2015), which involved Lehn's violation of Rushville policies by his possession of gaming and entertainment systems and his subsequent punishment. But Illinois gives preclusive effect to a prior lawsuit only if (1) a court of competent jurisdiction rendered a final judgment on the merits, (2) the new lawsuit involves the same "cause of action" as the old, and (3) there is an identity of parties or their privies between the suits. *Arlin-Golf, LLC v. Village of Arlington Heights*, 631 F.3d 818, 821 (7th Cir. 2011). As Lehn argues in his appellate brief, which was already filed, the two suits involve different causes of action because they do not "arise from a single group of operative facts." *River Park, Inc. v. City of Highland Park*, 703 N.E.2d 883, 893 (Ill. 1998). Other than one letter attached to Lehn's federal amended complaint and referred to in the state decision, there is no mention in Lehn's federal amended complaint, or the over 100 pages of exhibits in support, that refer to the events referred to in the state decision. Also, it appears that only Scott was a defendant in the state suit, and he is not in privity with Rauner because under § 1983 they must be sued in their personal capacity. Preclusion is normally an affirmative defense and perhaps, once the defendants have a chance to respond, they may be able to meet their burden of showing preclusion. But on this record I think summary reversal is appropriate.

Moreover, Lehn does state a claim under the First Amendment. The state may not restrain a civil detainee's First Amendment rights unless the restraint is rationally connected to the state's interests. *Brown v. Phillips*, 801 F.3d 849, 853 (7th Cir. 2015). Because Lehn's complaint was dismissed before any response from the state, there is not yet any reason to think that the defendant's actions were rationally connected to the state's interests.

Accordingly, I recommend that the panel grant the motion for summary reversal and remand to the district court. I suggest that the order say:

IT IS ORDERED that the motion to summarily reverse and remand is **GRANTED**. This case is **REMANDED** to the district court for further proceedings on all claims. Lehn's due process claims must proceed in light of *Hughes v. Dimas*, 837 F.3d 807 (7th Cir. 2016) and *Hughes v. Farris*, 809 F.3d 330, 334 (7th Cir. 2015). Lehn's First Amendment claim must also proceed because, on this record, we cannot say that his claim is precluded. The mandate in this appeal shall issue forthwith.

Please let me know if you have any questions or concerns.

And here is how (omitting the caption) I think the order should have been written, to explain the grounds of decision clearly in language and syntax very likely to be intelligible to Lehn:

Plaintiff-appellant Donald Lehn, acting pro se, sued Illinois Governor Bruce Rauner and Greg Scott, director of Illinois's Rushville Treatment and Detention Center, under 42 U.S.C. § 1983. Lehn, who is civilly committed under Illinois's Sexually Violent Persons Commitment Act, 725 ILCS 207/1–99, alleges that the defendants violated his due process rights under the Fourteenth Amendment by not "providing treatment of sufficient quality and quantity to facilitate his release." Specifically, he alleges that several of his treatment providers have opined that he no longer presents a sufficient risk of sexual violence to be committed and/or that he should be transferred to either a halfway house or some other community-based treatment facility in order to build an adequate support network before release. But, Lehn says, the defendants refused to allow him to be treated in a community-based facility, telling him that the Act does not allow transfer to such facilities. He adds that his treatment providers called for him to acquire necessary vocational or educational skills before release but that Rushville offers no vocational or educational training. He adds that the defendants would not allow him to obtain his own vocational and educational books and asserts that this violates the First Amendment.

The district court dismissed Lehn's amended complaint for failure to state a claim, *see* 28 U.S.C. § 1915A. The court concluded that Lehn had no enforceable right to less restrictive housing and that his allegations that certain mental health professionals had recommended his release imply a federal habeas corpus claims rather than a claim under cognizable under 42 U.S.C. § 1983.

Lehn appealed, and this court recruited counsel for him and invited the Office of the Illinois Attorney General to file a brief in response. Rather than do this, however, the Attorney General's office has moved for summary reversal and remand to the district court. Thus there is no opposition to Lehn's appeal.

The two cases cited by the Attorney General in support of her position are dispositive. *Hughes v. Dimas* , 837 F.3d 807 (7th Cir. 2016), holds that allegations that a civilly-detained person is not being provided treatment designed to lead to his eventual release states a claim under the Fourteenth Amendment. And *Hughes v. Farris,* 809 F.3d 330, 334 (7th Cir. 2015), holds that the denial of vocational training recommended by treatment providers can violate the due process clause if the denial is not based on the professional judgment of a mental-health expert. Lehn's allegation that the defendants are refusing to comply with the treatment plan provided by mental-health professionals states a claim under § 1983 and the Fourteenth Amendment.

The Attorney General does not address the dismissal of Lehn's First Amendment claim, but I think it is appropriate to summarily reverse the decision on that claim too. (The two claims are actually two suits, though that's a detail of no importance.) The district court dismissed it on the ground that it is precluded by a previous suit of Lehn's in state court, *Lehn v. Scott,* No. 4-14-0415, 2015 WL 9590327 (Ill. App. 2015), which involved Lehn's violation of Rushville policies by possessing gaming and entertainment systems, and his subsequent punishment. But Illinois gives preclusive effect to a prior lawsuit only if (1) a court of competent jurisdiction rendered a final judgment on the merits, (2) the new lawsuit involves the same "cause of action" as the old, and (3) there is an identity of parties or their privies. *Arlin-Golf, LLC v. Vill. of Arlington Heights,* 631 F.3d 818, 821 (7th Cir. 2011). As Lehn argues in his appellate brief, which was already filed, the two suits involve different causes of action because they do not "arise from a single group of operative facts." *River Park, Inc. v. City of Highland Park*, 703 N.E.2d 883, 893 (Ill. 1998). Other than one letter attached to Lehn's federal amended complaint and referred to in the state decision, there is no mention in Lehn's federal amended complaint, or the over 100 pages of exhibits in support, that mentions the events referred to in the state decision. Also, it appears that only Scott was a defendant in the state suit, and he is not in privity with Rauner because under § 1983 they must be sued in their personal capacities. Preclusion is normally an affirmative defense and maybe once the defendants have a chance to respond they'll be able to meet their burden of showing preclusion. But on this record I think summary reversal is appropriate.

Moreover, Lehn does state a claim under the First Amendment. The state may not curtail a civil detainee's First Amendment rights unless the curtailment is rationally connected to the state's interests. *Brown v. Phillips*, 801 F.3d 849, 853 (7th Cir. 2015). Because Lehn's complaint was dismissed before any response from the state, there is not yet reason to think the defendant's actions rationally connected to the state's interests.

For the reasons explained, we have decided to grant Lehn's motion to reverse, and to remand the case for further proceedings in the district court on all his claims.

* * *

And three final, very short examples of inadequate staff attorney memos, the first involving a pro se appeal in a case called *United States v. Nellum*, No. 17-1694. Here is the order drafted by the staff attorney (and issued):

The government asks the court to summarily affirm Montel Nellum's appeal because his opening brief concedes that his sole argument is foreclosed by current precedent. Nellum pled guilty to a drug trafficking charge and the district court sentenced him based on its conclusion that he was a career offender pursuant to U.S.S.G. § 4B1.1(a) because of his prior felony convictions for causing bodily harm to a family or household member, *see* 720 ILCS 5/12-3.2(a)(1), (b). On appeal, Nellum argues only that his prior convictions should not be deemed crimes of violence. He acknowledges that his contention is contrary to current precedent, *see United States v. Waters*, 823 F.3d 1062 (7th Cir.), *cert. denied,* 137 S. Ct. 569 (2016) (declining to overturn *De Leon Castellanos v. Holder*, 652 F.3d 762, 766–67 (7th Cir. 2011)). Nellum offers no compelling reason to overturn this precedent, but he has preserved the issue for possible further review. *See De Quijas v. Shearson/Am. Express, Inc.*, 490 U.S. 477, 484 (1989) (explaining that circuit courts must follow controlling precedent and leave to the Supreme Court to decide whether to overturn its decisions).

IT IS ORDERED that the judgment of the district court is summarily AFFIRMED.

And this is the order as I would have drafted it—a compressed and I think clearer version of the staff attorney's memo:

The government asks us to affirm Montel Nellum's appeal because his opening brief concedes that his sole argument is foreclosed by precedent. He pleaded guilty to trafficking in illegal drugs and was sentenced as a career offender pursuant to U.S.S.G. § 4B1.1(a) because of prior felony convictions for causing bodily harm to a family or household member in violation of Illinois law; see 720 ILCS 5/12-3.2(a)(1), (b). To us he argues only that those convictions should not be deemed crimes of violence, but the argument is wrong because acts that cause bodily harm, at least knowingly or otherwise inexcusably, are crimes of violence if bodily harm results. See, e.g., *United States v. Waters*, 823 F.3d 1062 (7th Cir. 2016); *De Leon Castellanos v. Holder*, 652 F.3d 762, 766–67 (7th Cir. 2011)).

The judgment of the district court is therefore affirmed.

My next example is the recent case of *Podemski v U.S. Bank National Ass'n*, No. 17-1927, another pro se case, in which the appellant seeks to stay her eviction from property once owned by her but now foreclosed. The staff attorney's analysis is sound, concluding that Podemski's motion to stay the eviction should be denied.

But the memo and accompanying order contain a number of stylistic errors, beginning: "presumably Podemski is seeking to stay her eviction." As there is no doubt that that's what she's seeking, there's no function served by "presumably." In the next sentence we're told: "The panel denied Podemski's initial stay motion with the explanation that Podemski did not set forth the issues she intended to raise on appeal"; the staff attorney should have said "that she had not set forth the issues she intended to raise on appeal." In the next sentence we read that "Podemski amends the stay motion"; it should read "she has now amended the stay motion." Later the staff attorney discusses a man named Jeffrey Stephan, a financial officer—and in the next sentence refers to him three times as "Stephen"; the staff attorney should have substituted "he" for those three Stephens.

In the next paragraph there is mention of a doctrine that "prevented [the district court] from essentially overturning" certain rulings; "essentially" does no work in that sentence. Later there is reference to foreclosure proceedings "that have been occurring for over seven years"; "been occurring" is not good English.

The last page of the memo/order begins with the staff attorney "respectfully" recommending denial of Podemski's motion for a stay; that's a pointless flourish. The staff attorney proceeds to note that the court had previously denied a motion by Podemski to "stay any action with respect to property in Indiana"; "to property" should be "to her property. Later we read that "Podemski also has filed her opening brief"; the "also" is superfluous. This is shortly followed by another superfluous "essentially." The last word in the order, "DENIED," should be preceded by "therefore," to produce closure of the statement "she hasn't demonstrated that she is likely to succeed on the merits of the appeal."

My last example is the even more recent case of *Bonty v. United States*, No. 17-2413, in which a pro se (in fact a prison inmate) has asked us to vacate his sentence, pursuant to 28 U.S.C. § 2255. The staff attorney wants us to deny his application. I have no quarrel with that recommendation, but I find the staff attorney's memo confusing.

First of all, although it says we denied a similar earlier application by Bonty, I can't find our ruling in the papers. Second, and more important, the first page of the staff attorney's memo has a very long, confusing, and unfortunate footnote, now becoming routine in staff attorney memos, about converting such memos to "staff attorney cover letters." Here's the footnote: "Recently the court decided that the orders resolving § 2244(b) applications should be expanded to include information about the applicant's litigation history (in addition to an analysis of whether the proposed claims warrant authorization). Information that used to appear only in the memoranda to judges, now appears in the draft orders. As a result the papers became repetitive. We therefore are experimenting with changing the memos to cover letters. The information we think is appropriate for a cover letter is (1) the type of case we are sending to you, (2) when the statutory 30-day period expires and an order must issue, (3) why we are presenting the application to this panel of judges, and (4) what documents we are sending to you. We welcome suggestions, comments, and requests." The oddity is that the five-point cover letter contains much less relevant information than the traditional memo, for the letter says nothing about the merits of the applicant's case.

Compounding the vagueness of the footnote, there is no promised cover letter, just the usual order, consisting of two half pages, equal therefore to one. The penultimate paragraph of the order contains a couple of verbal/grammatical infelicities: "rely" in the first line should be "relies," because the subject is "None," not "claims." And there is absolutely no reason to use the term "actual innocence" (in a sentence that states that "none of his [i.e., Bonty's] proposed claims relies on new evidence of his 'actual innocence'") instead of just plain "innocence," as the shorter and the longer form mean exactly the same thing. In the second line, "a new rule of constitutional law decided since" is not good English either, because a rule is enacted or promulgated or adopted, not "decided."

I am concerned with the poor quality of many of the staff attorney memos and orders (well illustrated by the drafts I've been discussing in this chapter). And puzzled too, since all of those documents are reviewed, or at least supposed to be reviewed, by supervisory staff attorneys. And surprised at the following reply of the chief judge to my criticism (in *Bonty* and other opinions) of the term "actual innocence": "The use of some terms, such as 'actual innocence,' cannot be avoided, because they have become terms of art, and they thus allude to a long line of Supreme Court decisions that don't need repeating in every order. 'Plain' innocence won't do the job, since it might mean that the person should have been acquitted for reasons that have nothing to do with what actually happened during the commission of the crime." To which I replied: "*Of course* the silly term 'actual innocence' can be avoided. Come on! Innocence is innocence. In the case you put of someone acquitted who was not innocent, this should be explained—he should not be called 'innocent'; the notion that innocence encompasses guilt is ridiculous. Think of the history of the term 'actual innocence.' Henry Friendly wrote a great article many years ago entitled 'Is innocence irrelevant?' He said no, which was certainly sensible. The Supreme Court picked it up but referred to 'factual innocence.' A couple of years later, however, the Court dropped the 'f,' thus creating the silly term 'actual innocence,' repeated incessantly for no reason at all except abject deference to our judicial superiors. I've never used the term and I've never been criticized for not using it. On the other hand I am not a model of deference."

* * *

I have been emphasizing cases in which the applicant for judicial relief is a pro se, but I don't want to leave the impression that they are the only cases in which staff attorneys make mistakes. Recently I discovered an order by our court, issued on July 28, in a case called *Gray v. Hardy*, Nos. 16-1129, -1222, in which the defendants (and possibly the plaintiff as well, although this can't be discerned from the order) were represented by counsel. The order in its entirety states that "Upon consideration of the **STATUS RE-PORT**, filed on July 28, 2017, by counsel for the appellees, **IT IS ORDERED** that counsel for the appellees shall file a further status report by August 30, 2017." No reason is given, no purpose assigned to the report, no suggestion offered for why only one side of the litigation should be required to file a status report in a month.

Either the order should have explained the "why" of it, or the staff attorney should simply have called up one of the plaintiff's lawyers and told him or her that the judges wanted a further status report in a month.

The order in the *Gray* case was one of a large number of orders, all dated July 28 or 29, that I received on July 31 of this year, and, though a few were complicated, all but *Gray* were uninteresting. Most involved just requests, which the order granted, for brief extensions of time for filing a brief; some were obviously untimely, outside federal jurisdiction, filed in the wrong court, or otherwise frivolous, notably *Sturdivant v. Krueger*, No. 17-1606), the appeal of a man claiming to be a "Private Aboriginal Indigenous Moorish American National." (Ain't no such cat.)

And why had I received this flood of orders? Because it had belatedly occurred to me that the only orders and opinions the office of the clerk of our court were sending me were ones in which I had been a member of the panel that had issued them. I decided that to do my job I should read or at least skim *all* the orders and opinions of the court; only then would I have a complete sense of what my court was doing, and how well it was doing it. The orders and opinions are issued by the clerk's office, and I asked my secretary to ask the office whether it could send me all orders and opinions, and it obliged, enabling me to discuss in this book interesting cases that I would not have known of had I not requested the flood.

But even before this I was being upbraided by the chief judge for publicizing staff attorney memos. "I am worried," she said, "about your [i.e., my] reference to detailed critiques of bench memos and draft orders written by our current staff attorneys. As I have said in other emails, these are internal court documents that should not be put in the public domain."

I had never before received an email or other communication on the subject. I am guessing that her email had been provoked by a previous email of mine in which I had said that my book (which she had not and has not seen—I have shown it to no one in the court except my law clerks—although later we'll see that someone gave her a copy of a preliminary draft of the book, which unfortunately I can't find in my files) "contains very detailed critiques of a number of bench memos and draft orders by our current staff attorneys." My reference to "a number of very detailed critiques" was off base, however, because at the time I had discussed only three such memos or orders (the bench memo in *Davis*, the response to the petition for mandamus in *Lewis*, and the response to the motion in *Lehn*—but since then three more—*Nellum*, *Podemski*, and *Bonty*, just discussed). I can't understand their being characterized as "internal court documents," since often such memos are incorporated or referenced in the order by the panel of judges disposing of the case, and that order, which goes to the litigant or litigants and is therefore not "internal," the litigant or litigants can do whatever he (or they) want[s] to do with it, including showing it to other people. I also don't understand why, other than in exceptional cases, internal court documents *should* be hidden from the public. I realize that the Freedom of Information Act is inapplicable, but its spirit is. The documents prepared by staff attorneys provide important information concerning the operation of the legal system. When the documents are defective, the public is entitled to know, so that it can understand and evaluate our legal system better.

I defer to Part Three of the book a more detailed consideration of the chief judge's criticism, but in the meantime I'll give a few more recent examples of staff attorney memos that yearn for correction. In the memo in *Aguado v. Godinez*, No. 17-1818, we read that "prison officials can be liable for deliberate indifference to an inmate's safety if they are subjectively aware of a risk to the inmate and disregard that inmate." What possible work is "subjectively" doing? One is aware or not aware. The identical phrase appears on the second page of the memo, and a few lines below that "were to allow" appears without the "to," making the phrase unintelligible. On the third and last page the staff attorney "respectfully recommend[s] denying his [the pro se's] motion to proceed *in forma pauperis* on appeal;" "respectfully" is a pointless flourish.

The reader is also told on that page that the pro se's motion for leave to appeal *in forma pauperis* is denied because he "has not raised a potentially meritorious argument that the district court erred" in rejecting his motion, yet there is no indication of what if any argument he'd made, and a few lines below that we're told that "Aguado shall pay the required docketing fee within 14 days, or this appeal will be dismissed for failure to prosecute"—yet the amount of the fee is not stated, nor whether he has the wherewithal to pay it. Also on this page, the suggestion to add "the following language in the order" is confusing. The first sentence suggested is not a sentence at all; there is no verb. In the next chunk of language that the staff attorney wanted to add, "raised" should have been "made." And finally in the last sentence the staff attorney talks about dismissing Aguado's appeal if he doesn't pay—but as the staff attorney is recommending dismissal of the appeal (i.e., affirmance of the district court's dismissal of Aguado's case) on the merits, the relevance of whether he pays or not is unclear.

I asked the staff attorney to redo her order disposing of the case. She did so, promptly, but unfortunately in several places the new order is also unclear. Although as we're about to see it denies on an adequate ground Aguado's motion for leave to appeal *in forma pauperis*, it goes on to say that unless he pays the required docketing fee (which in this case would be a fee for appealing to this court), "this appeal will be dismissed for failure to prosecute." But the staff attorney had already made a convincing case in her new draft that Aguado's attempted appeal had no merit, culminating in her statement that "the district court's summary judgment order is supported by the record and the law." The clear implication is that, the judgment of the district court being sound, the appeal should be dismissed without further ado. But the new order doesn't say that. It leaves the case in a judicial limbo.

In another case in the batch of staff attorney cases that I'm discussing in this chapter, *Riley v. Harrington*, No. 17-1853, the staff attorney sensibly recommends denial of the relief sought by the pro se, and also recommends adding to "the standard order" a sentence explaining the recommendation, but omits to explain what the "standard order" is. On inquiry I learn that it is: "This court has reviewed the final order of the district court and the record on appeal. We find no substantial showing of the denial of a constitutional right. *See* 28 U.S.C. § 2253(c)(2)." That doesn't tell me much; nor does the following variant, found in many orders in pro se cases (quoted earlier in this book, it's a favorite of the chief judge): "This court has reviewed the final order of the district court and the record on appeal. We find no substantial showing of the denial of a constitutional right." The memo in *Riley* should also have mentioned the pro se's 32-year sentence. There are some further variants, but the "standard order" will rarely exceed 10 lines of text. In one recent case, *Kamyk v. Berryhill*, No. 16-3647 (August 18, 2017)—an order issued the same day on which the pro se's appeal had been submitted to the panel of judges—the order was only four lines, with that pointless footnote (I've mentioned it elsewhere) stating: "We have agreed to decide this case without oral argument because the briefs and record adequately present the facts and legal arguments, and oral argument would not significantly aid the court." Given the first clause, the "an oral argument" footnote is completely superfluous, yet appears in countless orders.

I regard the standard order as pernicious. Recently I received from one of our best staff attorneys proposed standard orders in three pro se cases together with her recommendation to issue the orders. Two of the recommendations were a full page long, and the third a full page and a half long. They were excellent! I sent her a note saying: "you wrote three recommendation notes, which are excellent. But I take it—correct me if I'm wrong—that the pro se's won't get them. They'll get just the skeletal 'orders.' I think those orders—it's not your fault, they are rote drafts—are awful. They say nothing. I am sure they are unintelligible to the pro se's. Imagine yourself a poorly educated, low-IQ prison inmate receiving a document like that. All you would know was that you'd lost your case. I would like—this I know is quixotic—that every time a staff attorney recommends dismissal of a pro se's appeal, the staff attorney have done limited research to determine whether the pro se might have an alternative avenue of relief. Not knowing law, not having a lawyer, a pro se is likely often to miss the boat in deciding on what ground, with what references, etc., to base his appeal. I'm not like the other judges of this court. I don't consider pro se's trash. I want them to be treated fairly, in recognition of their handicaps. But maybe I'm missing some deeper point. I would be very interested in your thoughts. If you'd like to explain them in person, come by my office at a time convenient for you, but check first with my *secretary* to make sure I'm there."

In still another pro se case, *Pope v. Perdue*, No. 16-4176, the analysis in the staff attorney's memo is again fine, but there are several verbal infelicities any one of which could trip up the pro se should the memo be incorporated in the judges' order (as it should be) and thus be seen by the pro se. In the second paragraph of the staff attorney's memo we learn that the defendant "pleaded guilty to transporting an individual across states lines intending that she engage in prostitution"; "woman" would be better than "individual." Also we're told that the defendant "just wanted to relitigate the claim he brought in his first ... motion"; "he brought" should be "he had brought." Another infelicity is the assertion that "a guilty plea 'waives' errors with an indictment." For read literally though absurdly this means that the indictment is the weapon used by pleading guilty to waive errors; the staff attorney should have written "in" not "with." And there is more: In the third line of the third paragraph, "from the grand jury" is superfluous and so should be deleted, while in the fifth line "whatsoever" is superfluous and should therefore be deleted also. In the tenth line, "with" an indictment doesn't sound right. Also, I don't understand why the nonrequirement of a certification requires ("Accordingly") affirming the district court's decision. And finally the memo's lone footnote states that the age of the defendant's victim "did however impact his sentencing range." Instead of "did however impact" the memo should have said "influenced."

And last, in *Dingus v. Lashbrook*, No. 17-1039, the staff attorney again recommends adding a sentence to "the standard order" without explaining what the standard order is. What would a pro se make of such a statement?

* * *

Where oh where are the supervisory staff attorneys? They are letting a flood of mistakes in the junior staff attorneys' memos get through. Is this because the supervisory staff attorneys don't really know how to write well or edit well or that their juniors, the two-year staff attorneys, perhaps out of pride, tend not to accept the supervisory staff attorneys' suggested improvements?

Enough examples of mistakes by staff attorneys! I want now to explain a further problem with the chief judge's insistence on the privacy of staff attorneys' memos, draft orders, and other documents, a problem different from the denial of information to the public and, as or more important, to the judges and the pro se's. The further problem is the inconsistency of that insistence with the treatment of opinion drafts by law clerks. Most judges (not including me, however) ask their law clerks to prepare drafts of the opinions assigned to the judge; the judge edits the drafts, but rarely discards them and having done so rewrites them from scratch, and so the judge's published opinions will contain material, often a great deal of material, that was drafted by the judge's law clerks. I don't see the difference between that and the incorporation, in my revisions of the staff attorney drafts in *Davis, Lewis, Lehn,* and *Nellum,* of significant material written by the staff attorneys. I edited; I rewrote; but I did not discard most of the staff attorneys' work; I did not write from scratch. I worked with the staff attorneys in the same way that most judges work with their law clerks without thereby being criticized. What's the difference?

* * *

I need to remind the reader at this point of the memo sent to me in May 2017 purportedly by 17 unnamed staff attorneys of my court criticizing me for a memo I'd written. The staff attorneys' memo states that my memo "unfairly maligns" the work of the staff attorneys by asserting that "staff attorneys in this circuit are not attentive to the needs of pro se litigants." They call the suggestion "wrong and unfair." That's a misunderstanding, though one to which I've unwittingly contributed. My central criticism of our staff attorney program is that many of the staff attorneys' memos and other documents are poorly written (I just gave examples), for which I blame not them but, as I suggested earlier, law-school writing programs and the general culture of today's America. In addition the efforts made so far to improve the writing of newly hired staff attorneys are not well designed, though the final appendix in this book—"Judge Gilman's Writing Rules"—discusses a promising cure for this disease.

But what turned my remarking poor writing by staff attorneys into a criticism rather than merely an observation was that I was under the erroneous impression that an order by our court denying relief to a pro se appellant, petitioner, or movant *invariably* includes not only an announcement of the result with a one- or two-sentence explanation (often skipped, however, so that the entire order may just read "Petition Denied"—may, that is, just announce the result) but also the staff attorney memo that accompanies, and more fully explains, the denial of relief. I now learn that being intended for the judge the memo is rarely attached to or incorporated in the order denying relief and *hence is not seen by the pro se.*

And *that* is what I think a serious mistake (remember my discussion of that omission in *Kolar v. Berryhill,* pp. 55-57, *supra*), because it denies the applicant for relief essential information as to what if anything he can do next in an effort to obtain relief. And it is because I think it a serious mistake, and because I mistakenly believed that the order denying relief always includes the staff attorney's memo, that I criticized the quality of the writing in certain otherwise adequate staff attorney memos–not badly written in the usual sense—repetitive, ungrammatical, often too long, badly punctuated, etc.—but likely to be unintelligible to what I had thought, and what I strongly believe should be, the memos' principal intended audience—the pro se's who seek judicial relief. It's not enough for an order denying relief to a pro se to be legally correct; it (or a supplementary memo attached to it); it must also be intelligible to the pro se. And so recall how in discussing *Davis v. Moroney* I used the Flesch Reading Test to determine the pro se's competence to understand key evidence in his case. The staff attorney had recommended affirming the district court's denial of relief to *Davis*; the panel reversed in the opinion by me that included the staff attorney's memo—rewritten by me.

I don't expect elegance or profundity in staff attorney memos, or lament their absence. I want memos intelligible to pro se's, and I want those memos to be included with (whether attached to or incorporated in) whatever orders the court issues resolving pro se's appeals, petitions, motions, or other submissions to this court. And another thing I want, though it may seem quixotic, is for the court, when it rejects a pro se's appeal or related motion, to explain what if any alternative route to relief that pro se may have, thus enabling him, if there is such a route, to file a new proceeding in federal district court with a well-founded belief that this time he *may* (not that he is certain to) prevail.

Moving down my list of criticisms of, and suggestions of improvements in, my court's staff attorney program:

1. The program's top staff should endeavor to learn as much as possible about the staff attorney programs of the other twelve circuits. There may be—in fact undoubtedly are—practices of the staff attorneys of the other circuits that my court should imitate. I discussed the other programs at some length in Chapter 3, but in addition I launched a team of research assistants at the University of Chicago Law School to find out as much as *they* could about those programs, and I include in Appendix One to Part One, later in the book, a spreadsheet summarizing what they found together with what had been found and summarized by director Fridkin of our staff attorney program five years ago in a spreadsheet that captured the major operational differences among the different staff attorney offices/programs (staffing, types of cases handled, and the decision-making and review process). And I provide voluminous additional information about the other staff attorney programs in the succeeding two appendices.

As it happens, our chief judge met a few months ago with the other chief circuit judges, but her only report on the meeting that relates to staff attorneys is that the meeting confirmed her belief that ours is the best staff attorney program; we'll see later in this book that that claim appears to lack a factual basis.

2. A solid candidate for retirement is the boilerplate first footnote in the staff attorneys' draft orders, drawn from Fed. R. App. P. 34(2)(C) ("the facts and legal arguments are adequately presented in the briefs and record, and the decisional process would not be significantly aided by oral argument") cited mainly in cases in which the appellant does not request oral argument. A brief statement that he or she did not request argument could replace the

boilerplate. In cases in which the appellant does request oral argument but there are compelling reasons to deny the request, the reasons should be explained in the staff attorney's order, and thus fitted to the case rather than left to the boilerplate. And staff attorneys should be alerted to the fact that the boilerplate footnote is inapplicable to cases in which, as in *Myrick v. Greenwood*, 856 F.3d 487 (7th Cir. 2017 (per curiam), there is only one brief; yet the boilerplate footnote in the staff attorney's draft order in *Myrick* spoke of "briefs." Already the staff attorneys are instructed by the staff attorney office manual that when there is only one brief filed, the footnote should *not* refer to briefs (plural); but that directive is not always obeyed.

3. The term "peer review" in our staff attorney program refers as I noted earlier to review by a two-year staff attorney of a memo or draft order written by another two-year staff attorney, and it is generally agreed that the result of such review is to improve the memo or order and at the same time improve the writing/editing skills of the reviewer. In the case of briefs prepared by staff attorneys for short-argument days and Rule 34 conferences, peer review is coupled with review by a supervisor in the staff attorney program. Though peer reviewing is undoubtedly helpful, its value is limited, as suggested by the frequent deficiencies, discussed earlier, in staff attorney submissions to judges.

Every staff attorney is asked to submit to the supervisors both his or her draft order and the peer-review edits on the previous iteration of their draft. Supervisors periodically compare the two to see whether the peer-review edits have improved the draft. Almost always they do; they reveal that legal errors have been corrected, grammar and style improved, useless verbiage discarded. Yet as emphasized earlier in this memo, the drafts often remain unsatisfactory.

4. There is reason to doubt that an order drafted by a staff attorney should begin with the announcement of the result (generally a rejection of the appeal), for then the reader may not read the remainder of the order. Worse, announcing the result before the

analysis that leads up to and justifies it is presented to the reader creates the impression, whether or not justified, that the analysis was an afterthought—window dressing, a mere pretense. The announcement of the result should come at the end of the order, after the reasons for the result have been stated and explained and read by the intended audience. Preferable to the simplistic "We affirm" at the start of the order is an explanation in the order or in an attachment to the order of *why* we affirm. But in fairness to the staff attorneys, the "we affirm" (sometimes "we reverse") preamble is commonplace in our judicial opinions, and is merely being imitated by the staff attorneys with the approval of the judges (except of course me).

5.   An order addressed to a pro se should, if I may be permitted to reiterate a major theme, probably the major theme of this part of the book, be in simple English, not legal jargon, in deference to the fact that pro se's rarely are well educated or intellectually sophisticated or knowledgeable about law. Citations should therefore be kept to a minimum—and for the additional reason that the pro se reader may not have access to the opinions cited. In addition, efforts should be made to simplify citation formats where possible. There should be no fussing over italicized periods (which as I said can't be distinguished by the naked eye from roman ones) and no romanizing them by using a computer's find-and-replace function. These reforms are desirable aspects of the instructional program that I've been advocating in this book.

6.   Typically the staff attorney prepares a brief memorandum (a cover sheet, preceding the draft order and directed to the judge or judges who will review the order) explaining the draft order that he or she is submitting to the judge. But as I've indicated in this chapter and previous ones, the significant points made in such a memorandum should instead be incorporated into the draft order itself, because the memorandum is likely to include information to which the appellant or would-be appellant is entitled because he or she is entitled to be informed of *all* the considerations that went into the court's decision.

7. The Flesch [also called Flesch-Kinkaid] Reading Ease Readability Formula mentioned earlier should be applied to every draft order in a pro se's appeal to make sure the order is intelligible to the pro se. (On the nature and use of the test see, e.g., www.readability.com/flesch-reading-ease-readability-formula.php; or else simply just Google "Flesch.") Downloading the test from the Web, and using it, are as I mentioned free of charge. As also explained earlier, the Flesch test is a simple algorithm that estimates the difficulty of a given text by calculating the ratio of syllables to words and words to sentences; the higher that either ratio is (or both ratios are), the more difficult the text is to understand, other things being equal. The test is especially important for cases in which a party is pro se, often a prison inmate. It is unfair to pro se's to issue orders, denying their appeals, that they can't understand: the lesson of *Davis v. Moroney*.

8. Related to the preceding point, there are computer programs for transforming handwritten documents into printed documents. (The generic term is "Intelligent Character Recognition" (ICR); see, e.g., *Wikipedia*, "Intelligent Character Recognition," https://en.wikipedia.org/wiki/Intelligent_character_recognition.) Such programs should be used whenever the record includes poorly legible handwritten documents, normally by the pro se appellant, as they frequently do.

9. A "bunching" problem adversely affects the review of proposed orders by judges asked to issue them. Often as many as ten proposed orders will be delivered to a judge all at once, and the judge may feel overwhelmed. Some judges nevertheless prefer the bunching, which enables them to dispose of the orders in one sitting. Others, however, may prefer to have them spaced. The judges should be informed of the alternatives, and each judge permitted his or her choice. A possible though radical solution, which I mention without either endorsing or rejecting, would be to issue *all* approved orders as published opinions. That would both reduce the amount of rubber stamping and increase the judicial knowledge base. Provided that the order was either written by or carefully

reviewed by a judge, it would be as good as the ordinary opinion: shorter, no doubt, but brevity is a neglected element in most judicial opinions. I'm not clear why orders, provided they are carefully done under judicial supervision, should be allowed simply to disappear.

10. A problem that the court alone can't solve is the excessive cost to pro se's (even though, having no lawyers, they also have no legal fees) of litigating in the federal courts, including our court. Application fees for pro se litigants range from $100 to $505 (with appellate fees always higher than trial-court fees), though a prisoner unable to pay the normal costs of a lawsuit or a defense to a criminal trial can file a form disclosing how much money he has, in an effort to prove that he can't afford the application fee. Prisoners also have the option of filing their suit or appeal *in forma pauperis* (Latin for "in the form of a pauper"), though this merely permits them to delay payment of the filing fee; eventually they must pay it in full, though they can do so in installments. But if the court finds that three or more of a prisoner's lawsuits are malicious or do not state legally recognized claims, the prisoner is not permitted to file a civil action *in forma pauperis* unless he can prove that he's in imminent danger of serious physical injury unless allowed to sue.

The costs continue for the prisoner as his suit proceeds, for example with printing fees accumulating as he conducts his legal research. He is also subject to being fined if the court decides he's made too many excessively broad discovery requests. Prisoners considering pro se litigation are therefore repeatedly urged in their prisoner self-help packets to use the prison phone to try to find and hire a pro bono attorney to represent him in litigation.

11. There are virtually no African-American staff attorneys in my court. There have been a total of only two in the last 20 years—two out of about 160 (1.25 percent). Both were women; one of them, LaShonda Hunt, recently became a bankruptcy judge. The court is overlooking a potentially significant source of qualified staff attorneys, not only because there are many African-American lawyers but also because many pro se litigants are African-Ameri-

can and may relate better to lawyers of similar racial, and in some instances similar cultural, background. To increase our "take" of African-American staff attorneys, top staff in the staff attorney program, or perhaps one or more of the judges, should visit the deans of at least all the major law schools in Chicago—the University of Chicago, Northwestern, Kent, DePaul, and Loyola (and probably schools outside of Chicago as well)—annually to search out able African-American students at those schools who might be interested in a staff attorney position. Two years as a staff attorney is for many graduating law students an attractive alternative to the first two years at a law firm, which tend to be years of drudgery.

Efforts to improve the yield are ongoing, but Michael Fridkin reports that he has been "disappointed that [his] efforts to recruit African-American staff attorneys has yielded very little … . Every year I [i.e., Fridkin] speak at the University of Chicago and Northwestern law schools, directly to students, to recruit staff attorneys. This year I also have a trip planned to Harvard for the same purpose. I have also contacted the Black Law Students Associations at several top law schools to encourage applications. And I have relationships with the clerkships coordinators at the law schools; I use those relationships to recruit top law students, including African Americans. I will continue these efforts and develop others."

His approach is sound; the recruiter must not speak *only* to a dean or law professor about possible candidates for a staff attorney's position. There is apt to be a lot lost in transmission (transmission by a dean or a professor of what we say to the students). Better for the recruiter to meet directly with interested students, and also perhaps with racial or ethnic clubs in the law school.

Finally, it is worth consulting with judges who have had good luck in hiring African-American law clerks. One is our Judge Ann Williams, herself African-American (though unfortunately on the verge of retiring); another is Judge John Kane, a distinguished federal district judge in Denver whom I greatly respect. Doubtless there are others. A letter from Judge Kane to me discussing both the hiring of African-American law clerks and staff attorneys—and touching also on interns, whose use deserves consideration by our court as well (in fact a few of our judges use interns, who are law students who work part-time for judges)—follows:

I think the best instruction on legal writing comes from George D. Gopen, retired professor of rhetoric and law at Duke. His anchor book, *The Sense of Structure*, is one I give each incoming intern and we discuss at our weekly brown bag lunches in chambers. Prof. Gopen also teaches scientific writing. His short course at the U of Indiana/Purdue Medical Center in Indianapolis has produced significant increases in the number of NIH grants the researchers at that complex receive. (I'm told this is a big prestige item among medical schools. Many of the students I saw there were Asians and English is not the mother tongue of most, yet his instructions are enthusiastically received). I know that in part, my interns' grades have improved significantly because of exposure to Gopen's views. He also speaks tweet and other mutterings of the millennial so they are very receptive.

As for minority clerks and/staff attorneys, when I first joined this court in January, 1978, there were no minority law clerks. I was told by my new colleagues that there were no qualified African-Americans available. The comment was that because of affirmative action, the best of them were being snapped up by the big law firms. I called my friend Tony Amsterdam, a professor at N.Y.U. and received four applications almost by return mail. I hired two: one is now a professor at Rutgers and the other is a professor at Villanova. I have continued to hire minority applicants, but I don't have anything to do with OSCAR. My new law clerks each year come, almost entirely, from those who have been interns in my chambers. The two presently serving are from U.Va. and Vanderbilt. Last year the two were from Chapel Hill and Michigan. During the academic year almost all of the interns come from our two local schools, but in the summer I encourage and accept applicants from all over the country. This coming summer I will have four or five. One already accepted is a Chinese American woman from Boalt Hall.

War story: One of my former interns was an African-American graduate of U.C.L.A. He could barely write his name in the sand with a stick. He failed the Colorado and California bar exams so I persuaded him to stay for another semester and jammed him to the gills with Gopen and reading plays and poems aloud. He took a second try and passed both bars. He is now an equity partner in one of those megafirms that I don't like. More importantly, he is going through the chairs of the state bar association and I expect he will be (s)elected president in the next few years. Whenever I see him now, he routinely asks how J. Alfred Prufrock is doing. ["The Love Song of J. Alfred Prufrock" is one of T.S. Eliot's most famous poems.]

A final comment about prestige law schools. A professor of property law at Denver Univ. when I attended, had received a JSD from Yale after having practiced unsuccessfully in Denver during the 1930s. While doing his postgrad work at Yale, he served as an instructor. At a men's luncheon club I once attended, the professor was asked by another member, "You've taught at Yale and at D.U. What's the difference between the two?" He replied, "Our smartest students at D.U. are just as good as the smartest at Yale, but our dumb students are a lot dumber." I've had law student interns and law clerks from all over the country and I've found that statement to be as true as it is witty.

Judge Kane has been criticized for saying that his "African-American graduate of U.C.L.A" intern "could barely write his name in the sand with a stick. He failed the Colorado and California bar exams." The critics call this racist. Not so. It's a success story, for after a troubled beginning, which many whites as well as many blacks experience, the former intern is, as Judge Kane explains, "now an equity partner in one of those megafirms that I don't like. More importantly, he is going through the chairs of the state bar association and I expect he will be (s)elected president in the next few years."

12. Further recruitment complication: Phil Police, one of the supervisory staff attorneys, who report directly to Michael Fridkin,

is retiring, opening a slot for a new supervisor (who has now been appointed). A complication is that Police plans not to retire until January, five months from now, but the start date for the replacement is August, which is this month, potentially allowing for some overlap before Police retires; the budget of the staff attorneys office will support some overlap. (In addition it now seems that Police will be leaving in November rather than January.) A further complication is that another supervisory staff attorney, Mia Furlong, is retiring shortly, but her replacement has also been named and will start work soon.

13. One of my research assistants at the University of Chicago Law School, John McAdams, has reviewed a number of articles discussing the work that law clerks and staff attorneys do. I have read these articles and can report that McAdams has probably found everything that is out there. Unfortunately, as he notes, the discussion in the articles is mostly about how regrettable it is that law clerks and staff attorneys handle so much of the courts' work, rather than how to train them better. Here is the McAdams report:

> This memorandum provides an overview of the academic literature about staff attorneys in federal circuit courts. The vast majority of work that I found posed one question: is it bad that judges delegate decision-making to staff attorneys, or is it bad *and* unconstitutional? I found very little on how staff attorneys are hired or trained.
>
> There were a few articles that described the responsibilities of staff attorneys. The most thorough report described how their roles differed circuit by circuit, but that was from 1980 and as such I am not sure how much of it is still accurate.[1] A more recent article examined differences between some circuit courts' processes for deciding which cases the court will hear oral argument on and how staff attorneys

---

[1] Donald P. Ubell, "Report on Central Staff Attorneys' Offices in the United States Courts of Appeals," 87 *Federal Rules Decisions* 253 (1980). For example, the report includes no information on Federal Circuit staff attorneys because the Federal Circuit did not yet exist.

are used in that process.[2] The circuits were largely consistent in having staff attorneys write bench memos and draft orders for cases that are not granted oral argument.[3] However, they varied greatly in how they chose which cases to hear oral argument on. For example, the Second Circuit sorts by subject matter, rarely granting oral argument to immigration appeals but almost always granting oral argument in other cases.[4] The D.C. Circuit, on the other hand, has staff attorneys screen cases for merit, and decisions not to grant oral argument are discussed at an in-person conference with the judges before they are finalized.[5]

The sum total of what I found on staff attorney training comes from a passing mention in an article written by a career clerk on the Ninth Circuit. She said 'the staff attorneys' position might have been likened to a fourth year of law school where much time and effort was devoted to developing the attorney's legal writing and research skills, and based on today's standards, at a fairly leisurely pace,' when she began working there in the early 1980s, but that today, 'those writing and research skills are still critical to the position, but in addition, the staff must also have oral presentation and time management skills.'"[6]

One article went into somewhat greater depth about staff attorney hiring, but primarily lamented the dearth of available information.[7] The author observes anecdotally that staff attorneys "tend to have less paradigmatically elite qualifications than those who become appellate clerks," but that data to confirm that observation are lacking.[8] In

---

[2] Marin K. Levy, "The Mechanics of Federal Appeals: Uniformity and Case Management in the Circuit Courts," 61 *Duke Law Journal* 315 (2011). The article examines the D.C., First, Second, Third, and Fourth Circuits.

[3] See *id.*at 344–55.

[4] See *id.*at 349–50.

[5] See *id.*at 346–48.

[6] Cathy Catterson, "Changes in Appellate Caseload and Its Processing," 48 *Arizona Law Review* 287, 293–94 (2006).

[7] Penelope Pether, "Sorcerers, Not Apprentices: How Judicial Clerks and Staff Attorneys Impoverish U.S. Law," 39 *Arizona State Law Journal* 1 (2007).

[8] *Id.* at 53.

a speech, Justice David Stras of the Minnesota Supreme Court discussed how he prefers to hire staff attorneys with work experience and specializations for his court, but the speech does not delve into federal staff attorney hiring.[9]

The rest of the articles discussed the phenomenon of judges delegating decision-making to staff attorneys in response to increases in docket-size and its consequences. The academic opinions ranged from critical but understanding[10] to scathing.[11] The most widespread criticism was that staff attorneys write low-quality decisions. Some observed that the change in the federal rules permitting citation to unpublished opinions increases the likelihood that opinions written by staff attorneys could become binding precedent and thus lower the quality of the substantive law in the circuit.[12] Others observed that staff attorney opinions are inferior because they tend not to explain their reasoning. Another article argues that such delegation violates Article III.[13] It is worth noting that one article argues that pro se appellants do not appear to receive worse substantive outcomes from opinions written by staff attorneys than by judges."[14]

---

[9] David R. Stras, "Secret Agents: Using Law Clerks Effectively," 98 *Marquette Law Review* 151, 168–69 (2014).

[10] See, for example, Marin K. Levy, "Judicial Attention as a Scarce Resource: A Preliminary Defense of How Judges Allocate Time across Cases in the Federal Courts of Appeals," 81 *George Washington Law Review* 401 (2013); Shay Lavie, "Appellate Courts and Caseload Pressure," 27 *Stanford Law & Policy Review* 57, 65 (2016); Wade H. McCree, Jr., "Bureaucratic Justice: An Early Warning," 129 *University of Pennsylvania Law Review* 777 (1981).

[11] See, for example, Pether, 39 *Arizona State Law Journal* 1 (cited in note 9); Jeffrey O. Cooper and Douglas A. Berman, "Passive Virtues and Casual Vices in the Federal Courts of Appeals," 66 *Brooklyn Law Review* 685, 705–07 (2000); Katherine Macfarlane, "Shadow Judges: Staff Attorney Adjudication of Prisoner Claims," 95 *Oregon Law Review* 97 (2017).

[12] Pether, 39 *Arizona State Law Journal* at 8–10 (cited in note 9).

[13] Macfarlane, 95 *Oregon Law Review* at 118–22 (cited in note 13).

[14] Colter L. Paulson, "Will a Judge Read My Brief? Prejudice to Pro Se Litigants from the Staff Attorney Track," 76 *Ohio State Law Journal Furthermore* 103 (2015).

Chapter 7

The Massive Indifference of Most Judges and Staff Attorneys to the Plight of the Pro Se

The pro se—lawyerless, typically a poor person ignorant of the subtleties of law and with only a slight chance (because by definition he has no lawyer) of being allowed oral argument; usually poorly educated, often unhealthy mentally or physically or both, often not very intelligent and not intellectual and often a prison inmate or jail detainee—rarely engages the sympathy of my judicial colleagues, or of their law clerks or of the staff attorneys. Sometimes the pro se prevails on appeal, yet often to prevail is merely to delay defeat until the case is remanded to the district court or until a subsequent appeal by the pro from defeat on remand.

The *attitude* of the judges toward pro se's—a generally unsympathetic attitude shared by some though by no means all of the staff attorneys—is understandable. It resembles the common tendency to dislike one's "inferiors," with obvious exceptions such as pets, who are harmless, unthreatening, and "cute," which pro se litigants rarely are. They are aliens to judicial personnel and as such poor candidates for empathy, which is the ability to understand and share the feelings of another person. Lack of judicial empathy for a class of litigants wouldn't matter much if the members of the class had good, or even not so good, lawyers, because lawyers at all levels of the profession tend to be proficient at arousing at least some sympathy for their clients. But of course by definition pro se's do not have lawyers. As pointed out to me by a former staff attorney sympathetic to pro se litigants, "sometimes in the legal community (and within the court), those lawsuits [i.e., lawsuits by pro se's] are viewed as the least important, the least meritorious, and the least glamorous. I think that flawed perception exists for two reasons. First, people incorrectly assume that any person with a meritorious case can secure legal counsel. Second, there is an implicit bias against people who are incarcerated."

I believe I am [or rather was, when still a member of the court] the only member of my court who feels empathy for the pro se's. I admit that it's a relatively new feeling for me. I was nominated to the Seventh Circuit by President Reagan, a conservative Republican President, and confirmed (to my first, which is also my last, judicial appointment) by a conservative Republican Senate. At the time of my nomination and confirmation (late 1981), I had long been a conservative myself. That went back to the 1960s, when I had reacted very negatively to the urban riots of that decade by angry young blacks and whites and to the campus rebellions by radical students, but it was also the product of my association beginning in the same decade with brilliant conservative economists such as Milton Friedman, George Stigler, and Ronald Coase, an association that blossomed when I became a law professor at the University of Chicago in 1970, though I had gotten to know Stigler quite well the previous year, when I had taught at Stanford and he had visited there.

My conservatism was also nurtured by my strongly negative feelings in the decade of the seventies about Presidents Ford and Carter (but not about Nixon, who I still believe was a good president who should not have been forced from office over the break-in to the Democratic National Committee's Washington headquarters), and finally my positive feelings about Reagan, based not only on his politics and his charm but also on his having appointed as head of the Antitrust Division of the Department of Justice a law professor at Stanford whom I had gotten to know during the year that I taught at Stanford and greatly admired—William Baxter, who I believe was instrumental in my conversion from law professor to federal judge. But I suspect that my appointment owed less to either Baxter or President Reagan than to Edwin Meese, Counselor to the President and later Attorney General—a very intelligent, very shrewd, very conservative adviser to a president who needed good advisers.

And I confess that for the first 25 or even 30 years of being a federal judge I did not feel empathy for many litigants—and none for pro se litigants. They were nothing to me; they were alien; about half of then were prison inmates—criminals, and many of the other pro se's were ex-criminals; all struck me as failures. My interest in staff attorneys was also nil; they too belonged to a different world (I thought). I didn't cultivate them; I had minimal contact with the successive directors of the staff attorney program and even with the supervisory staff attorneys, and almost none with the two-year staff attorneys, whose recommendations—which were almost always to reject the pro se's claim—like the other judges I was for the most part content to rubber stamp.

So what changed me (beginning quite recently—March 2017)? I don't really know. Could it have been a delayed reaction to the election and reelection of Barack Obama, whom I, swinging left unexpectedly, voted for in both elections? (I had voted twice not only for Reagan but also for George W. Bush, also for his father, George H.W. Bush, who had run and been elected in 1989, succeeding Reagan); but I had become disillusioned with the Republicans because of their mismanagement of the economy that led to the great financial crash of 2008. And even earlier—I had voted for Bill Clinton in both his presidential campaigns in the 1990s.

In part my change of heart was a delayed reaction to the very disturbing procrastination of one of our cases, *Paine v. Cason*, 678 F.3d 500 (7th Cir. 2012), which involved the mishandling of a mentally disturbed young woman by Chicago police that resulted in very serious injury to her and great distress and expense to her parents. As a result of our procrastination, the appeal, though it had been argued to us on September 20, 2010, was not decided until April 26, 2012—and that decision was not final, but involved a remand to the district court for further proceedings (and meanwhile we amended our decision on May 17), culminating in a very thorough opinion by the district court judge, Judge Kendall, reported at 689 F. Supp. 2d 1027 (Oct. 11, 2012). Eventually the case was settled for $22.5 million. The protraction of the litigation was unconscionable, and it was all the fault of the appellate panel (of which I was a member, though I did not write the appellate opinion).

In greater part my recent "softening" was the result of the case of *Rowe v. Gibson*, 798 F.3d 622 (7th Cir. 2015), which I mentioned in Chapter 1—the case of an Indiana prison inmate who had a potentially fatal case of gastroesophageal reflux disease and was denied essential medicine for two years by the prison doctor. Rowe sued the prison for deliberate indifference to his medical needs, but had no lawyer and no medical (or other) witness and lost his case in the district court, yet appealed. I presided over the appellate panel and in the fall of 2016 wrote the majority opinion, reversing the district court's decision. One of the other judges dissented, defending the district court's unconscionable result in a long, heartless, formalistic opinion. (Both opinions are reproduced in my recent book *The Federal Judiciary: Strengths and Weaknesses* 317-343 (2017).) That was a wake-up call for me. Not that I had been a total reactionary. Though not in the least religious myself, I had long had a soft spot for members of fringe religious groups, who frequently challenged local ordinances designed to squelch them. But not for prisoners.

Most of the cases I was involved in in that era did not involve staff attorneys because most of the litigants had lawyers; The *Rowe* case was an exception, though I was unaware of that at the time. In pro se cases, which of course did involve staff attorneys, I was as I have indicated generally content, for lack of interest in such cases, to rubber stamp. But in the spring of 2017 I began noticing that the staff attorneys' memos and draft orders, submitted to panels of judges for approval, often seemed calculated to invite the judges to rubber stamp what were rather casual denials of relief, recommended by the staff attorneys. Not that such rubber stamping was new; it was my noticing it that was new, at least to me. It was typical for a batch of staff attorney memos to arrive in a lump on an afternoon; the temptation to rubber stamp them rather than to read them carefully one by one was very strong, and I had often yielded to it. Suddenly I woke up and realized, what should have been obvious to me years and years before, that each recommendation required careful consideration, and as I began to read each one carefully it became obvious to me that many of the recommendations were shallow, or, more precisely, incomplete.

Why did I have an awakening in the spring of 2017? The influence on me of *Rowe v. Gibson*? Turning 78 (on January 11, 2017)? Maybe and maybe, but, if I have had to guess, I would say that it was something else—different and rather banal. One Friday afternoon there arrived on my desk a batch of 10 memos or draft orders or both from staff attorneys, for me to approve. The documents would go to two other judges, the three of us constituting the panel to decide the case, and each of us would approve or disapprove. We all approved. I began to reflect that, because it was a Friday afternoon and there were ten memos to go through, I hadn't paid much attention to them. And I suddenly realized that that was terribly unfair to the pro se's, that we judges were frequently acting with lazy irresponsibility, and that it was time I took the staff attorney program and its clientele—the pro se's, half of them prisoners, remember—seriously.

But when I did that, I discovered that the real problem with the staff attorney program was not that the staff attorneys were recommending affirmance of wrongful denials of relief by district judges and other adjudicators. Usually, though of course not always, the recommendations, whether to reverse or more commonly to affirm, were sound. What was seriously amiss was that the staff attorneys' memos, which continued to be for the most part rubber stamped by the judges, were, even when well written (and many were not), not written at a level that most pro se's could understand. The memos were too legalistic; they were written for judges; and this meant that the court was not communicating with a large segment of its clientele. Improving that communication has been my major goal in regard to the staff attorney program. Its importance lies in the fact that the loss of an appeal need not be the end of the road for the pro se. He (rarely she) may have alternatives; he may have sued under the wrong statute; he may have sued the wrong people; he may have been ignorant of the most basic rudiments of litigation. We owe it to him to explain what his alternatives may be—how the next time he may prevail.

That recognition of the real, the deep, flaw in the staff attorney program, was the beginning, and this book the middle, of my efforts as yet only very partially successful, to improve the program radically. What the ending will be, I have no idea, especially since, having left the court, my influence on the judges, negligible so far as helping the pro se's are concerned, is now nil. All that is clear is that I've changed, that the change is very recent—in fact 2017, as indicated by the fact that a comprehensive (also the first, and possibly destined to be the last) biography of me,[1] published in 2016, does not so much as hint at the change I've been describing; and I've begun to wonder, what are the roots of that change? Was it a purely intellectual phenomenon? Or has it deeper roots in the past?

On May 17, 2017, I went to bed, as I always do, shortly after midnight, fell asleep promptly but awoke suddenly at 4 a.m. and did not fall back asleep. Instead I lay awake until about a quarter of 8, when I got up and dressed and had breakfast and went to my office. During those four hours of wide-awakeness I had a unique experience. My entire life to date, preceded by my parents' entire lives (both had been born in 1900), rolled through my mind. I was surprised and intrigued by how detailed my memory of their lives and my life was. I seemed to remember virtually *everything* that my parents and I had experienced, in their case between their arrival in the United States—in 1900 in the case of my father, age 3 months either when he left Jassy, Rumania, his birthplace, with his parents or when he arrived in this country, and in 1905 in the case of my mother, who had immigrated with her parents from Vienna to New York at the age of 5—and their deaths in 1990 (my mother) and 1996 (my father). My earliest recollection is of when I was 3 years old, in 1942, asked by my father to pluck some ears of corn from the garden of our summer house in Suffern, New York, for lunch guests—potential buyers of the house. Gasoline rationing had just been introduced because of the war and my parents could no longer afford to commute from Manhattan, their permanent home, to Suffern.

My parents had interesting immigrant lives, and I, their only child, have had an interesting life though not an adventurous one (no military service, no Himalayan mountain climbing, no level 4 surfing), and so, quoting the title of Vladimir Nabokov's autobiographical memoir, I tell myself: *Speak, Memory*.

---

[1] William Domnarski, *Richard Posner* (2016).

My parents were nominally Jewish, but in fact had no religious beliefs or interests whatsoever, being atheists strongly sympathetic to communism (my mother may have been a member of the Communist Party USA, though she denied it). My only scrape with Judaism came once (and once only) when as a child my parents took me to a Seder (a Passover dinner with prayer, commemorating the nonexistent exodus of Jews from Egypt in ancient times—for there were no Jews in Egypt, no Moses, no parting of the Red Sea, no divine assassination of the Egyptian first born; see Josh Mintz, "Were Jews Ever Really Slaves in Egypt, or Is Passover a Myth,?" *Haaretz*, Aug. 2, 2017). I was so bored by the Seder that I took to toasting matzos in a candle on the table, eating them—and getting a stomach ache, confirming my rejection of religion, although as I noted earlier I've always had a soft spot for the really marginal religions that I've encountered from time to time in cases, one of my favorites being the Black Hebrew Israelites of Jerusalem.

Though my parents had grown up in poverty on the lower east side in Manhattan, they were highly educated, spoke flawless English, were thoroughly assimilated and professionally successful— my father a lawyer and later a mortgage lender, my mother a public high school English teacher in an era in which New York had outstanding public schools.

So: no religion in my upbringing. No traces of the "old country." No foreignness at all. I remember when I was a teenager being told by a Jewish neighbor that I should associate with Jews more because, when I was an adult, only Jews would associate with me. I said nothing, but I thought—what utter nonsense; I'm just like everybody else; and in fact I've never experienced anti-Semitism *directed at me.*[2] I was however offended by a colleague at the Uni-

---

[2] The reason for what must seem a strange ending to this sentence is that when I was in college I used to go skiing in Stowe, Vermont, with some English friends (exchange students from Clare College, Cambridge, and we stayed at a very nice boarding house in Stowe. The landlady was a very nice person, but fiercely anti-Semitic. During meals she would be constantly denouncing the Jews. Of course she didn't know I was of Jewish origin, because I wasn't really any different from my English friends, and if I had told her that I was of the Jewish race I am sure she would have been terribly mortified at having denounced Jews in my presence. So of course I didn't reveal my origins and in private my friends and I just laughed about the landlady's spiel.

versity of Chicago who told me it must have been difficult for me to learn to speak without gesticulating with my hands, such gesturing being believed by her to be a Jewish trait. What nonsense! No one in my family was ever seen to be talking with his or her hands flapping.

Apart from not growing up religious, I also wasn't brought up to be a good neighbor, a warm-hearted humanitarian, a generous donor to honorable causes—in short a nice boy. I was brought up to be smart and successful—and independent, which I first manifested by being an obnoxious, though very successful, student first at Yale College (which I entered at the age of 16, having skipped my senior year of high school), from which I graduated summa cum laude, and then at the Harvard Law School, where I managed to offend the dean (Erwin Griswold) so successfully that he made strenuous though unsuccessful efforts to prevent the Stanford Law School from hiring me to teach there years after I'd graduated first in the class from Harvard despite the dean's (understandable) enmity toward me. At both Yale and Harvard I was unable or unwilling to conceal my dislike for particular teachers.

So where did I get my soft spot for pro se litigants, of whom about half have criminal records? Mainly from cases in which they were obviously being mistreated, whether by my judicial colleagues, district court judges, police, prosecutors, or staff attorneys. I am embarrassed that it took me a long time to notice the mistreatment and react to it, and that I don't know *why* it took a long time, and equally I don't know why it didn't take forever. But better late than never, and so a recounting of my efforts to make amends for earlier neglect of these unfortunate "clients" of my court, efforts that because of the indifference or hostility of my judicial colleagues have been only intermittently successful, occupies much of the book.

So read on, but before doing so consider this puzzle: why should I alone (I believe) of the judges on my court have acquired empathy for pro se's? As I've indicated, nothing in my background could have predicted that. But maybe empathy is just something one ages into. But why haven't my colleagues, none of whom is young, aged into it? I don't know, but can guess. To begin with, like many other judges, most of my colleagues (*former* colleagues, remember) are formalists. They think that a judge's role is to apply rules, not to do "justice" in a nontechnical, a humane sense. The pro se's have broken the rules, often the rules of lawful conduct and more often still the procedural rules of the judiciary. So to hell with them (not that a judge would say that out loud, or write it). They may be bad rules but they're our rules! Another possibility is that the judges have a nontrivial degree of work aversion. They say to themselves that hearing cases argued by lawyers and deciding how to decide those cases is enough; there should be a division of responsibility, with the non-argued cases largely consigned to staff attorneys; in other words, "leave us alone, pro se's, we're busy enough without having to think about you."

So what's different about me? I don't know for sure, but I do know that I'm not a formalist. I'm a realist, a pragmatist. To me a case is just a dispute, and the questions I ask are what's the most sensible resolution of the dispute and is that resolution—the decision that I'd like to render—blocked by statute or case law that I can't get around? Usually I can get around it by hook or crook, because our law is pretty fluid.

And remember what I said about being a difficult, even a somewhat rebellious, student at Yale and Harvard? Doesn't that make me just a bit like Winston Churchill, who happens to be my number-one hero? He was 14 when he entered Harrow, one of England's most prestigious public schools (schools that we would call private schools), in 1888, remaining there for four years. On the one hand, according to his housemaster, he was the "ablest boy in his form"—"in fact, remarkable." Yet at the same time "he was considered a hopeless pupil," a "baffling boy ... plainly uninterested in academic subjects. ... Of course he had always a brilliant brain, but he would only work when he chose to and for the matters he approved of." In short, "Churchillian stubbornness ...was the despair of his teachers." William Manchester, *The Last Lion: Winston Spencer Churchill: Visions of Glory 1874-1932*, pp. 157-160 (1983). I was no Winston Churchill. I was far more docile, yet I had and have a rebellious streak—visible, in this book, in my strong disagreements with judges and staff.

I also work harder than virtually anyone, judge or other, whom I know, but only because I *like* to work hard and don't value leisure. I imagine my work ethic grated on some of my judicial colleagues, not to mention staff. But I am what I am. I've been typing away since I got my first typewriter, at age 13, so why stop. But I have to admit, as bearing critically on my empathy for the pro se's, that I've gotten softer in the last year for reasons I can't *begin* to fathom. Could it be that I had simply gotten bored with my old routine, and needed something new? Could be. Or that I'd begun to take seriously a French quotation that Churchill took seriously (see Manchester, *supra*, at 245): "*Le coeur a ses raisons que la raison ne connaît point.*"[3] Or the following quotation from Simone Weil: "one must always be ready to change sides with justice, that fugitive from the winning camp."[4]

Manchester, *supra* at 404, calls Churchill "an intuitive rebel," who "being humane … was also genuinely appalled by the plight of the downtrodden," and who as Home Secretary in 1910-11 liberalized England's criminal laws and improved its prison conditions. *Id.* at 414-16.

Might I be just a *little* like him in these respects?

---

[3] In English, "The heart has its reasons that reason ignores."

[4] Manchester, *supra*, at 344, associates Churchill with the quotation, but must mean by this that he thought alone similar lines, not that he had invented it. Its invention has always been attributed to Weil, who was born in 1909, eight years after Churchill's parliamentary debut, which Manchester suggests led within weeks to Churchill's embrace of the thinking that led many years later to Weil's quotation.

Chapter 8

Rejection!

I had lunch with the chief judge of my court on Monday, June 5. The previous Wednesday, May 31, I had circulated to all the judges and staff attorneys of the court a memo that was a precursor to this book, presenting my plan to improve the staff attorneys' memos and draft orders en route to the panels of judges deciding pro se appeals, motions, and occasional other filings. I was surprised to have received no replies to my memo. I was especially curious as to how the chief judge would react to the principal suggestion in it—that I would review all the staff attorneys' memos and other documents en route to the judicial panels that would decide the cases to which those documents pertained. Having reviewed and if need be having revised the staff attorneys' documents, I would pass them on to the relevant judicial panels, urging the panels to include the documents in their decisions so that the pro se's would understand why they had lost (or won) and what if anything they should do next. The panels could and would, however, do what they wanted with my submissions: nothing, if they wanted to, for I would have no veto power.

I thought my proposal uncontroversial, and my sense from the lunch was that the chief judge, though she manifested no enthusiasm, would not oppose it, and I so informed Mike Fridkin that afternoon. I was therefore surprised, as well as very disappointed, to receive the following email from her the next day (June 6); I have boldfaced the portions of the email that I found disturbing, but I have also added in italics a few comments of my own.

> I just got a call from Mike Fridkin that made me realize, that I was not entirely clear with you at our lunch yesterday. What I meant to do at the lunch was, very simply,

to hear you out on your proposals. Some of those proposals seem very good to me and I've already talked to Mike about implementing them. Those include more frequent instruction in writing for the staff attorneys, more interaction between judges and staff attorneys (both for the Rule 34 conferences and the short argument days), and better recruitment tactics for minorities. *[Notice the absence of any suggestion that I would be involved in any of these implementation.]*

I did not intend to convey, however, that I agreed with your proposal to review virtually everything that comes out of the staff attorney's office before it reaches the Rule 34, short argument, or motions panel. In fact, I do not agree with it. I was trying to say *[obviously unsuccessfully]* that such a system is, in my view, **inconsistent with our structure as a multi-member court.** *[How so?]* To be clear, I am not going to tell Mike Fridkin to institute such a system. As I told you when you and Mike visited my office a few weeks ago, **there is a much more modest version of your proposal that I do think could work. If any particular staff attorney would like to have your input and guidance on something that he or she has written (something very like the example you put in your memo), then it is certainly fine with me for that staff attorney to approach you and to ask if you would be willing to engage in that teaching exercise.** The memo might be one prepared for a conference that already has taken place, or it might be for an upcoming conference. Any such sharing of the work product would also have to be done within the scheduling and other constraints that Mike and his deputies have imposed.

We obviously do not see eye-to-eye on a number of things, whether it is your overall view of the staff attorney's office or it is the television point [i.e., whether to allow oral arguments to be televised; *[I discuss that issue in the second part of this book]*. Until Diane Sykes takes over as chief, however, the final decision is mine. I read your 100-page memo very carefully and I made notes *[not shown to me]* in the margins. In those notes, I flagged which parts I thought were feasible and which were not, and I've tried here *[I can't find this, unless the reference is to the first boldfaced passage in the preceding paragraph]]* to let you know which is which. No other judge on the court has sent me any comments on the memo or has copied me on any comments possibly sent to you. If you do not agree with my decision, you are naturally free to ask the others if they support your proposals. **As I told you before, I am having a court meeting no matter what in September, to discuss the pending cases and the television proposal.** I realize that you do not like court meetings and think that they are worthless, but (setting those concerns to one side) there is nothing that would prevent us from discussing your memo. As far as I can tell, from what people have said to me over the years (i.e. not in any way connected to your memo), the judges are generally quite happy with **[I would say they are uninterested in]** our Staff Attorney's office and do not want to take any steps that would deter bright young lawyers from working there *[no explanation for why my proposed reform of the program would deter applicants]*.

I replied—angrily I admit—the same day, in the following email to her:

> Your statement "If any particular staff attorney would like to have your input and guidance on something that he or she has written (something very like the example you put in your memo), then it is certainly fine with me for that staff attorney to approach you and to ask if you would be willing to engage in that teaching exercise" doesn't make sense to me. The staff attorneys who are weakest in ability to communicate with pro se's will be the least likely to consult me, yet most in need of editing.
>
> Your reference to a multi-member court is irrelevant to what I'm proposing. As I explained to Mike in a phone

conversation this morning, my proposal is that I would review all staff attorney memos and draft orders other than perhaps a few that are procedural in the very narrowest sense unrelated to outcomes. On the basis of the reviews I've conducted to date, I would expect half of the memos and orders to be adequately written, and the staff attorneys responsible for those memos and orders would pass them on to the panel assigned to the case. The other half—the poorly written half—would be the focus of my efforts; I would edit each one in the presence of the staff attorney that had drafted it. My goal in editing would be to make the draft intelligible to a prison or jail inmate or other pro se. The memo would then go to the judges on the panel assigned to the case, and would include a recommendation to the judges on the panel on how to decide the case. If the judges found the memo and recommendation persuasive they presumably would (and would be encouraged to) forward it to the pro se together with any additional statement that the judges thought helpful. The judges would of course be free to ignore the memo and recommendation. I would have nothing to do with the judicial action in the matter unless I happened to have been assigned, presumably randomly, to the panel. My work on the staff attorneys' memos and orders and recommendations would be not as a judge but as an aide to Mike.

My goal would simply be to make all our communications with pro se's intelligible to them, as well as to help the staff attorneys make sensible recommendations for the disposition of pro se appeals and other filings. With or without me, there will still be peer review and review by supervisory staff attorneys, but experience teaches that that is not enough.

It would be a mistake to defer consideration of my proposal to a September court conference, because then the judges will have no concrete sense of the program I am proposing. Much better for the program to go into effect now *on an experimental basis*, so that there will be an evidentiary foundation for discussion at a court meeting.

If you 're unwilling to allow the experiment, I shall publish the memo, either as an article or online or both, as well
as circulating it widely throughout the federal judiciary,
and I may conjoin such an article with my thoughts on
allowing the routine (as well as "on request") televising of
federal appellate oral arguments, and thereby create a book.
I will also retire.

I should have retracted the last sentence: "I will also retire." (By
the way, it would have been better English to say: "Also I'll retire.")
I am 78 and a half, have been on the court for 35 and a half years,
am of course eligible to retire at full pay (as I have now done),
and could (now can) undoubtedly obtain academic employment,
continue writing books and articles, and spend more time with my
beloved wife, Charlene, and my famous cat, Pixie. I might also obtain a job as the manager of a cat shelter. (I am, unapologetically, a
"cat nut.") But in the days following my outburst I happened to be
preparing opinions of mine to circulate and realized that I still enjoyed writing judicial opinions (no longer, however). I wrote them
myself; I did not work from law clerks' drafts; my law clerks suggested improvements, often very good ones, in my opinion drafts,
but they were *my* drafts.

The rest of my memo was I think sound. As explained in its
opening paragraph, the staff attorneys most likely to approach me
voluntarily to help them to improve their memos or draft orders,
en route to submitting them to a panel of judges, would be the
ones who write well—who do not need my help. For those staff
attorneys know that when they get around to applying for new
employment to follow their stint as staff attorneys they can ask
me to write a letter of recommendation for them to prospective
employers and that I'll do it gladly because I'll be able to tell prospective employers frankly and truthfully that the staff attorneys
I'm recommending are stars. Some staff attorneys who are not stars
may nevertheless ask me for help with their memos because they
may expect or at least hope that my assistance will improve their
analytic and compositional abilities to the point at which they can
ask me for a letter of recommendation and realistically expect me

to agree, and to write a letter highly favorable to them. My fear is that the ones who *most* need my help will be *least* likely to seek it because of doubt that it will produce a letter of recommendation.

I was told (I forget by whom) that the chief judge was toying with the idea of permitting staff attorneys to ask me to help them with their memos only *after* a panel had already issued its order deciding the case. That seemed odd to me, because after the order is issued, requests for criticism and advice about a staff attorney's memo would threaten to undermine the order, for the criticism and advice might constitute powerful evidence that the order was erroneous—though if the order had been issued and the case therefore decided, it would be too late to correct errors. Criticism and advice need to precede, and shape, the order.

Stated differently, what could a judge (or panel of judges) be expected to do when after issuing an order the judge gets a revised staff attorney memo? The case having been decided, wouldn't the judge look absurd if he mailed it to the pro se, saying "very sorry I didn't have this when I decided your case, and now it's too late, but maybe you'll enjoy reading it or find some other use for it the next time you file an appeal with us." The sequence suggested by the chief judge—first the order, then the memo on which the order is purportedly based—was thus hard to picture.

* * *

Moving on: Notice that in my reply to the chief judge's email I softened my proposal, changing it to a proposal merely to conduct an *experiment*, between now (that is, June 6) and the court meeting that she had decided to convene in September—an *experiment* in improving the staff attorneys' memos and draft orders. Without that experiment the meeting was I thought likely to be a flop, just like the court meeting held I think in February on the televising of oral arguments, as explained later. Had I had three months to work on improving the staff attorneys' writing I would have had *evidence* to present to the other judges before the September meeting for discussion at the meeting, and as a result the meeting would not be mere idle chatter.

The chief judge's suggestion that the September meeting would also take up the issue (the subject of Part Two of this book) of whether to allow televising of our oral arguments struck me as odd in the following sense: it was in mid-November 2016 that C-Span asked our court to allow it to televise two upcoming en banc oral arguments scheduled for November 30. The chief judge declined because one of the other judges thought two weeks too short a time in which to decide so momentous an issue (actually trivial not momentous, for as we'll see there are no plausible arguments against televising oral arguments).

One of the cases (*Hively v. Ivy Tech*) was decided early in April of this year (2017), the other (*United States v. Johnson*) in May. It was in February if I remember correctly that the chief judge had convened a meeting of the judges to discuss whether to permit televising of the court's oral arguments. Of course that was too late for *Hively* and *Johnson*, which had already been decided. And so far as the future was concerned, the meeting was inconclusive and the chief judge appointed a committee of judges to make a recommendation. As of today, August 6, 2017, the committee has not yet reported, but the chief judge has added it to the agenda for the September 26 meeting. This means that 10 months will have elapsed from the date of the oral arguments before the issue is resolved. That seems too long, which adds to my doubts that there will be a sound and timely resolution of issues relating to the staff attorney program either.

Another twist to the issue of the September meeting is that the average age of the court's judges is 73 and the median age 74.5; only the First and Fifth Circuits have higher average (74 and 86) and median (76 and 85.5) ages; and it's a fair conjecture that the older a judge, the less likely he or she is to take an interest in administrative details; also the less likely to take an interest in the staff attorney program. (I'm a 78.5 year-old exception—but no longer a judge.) At present there are three vacancies on our court, and of the sitting judges all but two are eligible for retirement at full pay right now. Soon there will be a fourth vacancy because one of the judges eligible to retire, Ann Williams—a very fine judge, one of my favorites—is planning to retire in November. If more peel off soon and the appointment of successors is delayed, the court may find itself unable to manage the staff attorney program.

A further puzzle about the meeting scheduled for September 26 was its raison d'être in light of the judges' unanimous decision (unanimous except for me and Judge Williams, the two absentees) in response to the chief judge's judge-by-judge inquiry on June 6 concerning reaction to my proposed experiment. Given that unanimity, I couldn't see the point of a meeting to decide the identical issue. However, later the chief judge explained that she was planning over the summer to alter the staff attorney program, as I will explain later in the book.

Here's another puzzle concerning the extinction of my planned revamping of the staff attorney program: apparently none of the judges was *relieved* to learn that I was willing to shoulder the principal judicial burden of the staff attorney program. In part because of their age, many of the judges do not want to be workhorses and as a result usually welcome measures that reduce their workload— as my shouldering a significant part of the judicial involvement in the program would have done. It's not as if the other judges were or are *interested* in the staff attorney program; generally they are not, and are happy to relinquish control of the program to the staff attorneys. They knew me to be a fast, competent, *experienced* writer; did they doubt that I could improve the staff attorneys' memos? Or did they think me a softy, enamored of pro se's and bound therefore to try to empty the prisons? Or were they afraid that I'd overshadow them if given such an assignment? I'd known these judges a long time, but we didn't seem to understand each other.

My guess—no more than that—is that the chief judge indicated in her conversation with the other judges that she didn't want me to review the staff attorneys' memos and draft orders, and that the other judges fell in line, not having strong feelings about the issue. Yet had Michael Fridkin, the director of the staff attorney program, simply said to me: "Dick, please help the supervisory staff attorneys edit the two-year staff attorneys' memos and draft orders," and I had agreed to do so, would any of the judges, including the chief judge, even have *known*? And had they eventually found out, *cared* (with the possible exception of the chief judge)? I doubt it.

Recurring to the issue of the September meeting, I had no high hopes for it—for the additional reason that it was apparent that the chief judge had not suggested to any of the judges whom she had talked to on June 6 that they talk to me about my proposed experiment, and in fact no judge did ever call or email me to inquire into my response to the chief judge's email. Indeed no judge ever called or emailed me about the memo that I had emailed to all of them on May 31. I began to wonder whether the court has ceased to be a collegial body—and whether I was becoming a pariah, an outcast. But not to worry; for what would I have been an outcast of? A court seemingly in decline, given the high average age of the judges, the number of vacancies—all to be filled by Trump nominees—not a happy prospect—and the disarray in the staff attorney program.

Her long email that I quoted earlier seems to me to have weakened at the end, with its references to the judges' happiness with the current staff attorney program and its invocation of fear of losing applicants for the program if their writings were subject to review by me. In truth the judges, irrespective of age, are already largely indifferent to the program, and tend as a result to rubber stamp the recommendations of the staff attorneys rather than examine them critically, let alone edit them. This is related to the "bunching" problem that I referred to earlier. Occasionally a judge—this certainly has happened to me often enough—will receive ten staff attorney memos all at once, and the desire to dispose of them at once by rubber stamping them rather than studying them carefully is well-nigh irresistible.

What is more, until I became interested in the staff attorney program in the late winter/early spring of this year (2017) I'm pretty sure I'd never even discussed it with another judge. I can think of only three respects in which I'd been involved with the program before then. First, when I became a member of the court at the end of 1981, and shortly afterward rewrote a staff attorney's proposed order or opinion, the then director of the program told me that a judge is not permitted to rewrite a staff attorney's document. I knew that was absurd and ignored it, and the issue never arose again. Second, when I was chief judge (1993-2000) there was a sudden surge of pro se appeals and the then director of the staff attorney program (not the one I had told off years earlier) was overwhelmed by the surge and at my urging resigned and was replaced. And third, occasionally a nonsupervisory staff attorney would be semi-permanent rather than serve for only two years. I recall a staff attorney who was a genuine expert on medical problems (in part because she had such problems herself), and I considered her a major asset of the court and consulted her frequently. But a decision was made (this was before I was chief judge) not to have any permanent staff attorneys below the supervisory level (for all I know it's still the rule, but if so it's a bad one, which I believe is not in force in the staff attorney programs of the other federal courts of appeals), and so she was forced to retire, which I thought and still think was very unfortunate both for her and for the program.

The staff attorney program chugs along, but lacks energy. I had hoped to be allowed to give it a boost, but that hope was shattered on June 7, the day after my exchange of emails with the chief judge, when she sent me another email, of which the gist was that "I cannot agree to have you look at *all* of the staff attorney memos and draft orders *before* they are submitted to the assigned judge or panel, for your review and editing. As I have explained to you in the past [sounds like teacher talking to student], I regard this as fundamentally incompatible with the fact that we are a multi-member court on which each judge has equal responsibility for the court's work. That is why I cannot endorse this idea even as an experiment. I should add that I have asked every one of the other judges on the court (save Ann [Williams], who is in Africa and who has one foot out the door anyway [remember that she'd announced that she would be retiring at the end of the summer—yet could easily have been reached in Africa via the Internet, as she is tech-savvy and goes nowhere without her cellphone] whether they think that I should approve your proposal, and they all agree with my position." The "I have asked" statement was presumably a reference to her communications with the judges on June 6. She has not indicated what they said to her. Did she mention to them that any changes I suggested in a staff attorney's memo would not be binding on the panel of judges who received my edited draft? Had she told them that I can't believe they'd have objected. More than that, her reference to the other judges "agree[ing] with my [that is, her] position" suggests that she announced her position to them at the outset of the communication, correctly assuming that they wouldn't try to buck her.

Her first point, about each judge having "equal responsibility for the court's work," is misleading because even if each judge *has* equal responsibility for the court's work (which is not true, since some of the judges are on senior service and work only part time, as judges on senior service are permitted to do, and all the judges have different interests, energies, and abilities), it is obvious to anyone acquainted with the court that the degree to which judges shoulder their responsibilities varies greatly. Some of the judges have senior status and work only part time. Among the active judges the degree of energy, work, and output varies depending in part on how much of the work a judge delegates to law clerks—and to staff attorneys. The chief judge has not to my knowledge endeavored to equalize responsibility for the court's work among the judges, and it would not be possible to do so.

But this is a side issue. What particularly disturbed me was her deciding to consult all the *other* members of the court (except Judge Williams) yet give *me* no chance to respond. I had the largest stake in my proposed experiment and more knowledge of and first-hand involvement with the staff attorneys than any of the other judges. I would therefore have expected her to bring me into her conversations with the nine judges (all but herself, Williams, and me) whom she consulted about my experiment. I would have expected her either to put me on the line when she talked to the judges (or on the email, if that's how she communicated with them), or summarize to me what they said, or suggest they speak to me. I have no idea what she told them about my proposed experimental program, or (with one exception, discussed below) what they said in response, or whether she suggested they speak to me, or to Fridkin, or to anyone else, about the issue of my role in relation to the staff attorney program.

I can understand why she would want me to speak last, that is, to add my two cents worth only *after* I had heard the opinion of each judge called or texted by her. But I have difficulty understanding her total lack of interest in what I might say in response to each of the judges who rejected my proposal—a response impossible without my knowing *why* they had rejected it and so without an opportunity to respond to any of them. I think it an equal dereliction of duty on her part not to have *told* the judges whom she consulted about my proposed experiment to tell me, and not just her, their reactions to the proposal.

* * *

Two days after my exchange of emails with the chief judge in the first week of June, I called one of the judges whom I know well to try to learn what the judges had told the chief judge in response to her inquiries of them about my proposal regarding the staff attorney program. To my surprise he said he didn't know what *they'd* said; they hadn't told him and she hadn't told him. I tried to explain that what my proposed experiment that she'd nixed—an experiment that was a weakened version of my original proposal—would have amounted to was simply telling Michael Fridkin that I would write a letter of recommendation for *any* staff attorney who allowed me to edit his or her memos or draft orders, and I would explain in the recommendation letters for the weak writers that they had voluntarily requested that I edit their memos/ orders, that by volunteering they had expressed a genuine interest in learning to write better, and that on the basis of that display of interest I considered them to have promise to evolve into effective lawyers. I don't like the "volunteer" approach, as I noted earlier in commenting on its advocacy by the chief judge; it was just an effort at compromise, but apparently it was the approach preferred not only by her but also by the judge I was talking to. I thought he was being naïve to be as confident as he was that the "askers" for my reviewing their writing would be the staff attorneys who don't write well. As I've explained, the askers are more likely to be the *best* writers, because having impressed me with their writing skills they'd be assured of being able to obtain from me a warm letter of recommendation to any prospective employer whom they would be interested in working for after the end of their normally two-year term as a staff attorney. I have written many such recommendation letters—all for outstanding staff attorneys.

This judge told me that my email to the chief judge had left her with no alternative to doing what she did, which was to interview the judges in my absence. Not true; she could have said: let's discuss this in a conference call in which *everyone*, including Posner, can explain his or her views. Why didn't she do that? In a further email to the judge I was corresponding with I said I didn't think the other judges understood, and I wasn't sure he did, that it had never been my intention to "take over" the staff attorney program. I was merely going to assist Fridkin (who has been with me every step of the way, but refuses to challenge the chief judge because he serves, or rather he thinks he serves, at her pleasure[1]) in regard to the quality of the staff attorneys' memos and draft orders. Those documents are merely inputs into the decision process by the panel assigned to the case. I have been emphatic that a panel can do what it wants with a case assigned to it, except that it should include in whatever order it issues a properly edited staff attorney memo, which is to say a memo edited to make sure it's understandable by the pro se appellant.

* * *

I'm disgusted by all this chatter behind my back by my "colleagues." But that said, I have to admit that I am not above occasionally engaging in such chatter, and that I've decided to note two recent clashes with colleagues, whom however I shall not name. The first involved a case, *Muhammad v. Pearson*, opinion not yet published at this writing, in which a person filed a suit in the federal district court in Chicago against police for false arrest. The plaintiff had indeed been falsely arrested; that was conceded. The police had gone to the wrong apartment at the address given them by an informant, thinking they'd find a dealer in illegal drugs who had a gun, and probably some of the illegal drugs as well, with him; they found and arrested a man they believed to be the dealer (mistakenly—for one thing, a thorough search of the apartment yielded no

---

[1] That isn't exactly correct. As noted earlier in the book, to fire the senior staff attorney (the formal title of the director of the staff attorney program), the chief judge requires the approval of the court.

gun and no illegal drugs). The police carted him off to the police station nevertheless, but released him after he'd been there for 15 minutes, realizing belatedly that they'd arrested the wrong man.

He lost his suit for false arrest in the district court and appealed to our court, and though I was the presiding judge and wanted to reverse the dismissal of his suit, the other two judges on the panel wanted to affirm, deeming the blunder by the police an excusable mistake, and so I assigned the preparation of the majority opinion to one of them (as the senior-most judge on the panel, I was responsible for assigning the majority opinion even though I was planning to dissent), and after receiving a second draft of the majority opinion I wrote a dissent from which I'll quote just a brief portion of the ending: "The biggest blunder that Pearson [the head of the police team] made was that, intending to arrest Carr [the drug dealer], he arrested Muhammad [the innocent one, who became the plaintiff in the false-arrest suit] *after* realizing that the description of Carr didn't fit Muhammad. Pearson didn't even ask Muhammad his name before dragging him off to the police station—he asked only for an I.D., which Muhammad, as an overnight guest, happened not to have on his person. I added that the kind of police misconduct, condoned first by the district judge and then by the two other judges of my court on this panel, that occurred in this case is serious because of its impact on the black community." I further noted that not only did officer Pearson arrest an innocent person and doubtless terrify all four occupants of the apartment, but so far as appears the police did not reimburse the residents of [the apartment] for breaking open the door to the apartment, as the police did, with their battering ram [how police love battering rams!]. In addition, I believe that the police never apologized for their mistakes. Compare my majority opinion in *Balthazar v. City of Chicago*, 735 F.3d 634, 636 (7th Cir. 2013), a case in which having broken into the wrong apartment by means of a battering ram the police promptly paid the occupant for the damage to her door. Those police, like the police in this case, were Chicago police, but civilized Chicago police.

I should add that the mistake the police made in confusing Mohammed with Carr could well reflect a common phenomenon: the tendency of members of an ingroup (e.g., white males) to have difficulty distinguishing among members of an outgroup (e.g., black males). See Edwin R. Shriver, *et al.*, "Class, Race, and the Face: Social Context Modulate the Cross-Race Effect in Race Cognition," https://www.researchgate.net/publication/5640070_Class_Race_and_the_Face_Social_Context_Modulates_the_Cross-Race_Effect_in_Face_Recognition. Of course the fact that a phenomenon is common doesn't make it excusable; it was inexcusable, which is a principal reason why I think Muhammad is entitled to the damages he sought in his false-arrest suit.

* * *

My second recent disagreement with a colleague concerns a piece of trivia; I have to admit that the clash doesn't reflect credit on me.

Some of our judges refer to the current chief judge, whose first name is Diane, as "Chief Diane." That strikes me as odd. I call her "Diane," and would expect all the judges of our court to call her that, and other members of the court family, such as her law clerks, to call her, as they doubtless do, "Chief Judge Wood." (Personally, I don't like formality; my law clerks have always called me "Dick," and indeed anyone who wants to call me that is welcome to do so.) Becoming impatient with the sobriquet "Chief Diane," I emailed the judges reminding them that since my appointment to the court in 1981 there had been before Chief Judge Wood five male chief judges in sequence—Walter Cummings, Bill Bauer, Dick Posner, Joel Flaum, and Frank Easterbrook—yet no one had heard anyone of them referred to as "Chief Walter," "Chief Bill," "Chief Dick," "Chief Joel," or "Chief Frank." In light of this history it struck me as odd that the first female chief judge should be addressed in such a way.

In retrospect, I cannot understand what moved me to email the judges concerning my felt oddness at the sobriquet, as the issue is one of incredible insignificance. But by doing so I unintentionally angered one of the male judges (unintentionally because I thought that on reflection all the judges, including the chief judge, would agree that "Chief Diane" was a silly mode of address—I was wrong) and the chief judge ordered me to apologize to him, which I did, but, I have to admit, not very graciously. I said in an email to him: "Diane Wood told me today that you had been offended by the email I sent discussing the sobriquet 'Chief Diane.' The email was intended to be primarily tongue in cheek, though I do think it ['Chief Diane'] a rather silly mode of address, also sexist because none of the male chief judges has ever been referred to as 'Chief [first name].' But what particularly amused me was the fact that there would be two 'Chief Dianes' in immediate succession when Diane Wood's term as chief judge expires [in about three years] and Diane Sykes's term [Sykes is next in line to be chief judge] immediately begins. I didn't mean to offend you or anyone else, but if I did, please accept my heartfelt apology. We have been judicial colleagues and friends for more than 30 years and I don't recall our ever having quarrelled, though we've sometimes disagreed about case outcomes." I have since apologized profusely for fussing over the term "Chief Diane" and, I am glad to say, good relations have been restored.

Appendix One to Part One

The Spreadsheets

This appendix contains a good deal of interview material, primarily obtained by my University of Chicago Law School research assistants Makar Gevorkian, John McAdams, and Theresa Yuan from interviews with staff attorneys of federal courts of appeals other than the Seventh Circuit. But the appendix begins with a pair of spreadsheets comparing the staff attorney programs of the different federal circuits. The spreadsheets may suggest ways in which the Seventh Circuit's staff attorney program might be improved—and it certainly needs improvement.

The light gray boxes in the first spreadsheet contain the results of research conducted by Michael Fridkin several years ago; the findings (which are very recent) of my research team at the University of Chicago Law are also shown in light gray, and the findings of that team that coincide with Fridkin's findings are shown in dark gray. The second spreadsheet contains essentially the same information but is colorless, yet makes up for the loss of color by being more legible. In the text of this book I focus on a subset of the federal circuits' staff attorney programs, primarily those of the second, third, fifth, seventh, ninth, and eleventh circuits; the spreadsheets provide information about the seven other circuits' programs, enabling the reader to trace similarities and divergences among all the circuits' staff attorney programs.

Circuit	1st	2nd	3rd	4th	5th	6th
Numbers						
Total SA's	17.5-21.5	35-36	23-30	40-50	39-45	32
Senior/Supervisory SA's	1 senior, 1 supervisory	6		1 senior, 4 supervisory	7 supervisory	
Non-Senior/Supervisory SA's	15.5-19.5 (.5 for half a term)	29-30		35-45	32-38	
Term SA's vs. Career SA's	Mostly career	All term	Half term, half career	40% term, 60% career	All career	Half term, half career
Active Judges on this Cir.	6	13	14	15	17	16
Length of Terms (if terms)	N/A, career	2 years, can re-enlist up to 5	1-2 years	1-2 years	2 years (can convert to career)	
Office Setup						
Unique features?/Other notes		In 2005, created a separate office handling only Board of Immigration appeals.			Don't prepare memos on diversity, Title VII, tax court, bankruptcy appeals	
Background/ Hiring						
Salary Range* (*self-reported or as listed on job postings over the last 5 years)	$71,538 - $84,556		$63,323 - $74,884	$60,495 - $70,903	$59,246 - $84,443 (Senior Staff get $113,735 – 147,887)	$85,177 - $93,357
EEOC Diversity		Mostly White/Asian				
Hire straight out of law school?	No (at least 2 years out)	Yes	Yes	Yes		Yes
Writing Sample in Job Application?			Yes	Yes	Yes	
Writing Exercise in Job Interview?		Yes			Yes	
Productivity						
# of Merits Recommendations Annually	300		660	2500	2500	600
Number of orally argued cases on which the office drafts merits recommendations (annually)	0		Only death/immig. Cases	0	0	Only death cases
% of cases from office published as precedential	1%		Very small	0%	Very small	3%

7th	8th	9th	10th	11th	DC	FC
16-21	17-20	75-80	19-21	60-70		4
	4 supervisory					
	16					
All term	Half term, half career	All term	All career	All term		Half term, half career
11	11	29	12	12	11	12
	2 years	1-5 years		2 years	1-2 years	Multiple-year extensions
				Jurisdiction Unit (reviewing appeals to determine appellate jurisdiction), Issue Tracking Unit (to track relevant legal issues), Motions Unit (to process substantive motions)		Very little turnover
$64,174 ($131,380 - $161,900 if Senior SA)	$59,960 - $61,010 (Supervisory SA gets at least $93,999)			$63,161	$61,977 - $138,148	
				Mostly White/Asian		
Yes			No	Yes	Yes	
Yes				Yes	Yes	
				Yes		
475	400	3660		1800		
120	0	0		0		
13%	Less than 1%	0%		2%		

Circuit	1st	2nd	3rd	4th	5th	6th
Types of Cases						
Immigration	Yes		Yes	Yes	Yes	Yes
Employment Discrimination	Yes, if pro se		Yes	Yes	Yes, if pro se	Yes
Direct Criminal Appeals	Yes		No	Yes	Yes	Yes
Prisoner Rights	Yes, if pro se		Yes, if pro se	Yes	Yes	Yes
Non-prisoner rights	Yes, if pro se		Yes, if pro se	Yes	Yes	Yes
Habeas (2241, 2254, 2255)	No		Yes	Yes	Yes	Yes
Social Security	Yes		Yes, if pro se	Yes	No	Yes
Commercial/ Contract	No		Rarely	Rarely	No	Sometimes
Intellectual Property	No		Rarely	Rarely	No	Sometimes
FTCA	No		Rarely	Yes	Yes	Sometimes
ERISA	No		Rarely	Yes	No	Sometimes
Antitrust	No		Rarely	Rarely	No	No
Description of Procedure	SA's screen non-argument cases, write memo and draft opinion for 3-judge panel; panel judges vote in "round robin" fashion (if 1 just wants it sent to argument, it is); "not unusual" for judges to substantially revise or totally alter draft opinion	SA's screen non-oral argument cases, SA's write memo and draft summary order, judges don't meet each other or SA's to discuss these; judges vote on a serially submitted voting sheet with 1-week deadlines	SA's don't screen cases for oral argument; SA's write memo and draft orders/per curiam opinions; judges don't meet but instead submit votes to the "administrative judge" on the panel with a copy to the other panel members in no particular order (to minimize judges ocraticing each other when casting votes)	SA's write memo to judges if a pro se litigant (who isn't permitted oral argument in the 4th Circuit) should get to argue the case; 40% of cases don't have judges conferencing in person (instead, they vote alone with one lead judge, randomly assigned, voting first, followed in no particular order by 2 other judges); 60% of cases involve SA's making oral presentations before a panel, SA's draft dispositions (but don't write memos), judges convene by phone twice a month with SA's to discuss cases and the judges decide 45-75 appeals in one go	SA's do the screening (classify cases as I or II if these cases are likely to get a per curiam opinion, classify cases as II or IV if they cry out for oral argument); SA's draft memos and proposed disposition and present to judge panel; panel consults SA about proposed disposition	SA writes memo and drafts order, no ocratiction between judges and SA (although in the 80's, the 6th Cir. Was committed to face-to-face communication)

7th	8th	9th	10th	11th	DC	FC
Yes	Yes	Yes		Yes		
Yes	Yes	Yes, if pro se		Yes		
Yes	Yes	Yes		Yes		
Yes	Yes	Yes		Yes		
Yes	Yes	Yes		No		
Yes	Yes	Yes		Yes		
Yes	Yes	No		Yes		
Yes	Yes	Yes, if pro se		No		
Rarely	Rarely	Yes, if pro se		No		
Yes	Yes	Yes		No		
Yes	Yes	No		No		
No	No	No		No		
SA recommend dispositions on lots of cases "including some of the court's most controversial"?; SA's attend weekly private conferences with 3-judge panels	SA's attend court sessions with their judge; other SA's in a central office in St. Louis handle motions, pro se cases, cases submitted without oral arguments				SA's write a memo and draft a proposed disposition and send to 3-judge panel; Judges hold biweekly conferences deciding 6-24 such cases with the supervising SA and the authoring SA; in non-argument cases that are "frivolous" SA's send a memo to the Chief Judge and then to 2 other judges on a panel who either agree with the proposed disposition or put it on the argument calendar	

Circuit	1st	2nd	3rd	4th	5th	6th
Routine Motions (Extensions of time, oversized briefs)	No		Rarely	No	No	No
Substantive Motions (Stays pending appeal)	Yes		Yes, if pro se, habeas, or immig.	Yes	Yes	Yes, if pro se or death
Petitions for mandamus, Class-Certification, Sec. 1252 Appeals	Yes		Yes, if pro se, habeas, or immig.	Petitions for mandamus; no class cert. orders	Yes, if pro se	Yes, if pro se
Jurisdictional Screenings	Yes		Yes	Yes	No	Yes
Requests for certificate of appealability, Successive Habeas Applications	Yes		Yes	Yes	Yes	Yes
Turnaround Time for CA Request?			30 days	50-70 days	Up to 90 days	30 days
Turnaround Time for Successive Application?	30 days		10 business days	1-2 weeks	2 weeks	30 days

Oral Argument Input

	1st	2nd	3rd	4th	5th	6th
Input on whether to have argument?	Occasionally		No	Yes	Yes	Rarely
Input on how much time to set for argument?	Yes		No	No	Yes	No

Judge Interaction

	1st	2nd	3rd	4th	5th	6th
How do panels interact?	Electronic web vote	Serially-submitted voting sheet	Email	Email	It varies	Email/phone/face-to-face
Are SA's present for panels?	No	No	No	No	No	No
SA's get face-time with judges?	No/rarely	No/rarely	No/rarely	Yes according to job listing (no from Fridkin's interview)	Yes according to job listing (no from Fridkin's interview)	No/rarely
Are released orders as detailed as internal recommendations?	No		Yes	No	No. Orders are not detailed.	No. Orders are less detailed.
Draft dissents/ concurrences?	Occasionally		Occasionally	No	No	Occasionally
Chambers borrow SA's?	Not recently		Sometimes	No	Rarely	Rarely

7th	8th	9th	10th	11th	DC	FC
Yes (paralegal does these)	No	Yes (paralegal does these)		No		
Yes (paralegal does these)	Yes, if pro se	Yes (paralegal does these)		Only IFP, appointment of counsel		
Yes (paralegal does these)	Yes, if pro se	Yes (paralegal does these)		Yes, for petitions for mandamus		
No	No	Yes (paralegal does these)		Yes		
Yes (paralegal does these)	Yes	Yes (paralegal does these)		Yes		
30 days		Up to 1.5 years		35 days		
2 weeks	2-4 weels	60 days		5 (days? Weeks?)		
Occasionally	No	Yes		Yes, in 300/year		
No	No	Yes		Rarely		
Face-to-face/phone	By memo	Face-to-face		Email/phone/rarely face-to-face		
Yes	Sometimes copied	Yes		No		
Yes	No/rarely	Yes		No/rarely	Yes	
Yes	No. Orders are less detailed.	Yes		No		
Occasionally	Occasionally	No		No		
Sometimes	Not recently	Sometimes		No		

Appendix Two to Part One

The Interviews

Fruits of interviews and other research conducted by my research team at the University of Chicago Law School, supervised by my chief research assistant, Theresa Yuan

CASA. The Council of Appellate Staff Attorneys (CASA) is a group of 60 to 70 staff attorneys at the state and federal level. (Many state courts, like federal courts, have staff attorney programs, but I don't discuss them in this book.) CASA is part of the American Bar Association's Judicial Division. It costs $130 per year to be a CASA member, although discounted rates are available if staff attorneys and judges form 5-person groups. CASA began in the early 1980's, when the first staff attorney programs were developing. About ¼ of the members work in federal courts and the other ¾ in state courts.

CASA's main focus is on ramping up attendance at the annual Appellate Judges Education Institute (AJEI), a 4-day conference. CASA members can get Continuing Legal Education credits for attending,[1] although as CASA board members have noted, this attendance has been on the decline since some courts stopped requiring Continuing Legal Education credits of its staff.[2] CASA members attend sessions on legal writing,[3] constitutional issues,

---

[1] Michael Roew, an 11th Cir. Staff Attorney, described the conference as "a great way to knock out a lot of CLEs at one time." (*CASA Quarterly*, Spring 2009)

[2] The two other reasons for declining CASA membership and conference attendance are that courts do not provide funding to travel to, say, Honolulu for a four-day conference, and "some judges have an anti-ABA sentiment since the organization grades potential judges." (*CASA Quarterly*, Spring 2014).

[3] "Writing programs are always popular at [AJEI], and this year there are two-one program to focus on writing in plain English, and the other program addressing effective editing." (*CASA Quarterly*, Fall 2009)

changing concepts of marriage/family, marijuana-legalization-related issues, and privacy/technology issues, among others proposed by the CASA members. They also have dinner together and get to know one another through a highly anticipated funny T-Shirt exchange.

During the AJEI conference, CASA members volunteer to speak to law students at a nearby law school about their work. They have five minutes to describe their job functions, five minutes to describe "other" attorney positions within their court, and five minutes to describe why graduates of mid- to lower-ranked law schools should work there. I have no information about what comes of these sessions, and what types of law student attend.

Diversity has been a prevailing concern since 2009, when one CASA board member noted that "we have problems with diversity because there are few diverse members in our profession and few of them seek staff attorney positions."[4] Since 2014, a few CASA members have volunteered at the Judicial Clerkship Program, which is the American Bar Association's diversity outreach program. Fourteen law schools select and pay for 2 to 6 students from racial/ethnic minorities to attend each year. These students are placed in groups of 5 to 6 and assigned to a panel of judges/law clerks/staff attorneys. The students receive a legal scenario resembling an appellate case and are directed to identify the legal issues, research the law, and write the first draft of an opinion. The judges/law clerks/staff attorneys provide feedback concerning these opinions and the students' resumes. I could find one mention of an outcome from this volunteering program, namely that a law student from the 2016 program was promptly hired directly by an unnamed staff attorney office.

To improve staff attorneys' writing, CASA board members have floated two ideas (neither yet executed): creating a primer on best practices for pro se appeals and updating a 20-year-old out-of-print opinion-writing manual. The primer idea was proposed in 2014 and the manual idea in 2016.

---

[4] *Casa Quarterly*, Spring 2009.

1. **Questions for Staff Attorneys from Interviews**

   i. How many years did you work as a staff attorney? An answer may help to establish a timeline of where in their legal career they worked as an SA, if they are comfortable about disclosing such information. Or were you hired as a staff attorney straight out of law school? Or did you work elsewhere before working as a staff attorney? Where did you work, if you worked elsewhere?

   ii. Did anyone at your law school work with you to make the decision to work as a staff attorney? Was there any publicity for working as a staff attorney coming from your law school's career services office?

   iii. Were you in contact with any former staff attorneys before beginning work as a staff attorney?

2. **Application Process**

   i. What do you remember about selecting a writing sample?

   ii. Was there a writing component to your interview? If you are allowed to say and if you remember, what did the writing component ask you to do?

   iii. Did you have group interviews, or solo interviews?

3. **Decisions**

   i. What made you choose to be a staff attorney?

   ii. Looking back, do you have new information now that would have changed your decision?

4. **Office Demographics**

   i. How was the staff attorney program structured? Did you get assigned to a single supervisory SA? How many other SA's worked under a single supervisory SA?

   ii. Were there law clerks in the SA's office, just for the SA's?

   iii. Were you matched with a more experienced SA for mentoring? Perhaps based on staggered terms?

    iv. EEOC Diversity
        a. Do you recall:
            1. The ratio of men to women?
            2. Which race was in the majority? Were there black, Hispanic, Asian, Pacific Islander, Native American, other ethnicities?
                a. Would you say that the racial diversity of the staff attorney's office reflected the racial diversity of the individuals' whose cases you handled as a staff attorney?
            3. Were there any staff attorneys openly self-identifying as LGBQT+?
            4. Were there any individuals with disabilities, to your knowledge?
            5. Were the majority of SA's in their 20's? 30's? 40's? 50's? 60's?

5. Work Itself (Especially Related to Writing)

    i. How many of the cases were routine motions (extensions of time, oversized briefs) vs. substantive motions (e.g., stays pending appeal)?

    ii. Can you walk me through what happened from when you were first assigned a case to when you handed it off?
        a. Was there a deadline for each case?
        b. Would you get briefs, read them, and then write something up? What would you be writing up?
        c. What outside research did you need to use?

    iii. Did the SA's office screen cases for oral argument? Or did you receive only cases that definitely wouldn't get oral argument?

    iv. What were you writing for the judges? How long were the briefs?

    v. What kinds of case did you have to work on?
        a. What was the most common type of case?
        b. What was the most complicated or time-consuming type of case?

    vi. Did specializations occur—for example, if some SA is best at handling one type of complicated case, did he or she tend to be assigned more of those?

   vii. Memo-Writing/Dispositions Questions
      a. Were there, as in the 7th Circuit, "cover sheets" accompanying each proposed order? In that court cover sheets are used to express doubts about, say, the 'real' reasoning for an order—i.e., how the sausage *really* gets made. Did you have such encounters at your court?
      b. What was your main audience when writing? The judges? The pro se litigants?
      c. How did memo writing as a staff attorney compare to what you'd done and learned in law schools? Did you feel prepared to be writing memos, or was it more "trial by fire", "sink or swim"?
      d. What about proposing dispositions (decisions) of cases? Did it get easier to identify what would be the best proposed disposition as you went on over time? Did a supervising SA tell you what to propose for each case?
      e. Did you tailor your dispositions for the panel based on your knowledge of how certain judges were prone to decide?
      f. Were there ramifications if a proposed disposition was rejected or swapped entirely?
      g. Did you receive guidance on proposing dispositions from others that weren't a Supervising SA?

  viii. Caseload Question
      a. Did caseload become noticeably heavier in the time that you were a staff attorney? In certain areas? Did it become lighter?

    ix. Were there any particularly memorable cases that you are able to discuss? (i.e, not pending cases!)

6. Presenting Work to Judges
    i. Did you meet with judges in person? By phone?
      a. How often?

      b. How would they get in touch if they had questions on a case?

      c. Did the judges meet face-to-face, by email, by memo to discuss these cases?

  ii. Did you keep track of how often the panels (or individual judges) adopted or revised your proposed dispositions?

  iii. How significantly do the judges revise draft orders, opinions?

  iv. Would you ever draft dissents/concurrences?

  v. Feel free to be as specific as you'd like for this questions: how true is the popular perception that judges "rubber stamp" the decisions that come to them from the Staff Attorney's Office?

  vi. Timing. The 7th Circuit has a bunching problem: a bunch of orders get sent all at once on a Friday afternoon to a judge (although some judges prefer their orders bunched). Was there such a bunching occurrence at your court?

  vii. Are you aware of how many opinions from the office were precedential?

  viii. Did the chambers ever borrow staff attorneys for certain types of work?

7. After Presenting Orders to Judges

  i. Did you ever hear back from the litigants after an order went out?

8. Experiences Learned and Compensation

  i. What did you learn about writing memos?

  ii. What advice would you give yourself starting out as an SA that would have been valuable?

  iii. If you'd be comfortable disclosing—what was your salary as an SA? Were there salary increases based on how long you had been there? How did it measure up against the cost of living in the respective city?

iv. How many hours a week were you working, approximately? Was the workload even? How often did you have to work on weekends?

9. If Applicable

i. When did you leave? August of 2014.

    b. Did you have the chance to convert being a term SA to being a Career SA or otherwise extending?

ii. Did your years as a SA allow you to skip years of grunt work as an associate?

iii. Had you always planned to go into private practice/gov't/public interest/other? How did your years as a SA impact this decision?

10. General Improvements

i. Were these any changes implemented to caseflow/case-management, or to your office structure, that made your work noticeable easier or more efficient?

ii. Are there any changes you would recommend?

iii. How would you recommend law schools recruit students to be SA's (if indeed you recommend that students become SA's)?

iv. Should individuals straight out of law school work first as SA's before moving on to private practice or other government roles or in public interest roles? Or should it be the other way around?

11. Conclusion

i. Is there anything you'd like to describe about being a staff attorney that you haven't yet had a chance to describe in this interview?

ii. Do you know anyone else who might be willing to discuss working as a staff attorney?

iii. Please let me know if you have any questions and feel free to reach out in the future if they come up. Thank you for your time!

Appendix Three to Part One

More Interviews, Plus Academic Literature on Staff Attorney Programs

This section of the book provides an overview of the academic literature about staff attorneys in federal circuit courts not limited to my court, as well as summaries of a few more interviews of staff attorneys in those other courts. The majority of work that I have found poses just one question: is it bad that judges delegate decision-making to staff attorneys, or is it bad *and* unconstitutional? I found relatively little on how staff attorneys are hired and trained and used, though those are the questions that interest me the most.

Some articles describe the responsibilities of staff attorneys. The most thorough article that I found described how their roles differed circuit by circuit, but that was from 1980 and I am not sure how much of it is still accurate.[1] A more recent article examined differences between some circuit courts' processes for deciding which cases the court will hear oral argument in and how staff attorneys are used in such cases.[2] The circuits are described in the

---

[1] Donald P. Ubell, "Report on Central Staff Attorneys' Offices in the United States Courts of Appeals," *87 Federal Rules Decisions* 253 (1980). For example, the report includes no information on Federal Circuit staff attorneys because the Federal Circuit did not yet have any.

[2] Marin K. Levy, "The Mechanics of Federal Appeals: Uniformity and Case Management in the Circuit Courts," *61 Duke Law Journal* 315 (2011). The article examines the D.C., First, Second, Third, and Fourth Circuits. Another article that provides good background on staff attorney programs is Elizabeth Armand and Malini Nangia, "Judicial Clerkships: Federal Staff Attorney Positions," *NALP Bulletin*, Dec. 2008. The article contains a valuable table that for each circuit lists contract and contact information, such as whether the court hires just-graduated law students for staff attorney positions, hiring timelines, application characteristics, and docket information.

article as largely consistent in having staff attorneys write bench memos and draft orders for cases that are not granted oral argument,[3] but vary greatly about which cases to hear oral argument in. For example, the Second Circuit sorts by subject matter, rarely granting oral argument to immigration appeals but almost always granting it in other cases.[4] The D.C. Circuit, on the other hand, has staff attorneys screen cases for merit, and decisions not to grant oral argument are discussed at an in-person conference with the judges before they are finalized.[5]

The most detailed description of a staff attorney program that I've found is that of the Fifth Circuit; I owe the description, which follows, to the director of the Fifth Circuit's staff attorney program, Michael Schneider: Here it is:

Fifth Circuit Court of Appeals' Staff Attorneys' Office

A. Role of the Staff Attorneys' Office

The Staff Attorneys' Office for the Fifth Circuit ("SAO") is under the administrative control of a supervisory circuit judge (or proctor) designated by the court. Staff attorneys work as an institution for the court rather than for individual judges in the manner of traditional law clerks.

The SAO is headed by a senior staff attorney. The senior staff attorney performs the duties assigned by the court, establishes policies and procedures of the office; supervises the work of the supervisors and staff attorneys; and assigns appeals and motions to staff attorneys.

Staff attorneys are assigned to a supervisor, and that supervisor reviews the staff attorney's memoranda and proposed opinions or orders, monitors personnel actions, trains, and solves problems

---

[3] See Levy, note 2 above, at 344–55.
[4] See *id.* at 349–50.
[5] See *id.* at 346–48.

related to the work supervised. A rotation in supervisors occurs approximately every six months.

The SAO functions as part of the court's case management system, primarily by assisting the court in screening appeals and deciding motions. Staff attorneys prepare screening memoranda and draft proposed opinions with respect to appeals and prepare memoranda and proposed orders with respect to certain motions filed in the court – staff attorneys recommend, judges decide. As part of the case management system and the Continuity of Operations Plan (COOP), the SAO can function totally electronically.

B. Screening Procedures for Appeals

Staff attorneys participate in the screening of direct criminal appeals, prisoner cases challenging conditions of confinement, habeas corpus cases, civil federal question cases, immigration cases, civil cases in which the United States is a party, civil rights cases except Title VII, and at times social security cases. Historically, staff attorneys have not prepared screening memoranda in diversity, Title VII, tax court, and bankruptcy appeals.

Screening is the appellate procedure by which each appeal is examined for the purpose of routing it to one of four decisional tracks: Class I, Class II, Class III (limited oral argument), and Class IV (full oral argument). The court's classification categories are described in *Huth v. Southern Pac. Co.*, 417 F.2d 526, 527 (5th Cir. 1969). The SAO classifies cases as either Class I, II, or III. Class I represents frivolous cases; Class II represents the court's summary calendar (cases raising issues that can be resolved without oral argument), and Class III cases often involve res nova issues and are considered during the court's monthly oral argument weeks. For cases that raise an issue that is currently pending before the court, an appropriate recommendation may be to hold screening of the case until the mandate issues in the pending case.

After a cursory review for jurisdictional problems by a jurisdictional attorney, the briefs are transmitted to the SAO from the Clerk's Office. The senior staff attorney reviews each set of briefs to determine if the appeal should be routed for oral argument. If the senior staff attorney determines that the appeal should be routed for oral argument, the senior staff attorney marks that recommendation on the routing form, provides a brief explanation for the recommendation, and returns the case to the Clerk's Office without a staff attorney memorandum. Civil cases are then forwarded to an initiating active judge. If the screening judge accepts the recommendation for oral argument, the case is placed on the next appropriate calendar. If the screening judge rejects the recommendation for oral argument, that judge's screening panel disposes of the case under the summary calendar procedure. Criminal cases that meet these criteria are placed on the calendar without being referred to an initiating judge.

If, upon initial inspection, the senior staff attorney determines that the briefs in a civil case do not clearly show the need for oral argument, the case is either forwarded to the court with a Class II, no (staff attorney) memorandum, recommendation, or it is assigned to a staff attorney for preparation of a screening memorandum. The Class II, no memorandum, recommendation is not used in criminal and pro se cases. This recommendation is used in counseled civil cases, which involve areas of the law in which the staff attorneys have no special expertise.

C. Case Assignment and Deadlines

The senior staff attorney assigns all cases. Cases are assigned to individual staff attorneys by the age of the case, with the oldest case received in the office being assigned first, except that direct criminal appeals, motions for release pending trial or appeal (i.e., bail motions), and motions to file a successive 28 U.S.C. § 2254 petition or a 28 U.S.C. § 2255 motion are given priority. These priority cases are assigned when received. Non-priority cases are assigned periodically throughout the month. When possible, appeals or motions involving a previous litigant are assigned to the staff attorney who worked on the previous litigation.

Direct criminal appeals are generally due out in 30 days. Civil and indirect criminal appeals are generally due out in 60 to 90 days. The precise due-out date (also known as the suspense date) is noted in pencil by the senior staff attorney on the routing sheet. Once a case has been assigned to a staff attorney, the records manager logs the case into the court's electronic case management system ("CM") to reflect the receipt and assignment of the case. The records manager then delivers the case to the assigned staff attorney. All cases, civil and criminal, must be placed in review a minimum of 5 working days prior to the due-out date.

After completion of the review process, the screening memorandum and proposed per curiam opinion (if required), together with the case materials received from the Clerk, are returned to the records manager to be logged out in CM. The screening memorandum (now called a "greenie" because it has been photocopied onto green paper), the proposed per curiam opinion (if required), together with the case materials, are returned to the Clerk's Office. The Clerk's Office then forwards the case to an initiating judge selected by rotation from a log maintained by the Clerk's Office.

If the initiating judge decides that the case warrants oral argument, the judge returns the case to the Clerk with instructions to docket the case on a Class III or IV oral argument calendar.

If the initiating judge decides that the case should be decided without oral argument, on the summary calendar, that judge prepares an opinion. The judge may use the proposed per curiam opinion prepared by the staff attorney. After the initiating judge has prepared an opinion, the judge forwards it with the case materials to the second member of the panel. If the second judge concurs in the opinion, he or she forwards the case materials to the third judge on the panel. Either judge may send the case to an oral argument calendar, or either panel member may discuss changes in the draft opinion with the initiating judge. If they do not agree on the full text of the opinion, the case is sent to an oral argument calendar. However, if the parties waive oral argument, summary disposition may include a concurring or dissenting opinion by a panel member.

D. Motions Procedure

The SAO reviews applications for a certificate of appealability (COA) - a jurisdictional prerequisite in state prisoner habeas corpus appeals, 28 U.S.C. § 2254; and in 28 U.S.C. § 2255 motions by federal prisoners filed after April 24, 1996); applications for leave to proceed *in forma pauperis* (IFP); applications for leave to file a successive 28 U.S.C. § 2254 petition or a 28 U.S.C. § 2255 motion ("successives"); motions for release on bond or reduction of bond pending appeal ("bail motions"); applications for interlocutory appeals; motions for the appointment or withdrawal of counsel; and motions for the preparation of transcripts at government expense.

Bails pending trial or appeal are due out in three working days, and applications to file successives are due out in 15 days. Other motions are generally due out in 30 to 60 days as noted in pencil by the senior staff attorney on the routing sheet; these motions must be placed in review a minimum of 5 working days prior to the due-out date.

After the review of the staff attorney memorandum and order is completed, the memorandum (also called a "greenie") and proposed order are returned to the Clerk's Office electronically for submission to the court, which is also done electronically. Most of the motions addressed by staff attorneys are decided by one judge. *See* 5TH CIR. R. 27.1 for a list of motions on which the court has authorized the Clerk to rule, and 5TH CIR. R. 27.2 for a list of motions on which a single judge may rule. For single judge motions, the initiating judge acts on the motion and returns it to the Clerk with an appropriate order. For motions requiring panel action, the initiating judge transmits the file to the next judge on the panel with a recommendation. The second judge sends it on to the third judge, who returns the file and an appropriate order to the Clerk.

E. SAO Work Product

For every assigned case, staff attorneys prepare a formal memorandum and a proposed opinion or order (if the recommendation includes a recommended outcome). The assigned staff attorney prepares a "screening memo" when screening an appeal or a "memorandum of staff counsel" when addressing only a pending motion. All memoranda state the relevant facts with record citations, describe the issues, analyze the record and authorities cited (frequently including authorities beyond those cited in the briefs), and explain the staff attorney's recommendation to the court as to classification (if applicable) disposition (affirm, reverse, vacate, or hold).

The staff attorney's initial review includes the following considerations:

- jurisdiction (e.g., final order)
- timely notice of appeal
- mootness or changed circumstances
- waiver of appeal
- abandoned or inadequately briefed arguments
- arguments raised for the first time on appeal
- liberal construction of pro se pleadings
- procedural posture of the case
- standard of review (including plain error)
- prior sanctions or "strikes" if applicable
- outstanding motions or other submissions
- application of the rule that parties may not incorporate other pleadings into briefs.

F. Organization of memoranda

Generally, memos are divided into functional sections: heading, facts, discussion, and recommendation. The office has developed Word templates which contain the format for a screening memos and memoranda of staff counsel. The heading includes the case caption, the case number, the name and email address of the writing attorney, the telephone number for the judges (only) to use, the ruling appealed from in the case of appeals (or the proceeding below in the case of a motion), the district court and judge, jury or nonjury trial (if appropriate), any pending motions in the case of an appeal, the issues in summary, the parties' requests for oral argument (for screening memoranda only), and the recommended disposition. The ruling appealed from should give a statutory reference. For example, 42 U.S.C. § 1983 (civil rights); 21 U.S.C. § 841(a)(1) (drug convictions). If the case is designated for Conference Calendar, the heading also includes a "Conference Calendar" designation at the top of page one.

The statement of issues should be accurate, concise, and stated in terms of the facts of the case. The issue statement should generally follow the appellant's formulation of the issues, but ultimately the issues must be formulated as necessary to decide the case. If you list an issue not raised by the parties, place "(raised by staff attorney)" after that issue. The standard of review should be incorporated into the formulation of the issues, if possible.

In a screening memorandum, the recommendation must provide the calendaring class and, if not Class III or IV, the suggested outcome. Class I involves cases so lacking in merit as to be frivolous and subject to dismissal or affirmance under FED. R. APP. P. 34(a)(2)(A) and 5TH CIR. R. 42.2.

Pursuant to FED. R. APP. P. 34(a)(2)(B) or 34(a)(2)(C), a Class II classification should be recommended for clear-cut decisions; for cases where the issue is sufficiency of evidence and the record demonstrates sufficient evidence; for cases applying well established rules of law to recurring fact situations; for cases involving discretionary acts by a district court where the record demonstrates a rational basis for the exercise of discretion; and for cases presenting straightforward, well defined legal questions requiring decision but not refinement at oral argument. A Class II recommendation may also be appropriate for a case that presents an issue (i) which is res nova in this circuit (and therefore requires a published opinion) but which has been decided by at least two other circuits in the same way, (ii) which does not involve an existing circuit conflict, and (iii) as to which (in the opinion of the SAO) this court is unlikely to differ from the other circuits that have pronounced on it. Staff attorneys should include a publish recommendation in the recommendation line. E.g., Class II, affirm (publish). If the case presents a close question, a notation should be placed in the recommendation indicating that there is a close issue and offering to revise the opinion if the panel wishes. E.g., Class II, affirm (Issue 2 is a close issue; staff counsel can revise the opinion if the panel desires).

A case of first impression in this circuit, a case having issues with little or no controlling authority, or a case involving facts which present a close question may warrant Class III treatment.

A Class III recommendation also requires a recommendation as to oral argument. In criminal cases, if one of the parties is pro se, oral argument is not favored. In civil cases, if one of the parties is pro se, consider whether the appointment of pro bono counsel would be appropriate. In general, a Class III, no oral argument, recommendation is disfavored. Often, such cases may be screened Class II, with either a publication recommendation or an identification in the recommendation line of the close issue presented in the case.

When staff counsel is recommending Class III treatment for a case, staff counsel should also consider whether to recommend supplemental briefing. Supplemental briefing may be appropriate when staff counsel has raised an issue in the case that has not been briefed by the parties, such as when there has been a change in the law since the briefs were filed or there is a jurisdictional issue not noted by the parties. If staff counsel determines that supplemental briefing could be helpful to the panel, staff counsel should address that at the end of the memo and add that recommendation to the memo's recommendation line. A Class III recommendation is also more than just a recommendation for oral argument as the Class III classification constitutes a different decisional process than a Class II classification. In a Class III calendar case, all three judges on a panel prepare for a decision separately but simultaneously in chambers, with each usually receiving a bench memorandum from one of his or her law clerks. Cases on a Class II calendar, in contrast, are decided serially by the screening panel.

In a memorandum of staff counsel (for motions), there is no recommendation as to classification but simply a recommended outcome (grant, deny, or hold).

All outstanding motions must be addressed in the memo and the opinion or order. If a motion is moot because the request for a COA is denied or a judgment is affirmed, both the memorandum and the opinion or order must deny the motion as moot.

G. Special Memorandum Types

Every other month, the court holds an electronic conference calendar to consider *Anders* cases designated for Conference by the writing attorney, in consultation with his or her supervisor. The designated weeks and panels for Conference Calendar are listed on the SAO website under calendars. All Conference Calendar records are kept with the SAO until Conference is concluded. Because the judges conduct their review electronically, there are no presentations to the panel by the writing attorneys. Writing attorneys, however, may receive email or phone inquiries from the judges or their chambers.

Certain direct criminal appeals may be treated in an expedited, summary manner. There are two types of summary treatment cases. In a summary affirmance case, the appellant files a blue brief, and the Government moves for summary affirmance, arguing that the issue is foreclosed. Even if the appellant has not conceded that the issue is foreclosed, the case may be treated summarily, if in fact, the issue is foreclosed. In a summary disposition case, the appellant files a motion and a letter brief, asserting that the issue is foreclosed.

An application to file a successive 28 U.S.C. 2254 application or successive 28 U.S.C. § 2255 motion should be placed on the Augean Calendar if it is straightforward and if the Augean panel will consider the application close to the 30-day period permitted to consider such applications. The Augean Calendar is conducted electronically once a month, typically. If a case presents a close question or is somewhat complicated, it should not be directed to Augean. There are no presentations on applications put on the Augean Calendar.

H. Hyperlinking

The Clerk's Office has developed an automatic hyperlinking program, Citelink, which adds hyperlinks to our memoranda using a specific citation style. Staff attorneys may also manually insert hyperlinks to necessary case information, such as citing to the Bureau of Prisons' inmate release date information. Cited material that cannot otherwise be hyperlinked may be uploaded to the private docket sheet of that case so that it can be hyperlinked using Citelink.

I. Staff Attorney Proposed Opinions and Orders

When an appeal is classified as Class I or Class II, in addition to preparing the screening memorandum, the staff attorney also drafts a proposed per curiam opinion (PC) that is consistent with the recommended outcome. Proposed opinions in cases that will be considered at Conference Calendar must include a reference to Conference Calendar (rather than Summary Calendar) in the caption and the judges assigned for that conference. For motions, the staff attorney drafts a proposed order. Attorneys must use the official templates which contain the format for per curiam opinions, conference calendar opinions, successive habeas orders, successive § 2255 orders, and other miscellaneous orders and opinions.

In drafting orders and opinions, the key consideration is brevity. Each issue (or group of issues) should be disposed of in a sentence with citation to applicable authority. The appellant is generally identified by name rather than by "appellant." The judgment appealed from is identified, each issue and its disposition is stated, and authority for the disposition of each issue is cited. When citing a published case as authority for the disposition of an issue decided on its merits, choose a case that states the relevant standard of review. If an issue is not decided on its merits, state the reason and cite a case. E.g., issue not adequately briefed. Appellate courts do not make findings but rather make conclusions of law. Accordingly, in drafting an opinion, use "conclude" or "hold" but not "find."

All outstanding motions must be addressed in the PC or order.

J. Special Opinions or Orders

Anders per curiam opinions do not list issues, but they must specifically grant or deny the motion to withdraw. The opinion must identify the Federal Public Defender (FPD) when the FPD submits an *Anders* brief. The opinions must also mention whether the defendant has filed a response to counsel's motion to withdraw. When an appellant responds to counsel's motion to withdraw in accordance with *Anders* and raises the issue of ineffective assistance of counsel or a claim that his guilty plea was made under coercion and duress, the opinion should state that the record has not been adequately developed for the court to consider the argument on direct appeal if the issue is not being decided.

Draft opinions recommending vacate and remand have a more detailed analysis than opinions that affirm or dismiss as frivolous.

Parties who are proceeding *in forma pauperis* should be cautioned when their appeals are dismissed as frivolous. When the appellant is a prisoner, use the appropriate sanctions language developed pursuant to 28 U.S.C. § 1915(g). When the appellant is a nonprisoner, the appellant should be cautioned that any additional frivolous appeals filed by the appellant or on the appellant's behalf will invite the imposition of sanctions. The nonprisoner appellant should also be advised to review any pending appeals to ensure that they do not raise arguments that are frivolous. A sanction may be imposed the second time that the appellant has an appeal dismissed as frivolous.

K. SAO Legal Research Tools

In addition to Westlaw and LEXIS, the SAO also uses West Knowledge Management (KM), a West software package that indexes recent SAO memoranda, proposed opinions and orders, and published and unpublished opinions. West KM is a full text retrieval program that works similarly to Westlaw and LEXIS. Using West KM, staff attorneys may locate prior SAO memoranda written on specific issues as well as unpublished, possibly precedential authority. West KM is an excellent tool for locating pending Class III issues or other appeals raising similar or related issues currently pending before the court.

L. Supplemental Work Requests from Judges

A judge may request a supplemental memo or other additional work after the staff attorney has prepared a greenie in a case. The senior staff attorney will direct that the case be logged into the office again, if necessary, and the case will be reassigned to the staff attorney who did the initial work. The staff attorney should give the assignment priority—after bail and direct criminal cases, before other assignments. Other times a judge may make a call or send an email to resolve a simple issue.

* * *

I want to turn to some of the other first-class staff attorney programs, beginning with the Eleventh Circuit—the court with the second-largest number of staff attorneys (after the Ninth Circuit), 70, compared to the 24 or so of my court. Its program is entitled "Job Details for Staff Attorney," www.uscourts.gov/careers/current-job-open-ings/83-709, and includes the "Position Description" quoted by me on page 57 of this book (I acknowledge that this section of the chapter contains some repetition of my discussion of staff attorney programs in Chapter 3), where we learn that the principal task of the staff attorneys office is to assist in the disposition of appeals through the preparation of legal memoranda. The types of cases the office presently handles include (1) direct criminal appeals involving sentencing guidelines and guilt/innocence issues, (2) all pro se appeals, including collateral attacks on criminal convictions by state and federal prisoners, and civil rights suits under 42 U.S.C. § 1983, (3) employment discrimination cases, (4) immigration cases, and (5) social security appeals. There are also three specialized units within the office. The Jurisdiction Unit assists the court in the initial review of all appeals filed for the purpose of determining appellate jurisdiction. The Issue Tracking Unit serves to track and catalog relevant legal issues. The Motions Unit possesses certain substantive motions, including those for *in forma pauperis* status, certificates of appealability for 28 U.S.C. § 2254 and § 2255 appeals, transcripts at government expense, and motions to appoint withdraw, and/or substitute counsel.

The staff attorneys at the Eleventh Circuit interviewed by my research team said they planned to stay in government employment, though it was too early in their respective careers to know whether they had really ruled out private employment. Interestingly, one staff attorney explained that her main interest in becoming a staff attorney had derived from her law school internships in Tanzania and Bangladesh, where she had seen stacks and stacks of pending cases, some twenty years old, languishing in courthouse closets. She wanted to see how the American court system manages its heavy caseload so relatively expeditiously.

For research tools, line staff attorneys mentioned several in addition to Westlaw: six spiral-bound case-law books specific to each of the six subject-matter areas referred to above, and an online database of every staff attorney decision ever made in the Eleventh Circuit. The staff attorneys primarily understood their task to be translating the irrelevant, unverified, and often illegible facts cited by pro se appellants into legal arguments that could be understood and accepted by judges. Their primary audience was thus not the litigants but the judges on each panel (though they did not know which judges would be assigned to which case). Memos were reviewed by an "editing buddy" of the staff attorney's choice and a supervising staff attorney. Supervising staff attorneys had the final say on proposed dispositions, though they would first have long discussions with line staff attorneys, who knew each case more, before deciding on a disposition.

Once the memos leave the staff attorneys' office, staff attorneys receive no feedback on any of their cases unless they take it upon themselves to track the outcome, as one of the interviewees did. Occasionally, poorly written memos and senseless proposed dispositions provoke a stern phone call from a judge; staff attorneys have no other contact with judges.

In the Sixth Circuit staff attorneys make recommendations in more than 50 percent of the court's cases (earlier I noted that the corresponding figure in the Seventh Circuit is 50 percent, hence at least slightly lower than in the Sixth); yet "there is generally no interaction between the staff attorneys and the judges in the vast majority of the cases" in which staff attorneys submit memos and proposed orders to the judges.

"The Fourth Circuit presents an interesting contrast: its judges discuss each case with the responsible staff attorney before the case is decided."[6] Yet despite being the third largest staff attorneys' program in the federal system, with 40 to 50 staff attorneys, the Fourth Circuit has (or at least had as of a few years ago—I don't have current figures) the highest percentage of unpublished opinions of any federal court of appeals. See Laural Hooper *et al.*, "Case Management Procedures in the Federal Courts of Appeals" (2d ed.), *Federal Judicial Center* 31 (2011). And some of these opinions,

---

[6] Colter Paulson, "Sixth Circuit Appellate Blog: Case Management at the Sixth Circuit: The Role of Staff Attorneys," *News and Analysis*, Aug. 12, 2011.

unsurprisingly, are as perfunctory as so many of my court's unpublished opinions, often saying little more than "We have reviewed the record and find no reversible error. Accordingly, we affirm for the reasons stated by the district court." *Pickens v. Shanahan*, et al., 2017 WL 1040540 (March 17, 2017).

On the training of staff attorneys, the sum total of what I have found comes from a passing mention in an article written by a career clerk on the Ninth Circuit. She said "the staff attorneys' position might have been likened to a fourth year of law school where much time and effort was devoted to developing the attorney's legal writing and research skills, and based on today's standards, at a fairly leisurely pace," when she began working there in the early 1980s, but that today, "those writing and research skills are still critical to the position, but in addition, the staff must also have oral presentation and time management skills."[7]

One article went into somewhat greater depth about staff attorney hiring, but primarily lamented the dearth of available information.[8] The author observed anecdotally that staff attorneys "tend to have less paradigmatically elite qualifications than those who become appellate clerks," but noted the absence of data to confirm that observation.[9] In a speech, Justice David Stras of the Minnesota Supreme Court discussed how he prefers to hire staff attorneys with work experience and specializations for his court, but the speech does not delve into federal staff attorney hiring.[10]

The rest of the articles I've read discussed the phenomenon of judges delegating decision-making to staff attorneys in response to increases in docket-size and its consequences. The articles ranged

---

[7] Cathy Catterson, "Changes in Appellate Caseload and Its Processing," 48 *Arizona Law Review* 287, 293–94 (2006).

[8] Penelope Pether, "Sorcerers, Not Apprentices: How Judicial Clerks and Staff Attorneys Impoverish U.S. Law," 39 *Arizona State Law Journal* 1 (2007).

[9] *Id.* at 53.

[10] David R. Stras, "Secret Agents: Using Law Clerks Effectively," 98 *Marquette Law Review* 151, 168–69 (2014).

from critical but understanding[11] to scathing.[12] The common criticism is that staff attorneys write low-quality opinions. Some observed that the change in the federal rules permitting citation to unpublished opinions increases the likelihood that opinions written by staff attorneys could become binding precedent and thus lower the quality of the substantive law in the circuit.[13] Others observed that staff attorney opinions are inferior because they tend not to explain their reasoning. Another article argues that such delegation violates Article III.[14] One article argues that pro se appellants do not appear to receive worse substantive outcomes from opinions written by staff attorneys than from opinions by judges.[15]

More on the Eleventh Circuit, and findings regarding the Third: The Eleventh Circuit trains new staff attorneys ("line staff attorneys") by assigning each one to a supervisory staff attorney in one of six subject-matter areas for one month: sentencing, direct criminal appeals, petitions for habeas corpus, employment cases, immigration cases, and civil rights cases. At the beginning of each month the line staff attorney is assigned easier cases, but progresses to more difficult ones. Throughout this training period and at the beginning of every two months, they receive in their mailboxes a stack of cases and must complete a fixed quota by the end of the two months. A line staff attorney who is nearing the end of her

---

[11] See, for example, Marin K. Levy, "Judicial Attention as a Scarce Resource: A Preliminary Defense of How Judges Allocate Time across Cases in the Federal Courts of Appeals," 81 *George Washington Law Review* 401 (2013); Shay Lavie, "Appellate Courts and Caseload Pressure," 27 *Stanford Law & Policy Review* 57, 65 (2016); Wade H. McCree, Jr., "Bureaucratic Justice: An Early Warning," 129 *University of Pennsylvania Law Review* 777 (1981).

[12] See, for example, Pether, 39 *Arizona State Law Journal* 1 (cited in note 9); Jeffrey O. Cooper and Douglas A. Berman, "Passive Virtues and Casual Vices in the Federal Courts of Appeals," 66 *Brooklyn Law Review* 685, 705–07 (2000); Katherine Macfarlane, "Shadow Judges: Staff Attorney Adjudication of Prisoner Claims," 95 Oregon Law Review 97 (2017).

[13] Pether, 39 *Arizona State Law Journal* at 8–10 (cited in note 9).

[14] Macfarlane, 95 *Oregon Law Review* at 118–22 (cited in note 13).

[15] Colter L. Paulson, "Will a Judge Read My Brief? Prejudice to Pro Se Litigants from the Staff Attorney Track," 76 *Ohio State Law Journal Furthermore* 103 (2015).

two months yet is not close to completing her quota may return to the pool to be randomly assigned additional cases in the hope that she'll be assigned simple cases, which can boost her number of completed ones—though she might instead get unlucky and receive an additional complicated case that will also need to be completed within two months of receipt.[16] In this way, as all the staff attorneys who were interviewed lamented, the quality of their performance was a function of the luck of the draw.

In the Third Circuit, an office separate from the staff handles immigration appeals. The circuit has no formal training program for writing or managing cases, but a wiki provides information on how to handle different types of case. Staff attorneys have no deadline, though the one that my research team interviewed reported working at a rate of 30 cases in 60 days. But the staff attorneys did not have face time with judges and were also unaware of panel composition.

In terms of future prospects, the one staff attorney interviewed reported having gone directly into private practice after completing his job as a staff attorney, and stated that his work as a staff attorney had played a significant role in attaining his current position.

Like the Fifth Circuit, the Third keeps meticulous voluminous records of its staff attorney program, as shown in these two files provided to me by Ms. Marisa Watson, the director of the program—records certainly unmatched by the Seventh Circuit and almost certainly also by several, at least, of the other federal courts of appeals. What follows is lengthy and intricate, but important:

Legal Division, U.S. Court of Appeals Third Circuit, File One:

Supervisory staff attorneys work closely with a different batch of 4-5 staff attorneys every six months, and they have the final say on proposed dispositions. The respondents overwhelmingly believed that supervisory staff attorneys' edits and contributions to proposed orders prevented any badly written or badly argued memos from being sent out of the office.

---

[16] One could play the odds to one's favor by heading to the "pool" after a Supreme Court decision just came down and a bevy of prisoners' cases, many of which poorly apply case law, can be quickly dispatched.

Time-sensitive cases (involving emergency motions) have deadlines but other ones have general due dates prioritizing older cases for completion. Staff attorneys write memos for unknown panels of judges (both standing motions panels and standing merits panels). They also draft a proposed order (around one-two paragraphs) or per curiam opinions. The per curiam opinions include a cover memo that includes additional analysis for the panel, but the text of the per curiam opinion itself is "drafted primarily for the benefit of the pro se litigant." Interestingly, in close cases, the office will provide alternative orders for the panel and argue for the best outcome in the cover memo. Additionally, "unlist" memos are written for supervisory staff attorneys. All in all, the staff attorneys interviewed overwhelmingly perceived their primary audience for memos as the panels, and most noted that the parties were the primary audience for orders/opinions.

Finished work products are sent to panels with levels of urgency based on the case type. Emergency motions are sent when they are ready, non-time-sensitive substantive motions are sent once a week, usually on Thursdays, in batches of 5-10, to each panel, and fully-briefed pro se cases are sent once they are ready (usually at a rate of two cases sent to each panel per week). Judges rarely call/e-mail staff attorneys with questions but the office strives to produce work that does not require further dialogue. Staff attorneys get the most feedback on their work from supervisory staff attorneys, rather than judges.

Finally, none of the responding staff attorneys had gone directly from law school to the office. Instead, about half had clerked at the state-court-level and the other half had worked in private practice. Only one staff attorney had moved to Philadelphia for the position; the other six were already living in Philadelphia. None of the responding staff attorneys weighed other circuits' staff attorney programs before taking up the position. Many noted that they took up the position either because they had enjoyed clerking and the work in the office was the closest match to that kind of work, or because they preferred not to practice.

Legal Division, U.S. Court of Appeals Third Circuit, File Two:

How many years have you been working as a staff attorney? SA 1: 6 Years, SA 2: 18 months, SA 3: 8 months, SA 4: A total of 5.125 years, representing two separate stints, SA 5: 17.5 years total, SA 6: 7-8 years, SA 7: 23 years.

Were you hired as a staff attorney straight out of law school or did you work elsewhere before working as a staff attorney? Where did you work, if you worked elsewhere? SA 1: I had worked for five years before joining the staff attorney's office, I 1 year as a clerk for a United States District Judge (E.D. Pa.),1 year as a clerk for a United States Circuit Judge (3d Cir.),3 years as a litigation/appellate associate at a large firm. SA 2: Before joining the staff attorney's office, I clerked for approximately 16 months for a Pennsylvania Court of Common Pleas judge. SA 3: Prior to my employment as a staff attorney, I clerked for Justice Lee Solomon on the New Jersey Supreme Court. SA 4: I was hired straight out of law school, worked here 4 years, then worked for a small firm for 3.5 years doing plaintiffs-side civil litigation in Pennsylvania/New Jersey, then returned to the SA's office in 2016. SA 5: I completed a state court clerkship before working as a term staff attorney. After completing my term, I worked for several years as a litigation attorney for a federal agency. I was then rehired by the court to fill an experienced staff attorney position. SA 6: I worked at a large law firm before working as a staff attorney. SA 7: An odd mix; worked in the legal office of the Defense Logistics Agency and ran a classical CD store while completing an SJD.

Marisa Watson (Director): We use the Online System for Clerkship Application and Review ("OSCAR") to post job openings for staff attorney positions and to receive applications. We send email notifications of our posting to the career services offices of well over 100 law schools. We update the email contacts annually. Other outreach efforts are taken as well (e.g., attendance at job fairs, letters to law student organizations and BAR associations, etc.).

Question to Staff Attorneys: Did anyone at your law school work with you to make the decision to work as a staff attorney? Was there any publicity for working as a staff attorney coming from your law school's career services office? SA 1: No. SA 2: No one influenced my decision to apply for a staff attorney position, and there was no publicity for such positions at my law school. SA 3: My law school and its career development services center did not promote or discuss the possibility of a career as a staff attorney. However, my legal research and writing professor at Widener Law was also a supervising staff attorney for the Third Circuit. After graduation, I expressed an interest in working as a staff attorney, and he assisted me in the application process. SA 4: no. I believe the posting for a position with the office was passed on to me via career services, but nothing more. In fact, a staff attorney had never participated in my school's "clerkship panel" (at which law students could ask current clerks questions about their experiences) until I did so the year after I graduated. SA 5: No to both questions. SA 6: N/A. SA 7: No. The only publicity I saw for the job was an ad on a notice board (this was before the internet took off).

Were you in contact with any former staff attorneys before beginning work as a staff attorney? SA 1: Yes. A friend at the law firm I worked at had previously worked at the staff attorney's office. He told me about the office. SA 2: No. SA 3: See above. SA 4: no. SA 5: No. SA 6: No. SA 7: No.

Did you move from another city for this job? SA 1: No. SA 2: Yes. SA 3: No. SA 4: No. SA 5: Yes, for the term position. SA 6: No. SA 7: No.

Did you compare the merits of working at different circuit courts before committing to the Third Circuit? SA 1: No. My whole career had been based in Philadelphia, and I intended to stay here. SA 2: No. SA 3: No. SA 4: No, I did not seriously consider leaving the Philadelphia area. SA 5: No, I only applied to the Third Circuit. SA 6: No. SA 7: No.

Application Process: What do you remember about selecting a writing sample to send in with your résumé and cover letter? SA 1: I used an appellate brief I had drafted while in private practice. SA 2: I selected a writing sample I authored for a state court judge in connection with a petition for post-conviction relief. SA 3: Because I had been out of law school for only a short period of time and had only worked at the Supreme Court of New Jersey, where I completed memos and opinions that I could not use as a writing samples, I selected a summary judgment memorandum project from law school as well as my law review note as my writing samples. SA 4: First application (2008): I used at least one writing sample from my 3L externship with a District Court judge in order to demonstrate my court-writing experience and familiarity with some aspects of federal practice. Second application (2016): I used (1) a bench memo prepared for one of the Third Circuit judges while I was working in her chambers; and (2) a short advocacy piece from private practice to show the office what I had been up to the last few years. SA 5: I don't remember much, because it was so long ago. I probably chose based on a balance of complexity of legal analysis and overall readability. SA 6: I chose a writing sample that conveyed my abilities as a clear and thorough writer, and a thoughtful and objective legal thinker. SA 7: I selected something I thought would not be boring to read and that showed some legal analysis.

Was there a writing component to your interview? If you are allowed to say and if you remember, what did the writing component ask you to do? SA 1: I was given a short problem and paper copies of several Third Circuit opinions and asked to draft a memorandum or opinion (I cannot remember which) analyzing that problem. SA 2: As best as I can recall, the writing sample presented a scenario in which a district court had dismissed a prisoner's inadequate medical care claim, which was predicated on a largely trivial medical condition. The question presented, I believe, was whether the prisoner should have been permitted to amend his complaint. SA 3: We were asked to write a memo recommending whether an appellant prisoner had satisfied the criteria for an appeal. More specifically, whether he had adequately stated a claim for an eighth amendment violation based on deliberate indifference to medical needs. We were given the shell outline of the memo, as well as copies of the applicable statutes and cases to apply SA 4: Within a set amount of time, draft a per curiam opinion based on a short fact pattern using excerpts of the law (I believe it was a mock Eighth Amendment case) that were provided in the materials for the writing test. SA 5: I was to present my written legal analysis and conclusion based on hypothetical facts.) SA 6: Yes. I was provided with a fact pattern and statute and asked to draft an objective memo. SA 7: The writing test presented a legal problem to be solved exclusively using print-outs of a few controlling Supreme Court decisions.

Did you have group interviews, or solo interviews? SA 1: Three separate 30-minute interviews with two people each. SA 2: I interviewed with 4 members of the office. SA 3: I had a group interview, which included a few staff attorneys, two supervising staff attorneys, and the director of the Legal Division. SA 4: First application (2008): Multiple small-group interviews; Second application (2016): One large-group interview. SA 5: Both. SA 6: Group Interviews. SA 7: Three one-on-one interviews and one two-on-one interview.

Decisions: What made you choose to be a staff attorney? What did you envision about your career arc back then for which deciding to be a staff attorney was the right choice? SA 1: I liked reading cases, analyzing the law, and writing. I didn't like trying to get clients or doing the nitty gritty of trial work. I believed (correctly) that this job would allow me to focus on the parts of law I most enjoy. SA 2: I decided to apply for a staff attorney position largely to gain federal court experience. SA 3: After working for the New Jersey Supreme Court, I realized that I thoroughly enjoyed working for a court and interacting with court staff. As a clerk and editor in chief of my law review, I realized that my greatest strengths were legal research, drafting memoranda and opinions, and editing memoranda and opinions. I'm also that rare individual that thoroughly enjoys the Bluebook and applying its quirky rules. After working in a law firm as a paralegal for eight years, I was also pretty sure that I didn't want to litigate. SA 4: ? I chose to take a job as a staff attorney out of law school, in 2008, because I generally believed it was a better opportunity career-wise than others that were offered at the time, and because I did not have an affinity to a particular area of the law and thought working on different kinds of cases would bring into focus the kind of work I wanted to pursue as a practicing lawyer. I signed on for a two-year term and did not think I would stay longer. But I did, for two more years, largely because I really enjoyed my colleagues and the quality of life. I returned to the office in 2016 because by that time my wife and I had two children and my priority was to have a job that offered what I consider to be a good work/life balance. SA 5: I was and still am committed to public service and the mission of the office. Having been both a former law clerk and a litigator, I knew that I preferred writing for the judiciary than for advocacy. SA 6: I chose to be a staff attorney because I had previously served as an appellate clerk and enjoyed the work. SA 7: Wanted a job within the judiciary as part of the decision-making process rather than as an advocate.

Office Demographics: How is the office structured? Are you assigned to 1 supervisory SA? Marisa Watson (Director): Yes, but assignments change, generally every six months; reassignments can be made more frequently if the needs of the office require it. How many other SA's worked under a single supervisory SA? Currently, each supervisory staff attorney works with 4 or 5 staff attorneys Do you get an "editing buddy"? Or are you matched with a more experienced SA? n/a. Are there law clerks in the SA's office, just for the SA's? No. How many career SA's vs. term SA's are there? Approximately 50-50 split. How many years are in a term for an SA? Two year terms are preferred, though one year terms are sometimes offered. We (this is Director Watson speaking) have on rare occasions hired attorneys for temporary short terms, of approximately three or four months when the needs of the office have warranted it. Term extensions are possible.

Approximately how many staff attorneys work in the Third Circuit office? Marisa Watson (Director): Currently, there are 29 members of the legal staff.

EEOC Diversity: What is the office's ratio of men to women?

Marisa Watson (Director): Approximately 50-50 split among legal staff members.

What is the breakdown of racial backgrounds? The racial breakdown varies from year to year due to the turnover of term staff attorneys. Currently, about 17% of the legal staff members self-identify as non-white. Would you (Ms. Watson) say that the racial diversity of the staff attorney's office reflects the racial diversity of the individuals' whose cases you handle as a staff attorney? No. Are there any staff attorneys openly self-identifying as LGBQT+? Yes. Are there any individuals with disabilities, to your knowledge? Not at this time.

What is the age distribution of the office? Are most SA's in their 20's, 30's, 40's, 50's, 60's? About evenly split between two age bands: 20's-30's and 40's-60's.

Training: What kind of introductory training/orientation is given to staff attorneys when they start out? What kind of training related to writing happens?

Supervising Staff Attorneys hold "orientation/training" sessions with new attorneys in the substantive areas in which the office works most frequently: habeas corpus; immigration; appellate jurisdiction; and *in forma pauperis* procedures. Training related to writing occurs on a one-on-one basis between each attorney and his or her supervisor, with more or less feedback and training provided, depending upon the skill level of the attorney. Writing training/ development is part of a Supervising Staff Attorney's responsibility and is one-on-one in the context of assigned cases. New staff attorneys are encouraged to review the writing component of the online orientation module developed for law clerks. Budget permitting, staff attorneys sometimes attend court-funded writing seminars. In the rare occasion when an attorney is hired outside the typical hiring cycle, the assigned supervisor will conduct all training one-on-one.

SA 1: There are training sessions on (a) office practices and procedures, (b) the substantive law we work with the most, and (c) writing. The writing training was given by a supervising staff attorney who taught us some of the basics of opinion writing. After that, there was essentially one-on-one training because all of our work is closely reviewed by a supervising staff attorney. SA 2: As best as I can recall, I was required to watch several orientation videos that covered writing "basics." Each supervisor also provided handouts with writing tips. SA 3: We were given concentrated orientation and training for the first two weeks of our employment. I received a packet on my first day with instruction on how to access my email, our office's database, CMECF, and the various court dockets. It also contained detailed step-by-step instructions on how to complete memos, find sample memos, docket the memos as submitted for review or completed, and how to keep track of our monthly case statistics. Within a few days, I attended library training and review, and a safety seminar. I was given my first very simple jurisdiction case that first week along with jurisdictional training. As we are exposed to new types of cases, we are given training in the area before our assignments. My most recent training was for immigration cases. We were not given specific training with regard to writing style, organization or tone. However, we were given tips at each subject matter training session regarding what to look for and include when completing certain memos/non-precedential opinions. SA 4: Introductory training/orientation was staggered during my first year (2008-2009) and was subject-specific. Training sessions were anywhere from 1 hour in to 2.5 hours in length and were led by the supervising staff attorneys. The first session was on appellate jurisdiction, and subsequent sessions tackled the IFP statute, habeas law, and immigration law/removal proceedings. I do not recall a formal training session on court-writing. The supervising staff attorneys all were highly experienced, skilled court-writers. They provided informal 'training' with regard to court-writing (and the finer points of legal writing generally) on a regular basis. SA 5: Back when I started, there was little orientation or training. These days, there are some court-orientation sessions and some substantive overviews. Most of the training is on-the-job, including writing feedback, given by supervisory staff attorneys. SA 6: Senior staff attorneys provide training to the new attorneys in the major substantive areas of law we work with. Senior staff attorneys also work closely with new attorneys on an individual basis to improve their writing. SA 7: When I joined the office I received none; it was learn-as-you-go, which I still believe is the best way to learn. Now the office provides brief introductions to the core subject areas of the office (jurisdiction, PLRA, habeas, immigration).

Are CLE credits required at the Third Circuit? How often do you take CLE classes, and what are the names of the classes you take? CLE credits are not required. Time off is permitted to accommodate CLE classes. In addition, staff attorneys are encouraged to attend legal conferences presenting subject matter that is pertinent to the work of the office, such as the bi-annual FJC conference for staff attorneys and the annual conference of the National Association of Appellate Court Attorneys. Financial sponsorship by the office is provided, budget permitting. SA 1: To maintain my Pennsylvania license, I must complete 12 hours of CLE each year. I am involved with the National Association of Appellate Court Attorneys, and typically get my credits at its annual conference. Each year this includes summaries of the Supreme Court's past term, among other things. SA 2: I do not believe that CLE is required, but I generally take CLE every six months or so, mostly in the area of prison or civil-rights litigation. SA 3: CLE credits are not specifically required at the Third Circuit. We are given the opportunity to attend CLE's for a nominal fee almost every month pertaining to research issues, ethics, etc. I take advantage of as many as a can. The most recent CLE that I attended was called: Court Web: Thorny Issues in Prisoners' Rights Cases. SA 4: To my knowledge, the Third Circuit does not require anything but good standing with a licensing jurisdiction in order to practice at, or be employed by, the Court. I have always taken regular CLE classes to keep in good standing with the jurisdictions in which I am licensed to practice. The subjects of the CLE classes are varied. Also, our office provides opportunities to participate remotely in FJC-sponsored programming to earn CLE credit. In addition, the office has in the past facilitated staff attorney attendance at the annual conference for the National Association of Appellate Court Attorneys, at which one can earn a substantial amount of CLE credit. SA 5: CLE is required by the state, not by the Third Circuit. Each state has its own requirements. I take CLE classes whenever I need to meet my state's requirements, generally a few times per year. Classes can be on any topic. SA 6: CLE credits are not required. SA 7: CLE credits are not required beyond the extent to which they're required for bar membership.

Work Itself (Especially Related to Writing): Approximately how many of the cases are routine motions (extensions of time, oversized briefs) vs. substantive motions (stays pending appeal)? Staff attorneys in the Third Circuit work on substantive motions and fully briefed cases; much of the work involves case-dispositive analysis and recommendation. While the litigants in these cases are primarily pro se, our work in immigration and habeas cases regularly includes appeals and motions filed by counsel. Procedural motions such as motions for extensions of time are handled by staff attorneys only when accompanied by a substantive motion. Normally, case management staff (i.e., case managers, legal assistants, and attorneys) in the Clerk's Office handle the procedural motions.

Does the SA's office screen cases for oral argument? Marisa Watson (Director): No. Can you walk me through what happens from a case's assignment to you and your handing it off to a judge/supervisory staff attorney? SA 1: After the case is assigned to me, I read the record materials, conduct the necessary research, and prepare a memo or draft opinion. Then I give my document to a supervisory staff attorney for review. The supervisory staff attorney will give me edits. Once I have changed the document to that attorney's satisfaction, the document will be transmitted to a panel. SA 2: I work up the case independently, and then present it to a supervising attorney. Typically, he will recommend some edits. After incorporating the recommended edits, I submit the case to a panel for disposition. More difficult cases might go through more than one round of edits. SA 3: After we are assigned cases, I generally look each one over for time constraints. Before I start each memo, I discuss them with my supervising attorney to ensure that I'm on the right track. When I've completed the first draft, I submit the memo to my supervising staff attorney for review. I make changes based on his edits, and submit for review again if necessary. If not, I submit the memo as completed, and it is forwarded to a panel for consideration. SA 4: After the case is assigned, I review the record and the parties' arguments and then draft a memo or opinion proposing a disposition. I docket on CM/ECF that I am handing the work product off to the supervising staff attorney for his/her review. I revise the work product based on any feedback received from the supervising staff attorney and based on any additional edits I think are appropriate. I then docket on CM/ECF that I have completed the memo. After that I move the digital file of the memo to a particular computer directory folder for completed memos (for hyperlinking, formatting, etc. by an administrative assistant), and, lastly, send a copy of the completed memo to the Senior Staff Attorney.

Is there a deadline for each case? Time sensitive cases have firm deadlines; non-time-sensitive cases have general due dates that are set to ensure that the oldest cases are prioritized. Due dates are flexible to help ensure that the attorney has sufficient time to complete his or her work in satisfactory fashion. SA 2: Yes. SA 3: We are given a "delinquent date" that can range anywhere from 1 ½ weeks to two months depending on the urgency of the matter or nature of the motion. This can be extended in certain circumstances if the case requires. SA 4: Each case assignment comes with a "delinquency date," which may be altered based on, inter alia, extensions of the parties' filing deadlines or a need to request records from a state court (it typically takes a fair amount of time to receive such records). SA 5: Yes, internal deadlines set based on case age and case type. SA 6: Yes. SA 7: Usually no.

Where are you conducting your research? (Westlaw, internal databases such as some courts' electronic databases of every staff attorney order ever written, handbooks describing all the case law in the relevant subject area, etc.). SA 1: I mainly use Westlaw. Sometimes also WestKM, which is a database that stores all the memos that my office has created. SA 2: I use Westlaw and the Court's WestKM database, which contains all of our opinions and memoranda. SA 3: I conduct most of my research on Westlaw as well as our court database, WestKm, which includes memoranda and non-precedential opinions that staff attorneys have written. I've done minimal research with hardcopy treatises from our library. SA 4: All of the things in parentheses, plus books on occasion (habeas treatises in particular). SA 5: Westlaw, internal database, satellite library materials. SA 6: Primarily Westlaw, and also internal database of staff attorney work. SA 7: Primarily Westlaw and internal databases. Do you make use of stylistic writing guides? (Garner and Scalia, Strunk and White, etc.) If so, what are they? SA 1: I use Garner's Guide to Modern American Usage. SA 2: I use Garner's "Modern American Usage" and "Elements of Legal Style." I also use "Point Made" and "Point Taken" by Ross Guberman. SA 3: The New Jersey Supreme Court Justice that I worked for recommended "Thinking Like a Writer," by Armstrong and Terrell; I still reference it occasionally for help with organization and roadmapping. SA 4: Yes. Mostly Garner's *A Dictionary of Modern Legal Usage*. Sometimes *Chicago Manual of Style* or *Elements of Style*. And occasionally I'll see what Fowler had to say about a particular writing convention. SA 6: Occasionally. SA 7: I don't, though I sometimes consult Garner's *Modern American Usage*.

Did law school or a previous work experience prepare you to write these memos? Or did you learn how to write them on the job. SA 1: The memos are similar to those I wrote during my clerkships. SA 2: My previous clerkship prepared me well to write the memos and opinions I write here. SA 3: All of my prior work experience, law school, and the New Jersey Supreme Court helped to prepare me for writing a well-organized and effective memo. I learned the specific style and format needed for the Third Circuit through trial and error on the job. SA 4: I interned/externed in the chambers of trial-level judges throughout law school, and that experience helped to prepare me for court-writing generally. As far as appellate court-writing, my experience during law school had only been in an advocacy role (writing briefs supporting criminal appeals in the Third Circuit), so I did have to learn "on the job" to an extent. SA 5: Both previous work experience and on the job. SA 6: Law school and previous work as a litigator prepared me to conduct legal research and write legal memos, but I honed those skills on the job, learning quite a lot during my first year as a staff attorney. I continue to refine my writing skills year after year. SA 7: Primarily the latter.

Who is the principal audience for each memo? The panel? An individual judge, if you know who is on the panel? The appellants?

Marisa Watson: The principal audience of our work product varies, depending on the type of case. Much of our work is submitted to standing motions panels that decide motions and threshold questions in appeals that have not been fully briefed. Fully briefed cases are submitted to standing merits panels. In certain cases that are submitted to motions panels (e.g., COAs, appellate jurisdiction issues, motions for appointment of counsel, motions to stay, for transcripts, and for bail) a staff memo is written for the judges and a proposed order is drafted for the litigants. The orders are usually fairly short (one or two paragraphs), although judges sometimes ask that additional details be added. Staff attorneys draft per curiam opinions in cases that are submitted to motions panels for possible summary action, in petitions for writ of mandamus, and in cases requiring review under 28 U.S.C. §1915 (e)(2)(B), or to merits panels in fully briefed pro se appeals. These per curiam opinions are drafted primarily for the benefit of the pro se litigant. A cover memo is attached to the draft PC and includes any additional analysis that would benefit the panel. SA 1: For memos, the audience is the panel of judges to whom the memo will be submitted. We do not know the composition of the panel in advance. For draft opinions, we write for both the judges and the litigants. When the litigants are pro se, we try to use simpler language. If there is a complicated legal issue that we wish to analyze for the judges, we might do that in a cover memo that is not made public. SA 2: The principal audience is the panel. We generally do not know in advance of writing which panel a memo will go to. SA 3: The principal audience for the memos or non-precedential opinions are the panel. Certain "unlist" memos are written primarily for supervising staff attorneys. SA 4: Memos are internal work product drafted exclusively for judges on the panel; we do not know who is on the panel in advance of submitting our work unless the work submitted is a post-submission supplemental memo). However, the memos typically include proposed order language, and I write that part specifically with both the judges and the parties in mind as the audience. SA 5: It's a mix. Internal memos are addressed to the panel. Although we draft proposed orders and opinions for the panel's use, the ultimate audience is the litigants. SA 6: Each memo is directed to a panel of judges, although I do not know which panel will ultimately receive a given memo. When I draft an Order or NPO, I write it with the litigants themselves in mind, particularly if it is appropriate to explain an issue to a pro se litigant. SA 7: The sole audience of the memos we write is the panel. The audience for our orders and opinions consists primarily of the parties.

How long are the memos? Marisa Watson explains:

Upon direction of our Court, staff memos should generally be 5 single spaced pages or less. Some cases require more. Also, upon the direction of our Court, per curiam opinions should generally be 5 double spaced pages or less. Again, there is flexibility, as more pages are sometimes needed in unusual or complex cases. SA 1: It varies, of course, but in a straightforward case, the memo should be less than five pages. SA 2: On average, about 5-10 pages. The longest memo I wrote was nearly 20 pages, but that was unusual. SA 3: 3-20 pages. SA 4: Typical memos are 3-4 pages. Complex cases often require double-digit page-lengths. Same for draft per curiam opinions. SA 5: Around 5 pages, but some can be considerably longer if the case demands it. SA 6: My memos typically vary from three to ten pages. SA 7: As long as necessary; depending on the issues and complexity it could be anywhere from one to a hundred pages. But the average is probably five.

Is there a uniform structure for each memo? Watson (Director): Yes. SA 3 & 4: Yes. Sections include: Recommendation to the Court, Facts/History, Analysis, Proposed Order. SA 6: The attorneys in the office follow a loose structure, with plenty of room for adjustment when necessary in a particularly complex case. SA 7: Usually, though sections tend to blend together in really simple cases.

Does your supervisory attorney have the final say on a proposed disposition leaving the Staff Attorney's Office? Or do you? SA 1: The Supervisory Attorney does. SA 2: The supervisory attorney has the final say, though I have never disagreed on a disposition with a supervisor. SA 3: Supervisory attorney. SA 4: It is expected that the proposed disposition reviewed and ok'd by the supervising staff attorney will be the same proposed disposition that will be submitted to the panel. I have not had an experience where my supervisor and

I were unable to agree in the end on a proposed disposition. SA 5: It's a non-issue, because we typically agree. SA 6: My supervisory attorney has the final say. SA 7: If there's disagreement, but only one is correct, the correct one prevails. If the answer isn't clear-cut, the analysis will make that clear and may result in the panel's being presented with alternative dispositions to choose from.

How much feedback do you get about changing a proposed disposition? SA 1: When we are asked to change a proposed disposition we always get fairly detailed feedback. SA 2: Significant feedback, if the supervisor believes that a change is appropriate SA 3: I have been given a great deal of feedback from my supervising staff attorney when changing a proposed disposition, including an informative discussion on why the change is needed to ensure that I understand the issue/concept and/or the procedures of the court. SA 4: If the supervising staff attorney thinks the proposed disposition should be changed, he/she will discuss with the attorney. Maybe the disposition will be changed, maybe after discussion it will not be changed. When a judge asks you to change a disposition, the degree of explanation accompanying the request varies. SA 6: I am always given detailed feedback. SA 7: This varies with the staff attorney's experience.

Are you aware of which judges are on the panel for each case? SA 1: We learn at the time that the memo is submitted. SA 2: Not in advance of writing. SA 3: We are not aware of which judges are on the panel for each case until we submit our memos/opinions. SA 4: Only after the original assignment is completed. SA 5: Usually, I am not aware while I'm preparing the case and only find out later. There are a few exceptions that occur. SA 6: No. SA 7: Almost never.

Do you need to tailor your dispositions of the preferences/past decisions that the judges had on similar cases? SA 1: We do not have panel information in advance. SA 2: Generally, I use our internal WestKM database to make sure that my disposition comports with past dispositions in similar cases. SA 3: I have always approached each memo/dispo-sition as a new and separate case, and I have never been counseled to tailor a memo a certain way, nor have I felt the need to do so. SA 4: No. SA 5: Not typically. SA

6: No. SA 7: There is a preference for analytic consistency, at least with court precedent. We are not expected to anticipate panels' stylistic preferences. Are there consequences if a proposed disposition is rejected or if a memo is "badly written"? SA 1: It would affect our reputation, our yearly review, and, for term attorneys, the ability to have terms extended. "Badly written" memos will be caught by the supervisory attorney and corrected before they leave the office, so the consequences are internal. SA 2: I have never had a disposition rejected, or received complaints about bad writing. I would imagine that, if either of these events occurred, a supervising attorney would take some corrective action. SA 3: I am not aware of any consequences if a proposed disposition is rejected or if a memo is "badly written." SA 4: Neither the judges nor the office responds in punitive fashion if a particular proposed disposition is ultimately rejected by the panel. I suppose the supervising staff attorney and the supervisee would discuss the matter constructively. I suspect that a "badly written" memo would not be approved by a supervising staff attorney. SA 5: N/A—this generally just doesn't happen. SA 6: A badly written memo would go through many revisions with senior staff attorneys until it was ready to leave the office. SA 7: Do you mean rejected by the panel and deemed badly written by the panel? I am not aware of work being deemed badly written, and it is unusual for a disposition to be rejected because the analysis is deemed wrong; rather, it's a matter of interpretation or disagreement.

What kinds of cases do you work on? SA 1: Habeas cases, cases in which one party is pro se, and motions in immigration cases. SA 2: Generally two types: habeas corpus (§§ 2254 and 2255) and section 1983 claims. SA 3: Prisoner civil rights cases; habeas petitions; various civil cases, including employment issues; jurisdictional cases.SA 4: Any kind of case filed by a pro se litigant, and any requests for a certificate of appealability under 28 U.S.C. § 2253 (whether counseled or not). SA 5: Mix of habeas corpus, civil rights, immigration, appellate jurisdiction . What is the most common type of case? SA 1: Habeas corpus. SA 2: It is nearly a 50/50 split between habeas corpus and 1983 claims. SA 3: Habeas corpus petitions and prisoner civil rights cases. SA 4: Habeas corpus. SA 5: probably habeas corpus. SA 6: Applications for certificates of appealability in federal habeas cases; prisoner civil rights cases under §1983. SA 7: Habea corpus, prisoner civil rights, pro se merits, immigration.

What is the most complicated or time-consuming type of case? SA 1: Probably also habeas, although some pro se cases in substantive areas that we don't see too frequently can be difficult. SA 2: The most complicated and time consuming cases are probably § 2254 petitions that involve both (1) many claims and (2) procedural-default problems. SA 3: Merits cases involving prisoner civil rights and cases involving non-prisoner civil issues. These cases are usually briefed by the parties and counsel and often contain more complicated issues. SA 4: habeas is the most complicated; pro se merits cases (briefed cases not appropriate for summary disposition) are generally the most time-consuming. SA 5: Habeas cases. SA 6: An application for a certificate of appealability in a capital habeas case. SA 7: Capital habeas.

Is there much specialization, formal or informal? The 7th Cir., the 2nd Cir., and the 11th Cir. have specialized offices handling motions rather than writing orders, or handling certain types of case (immigration). Does your office have this? How are SA's divided into these offices? Does anyone 'generalize'/move between offices? Marisa Watson (Director): In general, there is no specialization. In theory, everyone works on everything, with two exceptions. Only experienced career staff attorneys work on capital cases. In the rare instances when attorneys are hired for short terms of three or four months, they are assigned only straight forward cases and in limited subject areas. New staff attorneys hired for one- or two-year terms do not work on all subject areas immediately upon arrival. Initially, their cases are pre-screened and they are introduced to one new subject area at a time, in each of the subject areas the office works in most frequently. Cases presenting a new subject area are added to a first year attorney's case list when the attorney has worked on a sufficient number of cases to develop familiarity with the range of issues typically presented in each area of law. By the end of the first year, a new staff attorney normally will have worked on cases in all of the office's core subject areas, as well as some additional areas that make up a smaller percentage of the office's case load.

Presenting Work to Judges. When a case leaves the staff attorney's office, what is the timing for its arrival on a judge's desk? (For example, in the Seventh Circuit, there's a "bunching" situation where often 10-20 cases arrive at a judge's desk on every other Friday. Is this the case at the Third Circuit?) Marisa Watson: The work produced by the office is submitted to standing pro se motions and pro se merits panels on different days of the week: (1) emergency motions are sent as they are ready; (2) non-time-sensitive substantive motions are submitted to motions panels once a week (typically on Thursdays) in batches of five to ten cases (these cases include COA applications, §1915(e)(2)(B) submittals, motions for stay of removal, appellate jurisdiction questions, motions for appointment of counsel, etc.); (3) fully briefed pro se cases are sent as they are ready, typically two cases per week, per panel.

Do you meet with judges in person? By phone? By email? Marisa Watson: Our judges primarily communicate with staff attorneys through email and by phone. Our judges' chambers are located throughout the circuit (Pennsylvania, New Jersey, and Delaware) and only a few active judges have chambers in Philadelphia. SA 1: Judges contact us by phone or email if they have questions or concerns about our recommendations. We also periodically see judges at luncheons or other court events. SA 2: Phone and email. SA 3: I have never met with a judge regarding a case that I'm working on. I have received phone calls or emails requesting small tweaks in language for an order or memo. SA 4: Not in person or by phone unless a judge has questions or feedback. And not by email unless a judge has a question/feedback. SA5: Rarely. How often? Marisa Watson: We regularly engage in dialogue with the Court through our written work product in a way that doesn't necessarily require feedback by phone or email. In close cases we provide alternative orders for the panel or explain in the cover memo why we believe the appeal should be resolved as set out in the draft opinion; we occasionally seek input from panels before drafting an opinion in a close case. It is our goal to present to the Court work product that is high quality and usable in its submitted form. SA 1: There are not regularly scheduled meetings between non-supervisory staff attorneys and judges. SA 2: I have been here for 18 months and have received not more than 5 phone calls and not more than 10 emails from chambers. SA 3: Twice in 8 months. SA 4: Not frequently, but not rarely either. SA 5: Rarely. SA 7: Very rarely.

How do they get in touch if they had questions on a case? SA 1: Mostly email, but sometimes on the phone. SA 2: Generally email. Less frequently phone. SA 3: Via phone/email. SA 4: Phone/email. SA 5: phone/email. SA 6: I rarely come into contact with judges. I do not meet with them in person. Every once in a while a judge will call me with a question or comment about a memo I have written. Occasionally, a judicial assistant calls or emails to request a minor editorial change to an Order or NPO. SA 7: Phone or email.

Do you meet with a judge's clerks? If so, how do you meet with them, and how often do you meet with them? SA 1: Some judges will call or email themselves when they have questions about a case. Some judges prefer to correspond through their law clerks. SA 2: I met once with a judge's clerk upon his request. He came over to my office to discuss a case. SA 3: No. SA 4: No. SA 5: N/A SA 6: No. SA 7: Almost never.

How often do the panels (or individual judges) adopt or revise your (i.e., staff attorneys') proposed dispositions? SA 1: It depends. Sometimes quite substantially, and sometimes very little. SA 2: Generally no revision occurs. SA 3: I have completed some 68 memos/non-precedential opinions in my eight months as a staff attorney, and I have been asked to make minor revisions in language to two memos/opinions and to provide more substance to an order. SA 4: Material revisions are typically done in collaboration with the staff attorney; it is rare to see a different-looking opinion at the time of publication unless the panel disagrees with the proposed disposition and a judge has opted to rewrite it himself/herself. SA 5: Not significantly, if at all. SA 6: N/A in light of preceding response. SA 7: Hardly ever.

Are the released orders as detailed as internal recommendations? SA 1: No. The internal recommendations include more detailed legal analysis and case citations, while the orders focus on the key grounds for decision. SA 4: The released orders are generally more detailed than the introductory recommendations in memos. SA 6: Yes. SA 7: No.

In the 7th Cir., there's a cover sheet describing issues about the case that gets left out of the order when it's issued. Is there a cover sheet for your circuit court? SA 1: No. SA 2: Our cover sheet contains only the list of attachments. SA 3: Yes. There is a cover sheet listing the attached docket entries as well as a supporting memo that gets left off the order. SA 4: Cover sheets for per curiam opinions sometimes offer substantive analysis that you want the Court to know but that is not necessary or appropriate for the opinion. SA 5: Depending on the case type, we write internal memos to the panels with proposed orders, or draft opinions for the panel and the parties. If needed, a cover letter accompanying the draft opinion addresses issues for the panel's information to explain why the opinion was written as it was. SA 6: Yes. SA 7: There's a memo (see above.)

Experiences Learned/Job Reflection: What have you learned about writing memos now, having worked as an SA, that you didn't after leaving law school? SA 1: As I have become more experienced I have gained an understanding of which issues need detailed discussion and which do not. SA 2: Be concise and eliminate boilerplate language. A 3: Because I was taught by a staff attorney in law school, and then worked as a judicial clerk, I feel that I was well prepared for my job as a staff attorney. However, I have learned brevity in my writing for the Third Circuit as well as added emphasis on organization. SA 4: Judges shoulder heavy caseloads: get to the point in your memos, but don't leave out anything important! SA 6: I have become a much more concise writer. SA 7: Focus, terseness.

* * *

Moving on: I have now discussed, in varying degrees of depth, the staff attorney programs of the following federal courts of appeals: the First through the Eleventh. That leaves only the D.C. and Federal Circuits, and they have very few staff attorneys—the D.C. Circuit has 10 to 14 and the Federal Circuit only 4.

Amplifying earlier discussions briefly, I note that the First Circuit, though the smallest in judges and caseload, has the same number of staff attorneys as the Seventh, most of them career rather than two-year staff attorneys. Despite the higher ratio of staff attorneys to judges than in our court, it appears that the First Circuit judges are more aggressive in revising opinions proposed by staff attorneys than our judges are. The Second Circuit is considerably larger than the First, and has nearly twice the number of staff attorneys; indeed, it has about 50 percent more staff attorneys—35-36—than my court does. The Third Circuit has 23-30, the Fourth Circuit 40-50, the Fifth 39-45, the Sixth 32, the Ninth 75-80 (the most of any circuit), and the Eleventh 60-70. The Eighth Circuit has the same number of staff attorneys as we, and half of them are career. The Tenth Circuit has the same number of staff attorneys as the Seventh and Eighth but they too are all career. The Tenth has as we know a tradition of face-to-face conferences with staff attorneys to decide cases presented to panels of judges—in effect an expansion of our Rule 34 conferences. In a variance of the Tenth Circuit's practice, the Ninth Circuit staff attorney in pro se cases review the record, research the law, and prepare a proposed disposition, which they then present to a panel of three judges during a practice we call 'oral screening'—oral because the judges don't see the briefs in advance, and because they generally rely on the staff attorney's oral description of the case in deciding whether to sign on to the proposed [by the staff attorney] disposition."

And notice finally that as one moves down the first spreadsheet in Appendix One, the differences among the circuit staff attorney programs diminish.

Part Two

Televising Oral Arguments

I have decided to include in the book a discussion of whether to permit the televising of our oral arguments. The issue has no direct connection to the controversy over our staff attorney program, but it has an indirect connection in further indicating what seems to me poor judicial management by the chief judge of my court. And a further connection, inasmuch as both (if we had both, which we don't yet) would reinforce the Seventh Circuit's transparency as a public institution; decisions that are readable by litigants help to educate them in the character of the judicial process, while televised courtroom hearings make the judges' encounters with litigators visible to the public.

My discussion of the issue is brief, however—not because I've run out of steam but because whether to televise appellate hearings is, or at least ought to be, as we'll see, a simple, straightforward issue.

I begin by asking: How can the average person (a non-lawyer, a non-judge, and a non-litigant) follow appellate courtroom proceedings? This chart summarizes the options for accessing oral arguments:

Circuit	Transcripts	Audio	Visual
1st	None.	All audio recordings are posted online (but judges on each panel are not identified directly).	None.

Circuit	Transcripts	Audio	Visual
2nd	None.	All audio recordings are posted online (but judges on each panel are not identified directly).	Since 1996, established members of the press or individuals affiliated with educational institutions can bring their own cameras to any non-criminal oral argument. There can be no more than 2 video cameras and 1 still camera.
3rd	None.	All audio recordings are posted online if the panel unanimously agrees to post. Judges on each panel are identified directly.	Since January, 2017, video recordings are posted online if the panel unanimously agrees to post.
4th	None.	All audio recordings are posted online. Judges on each panel are identified (but one would still need to recognize each judge's voice to know who is asking which questions).	None.
5th	None.	All audio recordings are posted online (attorneys are identified, but not the judges).	None.
6th	None.	All audio recordings are posted online (but judges on each panel are not identified directly).	None.
7th	None.	All audio recordings are posted online. Judges on each panel are not identified directly, although the case type is identified (prisoner, bankruptcy, civil, criminal, agency, etc.).	None.
8th	None.	All audio recordings are posted online (but judges on each panel are not identified directly).	None.
9th	None.	All audio recordings are posted online. Judges on each panel are identified directly.	All video recordings are on Youtube. Videos have been available since 2009. Additionally, there can be no more than 2 video cameras and 1 still camera for oral arguments.

Circuit	Transcripts	Audio	Visual
10th	None.	Select, "high-interest" oral arguments are posted online. Judges on each panel are not identified directly. To access other oral arguments, one can email the clerk's office and explain an interest in a particular case. The judges on the panel consider the request and respond within 10 days. If the request is granted, the clerk emails an MP3 of the oral argument.	None.
11th	None.	All audio recordings are posted online (but judges on each panel are not identified directly).	None.
DC	None.	All audio recordings are posted online. Judges on each panel are identified directly. Transcripts are also available by contacting the Clerk's Office.	None.
Federal	None.	All audio recordings are posted online (but judges on each panel are not identified directly).	

The appellate courts thus exist along a spectrum of different levels of public access to oral arguments, with the Ninth Circuit at the far end allowing the most access in varied forms and the Tenth Circuit offering the least straightforward level of access.[1] For circuits posting audio recordings without directly identifying the judges on each panel (by labelling each recording with the sitting judges), the only way to identify judges would be to listen to the entire oral argument in the hopes of catching an attorney or judge refer to a judge by name, or to wait until the opinion is posted, if it is posted. For circuits that directly identify the judges on each panel, one must still match judges' voices to their names (or, in the case of

---

[1] Some district courts will post all their oral arguments online as audio recordings, or on PACER (which costs individuals $2.40 to access each recording.) Before 2010, these recordings were accessible for $26 each. *Digital Audio Recording Project*, PACER, https://www.pacer.gov/announcements/general/audio_pilot.html.

the Ninth Circuit's video recordings, judges' faces to their names). Additionally, transcripts of appellate oral arguments are rare. None of the circuits hire court reporters. Parties can request a transcript, but they must know to order one ahead of time and pay for it and these transcripts are not posted on the court's website, PACER, or CM/ECF (and therefore not accessible to non-parties, even those willing to pay a nominal fee on PACER). In other words, there is no simple, low-effort way for members of the public to identify which judges are asking which questions in certain cases.

There is also no low-effort way for members of the public to understand the non-verbal communication that happens between judges. Exchanged glances, raised eyebrows, smiles, nods, shaking heads, and disapproving frowns (and not to mention, vacant stares when an attorney has altogether lost a judge's attention) are all left out of the public record, and all of these gestures can shift the meaning of the words judges and attorneys say during oral argument. An effort-intensive way to discover which judges tend to have which concerns, or to know which judges made which non-verbal communications, is physically sitting in on every oral argument. This method is limited by space constraints in the courtroom, an arbitrary criterion for deciding which individuals can have access to a public institution. As an attorney in a lawsuit challenging a 1952 law banning reporters from covering a high-profile murder case put it, "What if there are 125 seats in a courtroom and I'm the 126th and I can't fit in? The presence of cameras expands the gallery space infinitely. Should my constitutional access rights be contingent on seating arrangements in the courtroom?" An especially droll example of this arbitrariness can be found in Supreme Court oral arguments. When the courtroom gets too crowded, interested members of the public must rotate through the gallery in three-minute turns, ensuring that each individual only hears one small part of the argument and no one individual has the full context.[2]

In this informational void, the public relies on the media to report the worthiest snippets of courtroom proceedings (if the third branch's proceedings, especially at the appellate level, are

---

[2] This brings to mind the Indian fable of the three blind men touching an elephant and coming up with different definitions of "elephant" as a result.

mentioned at all in the news). This means that one of the popular arguments raised by judges[3] and scholars against televised oral arguments is already moot. At present, judges' statements in oral arguments can be excerpted at will by supposedly nefarious journalists. Compromising excerpts are currently difficult to verify, since only those physically in the courtroom at present are privy to the full context of every statement. Despite this, journalists have yet to excerpt compromising snippets that diminish judges' reputations, and this likelihood could only be diminished if complete transcripts and video recordings of oral arguments became widely available.[4] Any compromising excerpt could be easily debunked by interested individuals who read the transcript or watch a recording.

Opponents of televising courtroom arguments then argue that even if the public were given access to oral arguments, gavel-to-gavel, perhaps on C-SPAN or the short-lived Court TV, individuals would remain ignorant or, even worse, they would catch unrepresentative glimpses of a court in action. Even worse, the pre-

---

[3] Justice Stephen Breyer most recently said that he asks plenty of idiotic-sounding questions during oral argument and that televised courtroom proceedings could take these statements out of context. *U.S. Supreme Court Justice Stephen Breyer in Conversation with Associate Dean Alan Morrison* (American Constitution Society interview, June 8, 2017) (video available at https://www.youtube.com/watch?v=ksuRCixAto8). The late Justice Antonin Scalia had, and Justice Anthony Kennedy had and has, expressed similar reservations against televised court hearings. Robert Kessler, *Why Aren't Cameras Allowed at the Supreme Court Again?*, THE ATLANTIC, Mar. 28, 2013,https://www.theatlantic.com/national/archive/2013/03/case-allowing-cameras-supreme-court-proceedings/316876/). This concern is not new. Justice William O. Douglas in 1960 worried about the possibility of incomplete presentation. Douglas, "The Public Trial and the Free Press." And it is not a concern limited to Supreme Court Justices. See Molly Treadway Johnson and Carol Krafka, *Electronic Media Coverage of Federal Civil Proceedings: An Evaluation of the Pilot Program in Six District Courts and Two Courts of Appeals,* Federal Judicial Center, 1994, 24.

[4] A simple Google search for circuit courts' recent oral arguments yields no articles featuring irresponsible excerpts. Instead, oral arguments are written up as "play-by-play" accounts of proceedings by general-interest outlets like PBS *NewsHour*, the *New York Times, Fox News,* or specialized legal-news outlets like law firms' blogs or *The National Law Review.* The goal of the articles and news videos is to summarize proceedings for readers not present in the courtroom for the oral argument.

sumption is that the public would watch only for sensationalism and for entertainment. The late Justice Anthony Scalia had said: "The audio is not of interest to the 15-second take-out people, the 30-second take-out people."[5] But this leaves out the historians, legal scholars, reporters, watchdog groups, lawyers, and potential litigants for whom oral argument transcripts would reveal integral aspects of judicial decision-making that cannot be seen in any other work product emitted from courtrooms at present (the main one being, of course, opinions, which can hide behind legalese the true reasons for a judge's decision). That some individuals might watch oral arguments and not truly grasp every nuance of the proceedings is no reason to bar all who could benefit from watching. Or as the former *New York Times* reporter Walter Goodman wrote, "Punishing television for being too popular, too easy to switch on, too hard to resist is a perverse sort of logic; it rests on the assumption that public trials are all right as long as they are not unduly public."[6] Note also that at present "the public" allowed to attend oral argument is narrowly defined as those physically mobile enough and idle enough to sit in a courtroom during the business hours of the workweek.

Some time ago the judges of my court had a court meeting on the issue, prompted by a request by C-Span to be allowed to televise the *Hively* and *Johnson* en oral banc arguments. *Hively* was a particularly important case, requiring the court to decide whether the Civil Rights Act of 1964 forbids employment discrimination based on an employer's disapproval of lesbians. (We held by an 8 to 3 vote that it did. See *Hively v. Ivy Tech Community College of Indiana*, Apr. 4, 2017.) I think our chief judge should have replied to C-Span's request by telling it to go ahead, but instead she scheduled a court meeting for *after* the en bancs, and so had to reject C-Span's request. C-Span has made no further request to be allowed to televise a hearing or hearings of ours—not only to avoid a possible second rebuff but also because *very* few of our cases are sufficiently

---

[5] Alicia M. Cohn, "Justice Scalia: Cameras in the Supreme Court would 'miseducate' Americans" *The Hill*, July 26, 2012.

[6] Walter Goodman, "Court TV: The Case of the Curious Witness," *New York Times*, July 21, 1997, B5.

newsworthy to interest the national media, *Hively* being the rare exception.

The court meeting was a flop. My impression was and is that I was the only judge who had prepared for it carefully. The chief judge recently told me that she had too, and I have no reason to doubt that; but I don't recall her having disclosed her insights, if any, during the meeting.

I had prepared for the meeting by reading a brilliant article by Professor Sonja West[7] that the chief judge to her credit had cited on a page that she circulated before the meaning; by corresponding with West; and by conversing at length with Judge Alex Kozinski of the Ninth Circuit, a friend of mine. The Ninth Circuit has been televising virtually all of its oral arguments for the last 20 years, and according to Kozinski, who has been a judge of that court since 1985, there has never been an adverse incident—a threat to a judge seen on television, an assault, an insult, an angry letter—by someone who had seen the judge in a televised argument. On the contrary, he said, televising had increased the respect of the public for the court, because the judges come across on television as being dignified, well prepared, and polite. (If we ever have televised hearings, I will have to cultivate those qualities.) Besides the Ninth Circuit, the Second and Third Circuits also allow the televising of their oral arguments, though with greater restrictions. And all 50 state judiciaries allow extensive televising of their hearings, including most trials. As far as I've been able to determine, there has *never* been an incident resulting from anger generated by the sight of a judge on a TV screen.

But none of the other federal courts of appeals—and there are 13 in all—has followed the lead of the three that I mentioned, and this despite the fact that as long ago as the middle 1990s the Federal Judicial Conference recommended that the oral arguments of federal courts of appeals, and perhaps of other federal courts as well, should be allowed to be televised. Almost a quarter of a century later, the number seems to have stalled at three, unless my court gets off the dime.

---

[7] Sonja R. West, University of Georgia School of Law, "The Monster in the Courtroom," 2012 *B.Y.U.L.* 1953 (2012). See also Erwin Chimerinsky & Eric Segall, "Cameras Belong in the Court," 101 *Judicature*, no. 2, p. 14 (2017).

I don't know how many of the judges of my court knew or know all this, but I do know that at the meeting that I mentioned two of them expressed fear, groundless though it was, of appearing on television, lest they be assaulted or insulted if encountered on the street by someone who having seen them on television had taken a fierce dislike to them. Of course several of the Supreme Court Justices, though the Court does not allow its hearings to be televised, appear frequently on television. Shall we call them fearless?

One of the judges suggested at the meeting that the U.S. Marshals be consulted on whether it would be safe to allow our hearings to be televised. That was a natural suggestion to make, but in retrospect problematic—indeed unwise. Imagine yourself a federal marshal asked by a federal judge whether it is safe to allow the televising of judicial proceedings. The marshal will think: "it's probably, indeed almost certainly, safe; but suppose I tell them it's safe, go ahead—and unlikely though it may be, there is an unpleasant incident: I will lose my job, for having failed to protect the judge." Better to tell the judge: "I can't guarantee the safety of judges if they allow their hearings to be televised. There are 2.7 million residents of Chicago and they're not all sweeties."

But it's not our responsibility to protect the jobs of U.S. Marshals. Anyway the likelihood of an incident that would jeopardize the jobs of any of them appears to be infinitesimal based on the experience of the rest of the country with the televising of judicial hearings.

* * *

Four issues remain to be considered anent televising judicial proceedings. The first and least is money. If the only televising is by national media such as C-Span, they can be told to bring their television equipment with them into the courtroom on the rare occasions when they want to televise one of our oral-argument sessions, set it up, and operate it during the session. But if instead, as I certainly would prefer, and is the trend in the other courts of the nation, all our hearings were televised with the rare exception of hearings in which secret information has to be disclosed and the audience thus barred, then we'd have to buy our own equipment, and the chief judge is fearful that it would cost more than we could afford, because there's a movement afoot to reduce the budget of the federal judiciary, and the equipment would cost anywhere between $100,000 and $200,000. When she told me this I said I'd be glad to buy the equipment with my own money, and give it to the court (and I'd be glad to make the gift anonymously, although I don't think I mentioned this on that occasion). She turned down my offer without giving a reason.

And so by now the reader will have grasped a further reason for my deciding to fold the television issue into a book primarily concerned with the unrelated issue of proper management of the staff attorney program: The failure to progress on both fronts is attributable to the same person.

The second issue is the age of federal appellate judges. Their average age at present is 71, and is likely to rise because "the share of octogenarians and nonagenarians on the federal bench has doubled in the past 20 years,"[8] and this trend is likely to continue as Americans live ever longer. And remember that the average age of the judges of the Seventh Circuit court of appeals is 73. I think people tend to become more timid, more fearful, with age, and I worry therefore that if the question of televising our proceedings comes to a vote, a majority will vote against it.

The third issue, though it is not directly relevant to this court, is the televising (as yet forbidden) of the Supreme Court's oral arguments. (It is indirectly relevant, though, because a decision by the Supreme Court to allow its oral arguments to be televised would exert a strong influence on the courts of appeals to follow suit.) The case for that is stronger than it is for the lower federal courts because there is far more public interest in the Supreme Court than in any other court. Yet the Court has been adamant in refusing to allow any of its hearings to be televised. Justice Souter said televising of the Court's hearings would be over his dead body; what on earth could have precipitated such a silly statement? Well, he was something of a shrinking violet; the current Justices are not. Most of them appear from time to time on television talk shows

---

[8] Joseph Goldstein, "Life Tenure for Federal Judges Raises Issues of Senility, Dementia," *ProPublica*, Jan. 18, 2011.

or in presiding at mock trials that are televised, or make public statements that draw attention; why don't they want their hearings televised?

The reasons given for barring television from the Supreme Court's hearings no longer involve fear of assault or insult; indeed it's impossible to extract a cogent argument for the barring of television either from Supreme Court Justices or anyone else.[9] The principal, or at least most vocal, opponent of allowing the televising of the Court's hearings is nowadays Justice Breyer, whose arguments for his position are, as pointed out by Michael Dorf, bad.[10] He said (this is Dorf's paraphrase, not an exact quotation from Breyer) that "if the Supreme Court were to allow cameras in its courtroom, then other courts would fall under irresistible pressure to do the same. And in that event, he though, harm would be done in cases in which unwanted notoriety would befall people unlucky enough to be involved in legal proceedings." As Dorf points out, "Many trial court proceedings are already televised, and the lower courts—which are way ahead of the Supreme Court on this issue—have developed extensive guidelines on when to permit, and when to exclude, cameras." Breyer had a second response: "that televised oral arguments would give the public a distorted picture of how the Supreme Court functions because oral argument comprises only 'two percent of our decision-making process.'" Dorf pointed out in response that "under the current system—in which Americans learn about what transpires at oral argument from newspaper accounts that rarely take the form of full transcripts—the public has access to less than two percent of the Court's decision-making process," and television would "increase understanding of the Court's business." Dorf points out that "the real nub of the Justices' opposition to television coverage of oral arguments (and the handing down of decisions) stems from their desire to present themselves on their own terms." Right on!

---

[9] See, for a comprehensive analysis, Ronald Goldfarb, "Televising the Supreme Court," *Washington Lawyer*, Nov. 2004; see also "Democracy in America: Cameras at the Supreme Court—They Ought to Be in Pictures: Why Are the Justices So Camera Shy?," *The Economist*, March 25, 2014.

[10] Michael C. Dorf, "A TV Appearance by Two Supreme Court Justices Indicates How Much the Court Values Control," *FindLaw*, July 9, 2003.

The gold coin of the literature on whether the Supreme Court's courtroom proceedings should be televised is Professor West's article in the Brigham Young University Law School, cited earlier, and I need to say more about it. The article makes the following salient points. First, that the Court is not secretive, that it allows several avenues of public access to its process, making it a relatively open and transparent government body. And this makes it seem that West is going to argue that Court's allowing its oral arguments to be televised would be just icing on the cake. But no, her inference is that the Court's openness "makes it all the more curious why the Justices have drawn the line at cameras." She notes the paradox that Supreme Court nominces usually endorse televising the Court's proceedings, only to become opposed once they're seated on the Court, a notable recent example being Elena Kagan. And this despite the fact that, owing to improvements in the technology of televising, "no one has argued for years that the [television] cameras would be too loud or too big and thus a disruption."

West quotes a Supreme Court opinion that states that "a trial is a public event. What transpires in the court room is public property."[11] A hearing in the Supreme Court is not a trial, yet is as much public property as any trial. And, West points out, televising the Court's proceedings would "provide the public with more information about the [Court] ... and enhance accountability." Information the public needs, for as she also points out two-thirds of America's citizens cannot name a single Supreme Court Justice and 60 percent don't know the Court has nine members. She further points out that televising the proceedings would make the Justices come alive to the viewers, would make the Justices vivid in a way that reading about them or even hearing a recording of an oral argument would not (often the reader or, especially, the listener would have no idea which Justice he or she was reading about or listening to). And of course far more people watch television than read newspapers or listen to the radio.

The objections to allowing Supreme Court arguments to be televised come mainly from the Justices themselves and are feeble, as West points out. One argument is that having a television au-

---

[11] *Craig v. Harney*, 331 U.S. 367, 374 (1947).

dience will make the lawyers "grandstand," but as she points out they dare not do it as they will offend the Justices and as a result have a diminished probability of winning their case. She further notes that the courts, state and federal, that allow the televising of judicial proceedings have not encountered grandstanding. She quotes Tom Goldstein, a frequent advocate before the Supreme Court, explaining that the advocates' "only concern is persuading the Justices, not annoying them and potentially losing votes by grandstanding." West further notes studies that have found that televising the confirmation hearings of Supreme Court nominees did not cause the nominees to grandstand. And likewise she notes that the fear expressed by the late Justice Scalia and others that viewers of televised Supreme Court hearings would take away from them merely "30-second sound bites" has no basis in reality. And last she notes the fear of the unknown, emphasized by Justice Breyer and earlier by Justice O'Connor, an unknown that led Breyer to suggest that it's better to have what they say at oral argument interpreted by the press and for the public to learn about the oral arguments from the press. That is pretty condescending.

The fourth issue concerning the televising of oral arguments, an issue of particular relevance to the Seventh Circuit, is the precise format of the televising. I can think of nothing better than imitation of the Ninth Circuit, the leader in the televising of oral arguments in federal appellate courts. The Ninth Circuit posts all its oral arguments on Youtube.com, the video-sharing website owned by Google that clocks in as the second-most-visited website in the world (behind Google.com). The Ninth Circuit has posted 4,343 videos since joining YouTube in 2010, most of which are complete video recordings of its oral arguments.

Videos split into two screens. Attorneys are shown in the bottom right-hand corner, while the panels fill the rest of the screen. For most oral arguments, a few sentences accompany each video describing the case's main issues and allegations. YouTube allows viewers to interact with video-posters by commenting below each video and "liking" or "disliking" each video, but for most of the Ninth Circuit's videos, especially those drawing many views, comments and "likes"/"dislikes" are turned off, reinforcing the sense that these videos are posted for educational purposes and certainly not for any public feedback on courtroom proceedings.[12] Cases are posted within a week of being heard and at the Ninth Circuit, the last opinions and final orders for cases take about a month to be issued.[13] Given this timing and the settings for the Ninth Circuit's YouTube account, any panel's judge stumbling across the YouTube video of an assigned case before coming to a decision on it runs no risk of being influenced by this particular public forum.

What can be learned from the Ninth Circuit's YouTube page? While it is impossible to know who is watching which oral arguments without being the administrator of the YouTube account in question, it is possible to know which oral arguments get the most views. And since none of the Ninth Circuit's videos are frozen at "301+" views, the penalty YouTube imposes on video-posters who use bots to ratchet up their view counts to garner more ad revenue, it is safe to say that the Ninth Circuit's views

---

[12] Some of the Ninth Circuit's videos do let viewers "like" and "dislike" videos. For these videos, it is difficult to discern precisely why viewers are "liking" or "disliking" each video. Do they like one lawyer's argument? Do they like a judge's questioning? Do they like the fact that this case is being litigated at all? Or do they perhaps dislike some aspect of the case but appreciate the court's efforts in making it publicly viewable? These questions are impossible to answer without seeing the exact time-stamps for each "like" pressed. For example, viewers who approve that a class action lawsuit has been filed against an automobile manufacturer would probably press "like" before oral argument has even begun. Viewers who take one side in *National Abortion Federation v. Center for Medical Progress*, though, would wait until either the attorney representing their preferred side makes an excellent point to "like" (or "like" when the judge asks a pointed and unanswerable question of the opposing side.) Despite the inscrutability of viewer's "likes", one pattern emerges: for the videos receiving over 400 views within the last year, the "likes", when viewers bothered to register any reaction, overwhelmingly outnumbered the "dislikes." In an indeterminate order, people watch certain cases and they "like" those cases.

[13] Table B-4A Appeals—Median Time Intervals in Months for Civil and Criminal Appeals Terminated on the Merits, By Circuit, During the 12-Month Period Ending September 30, 2016, U.S. Courts, (2016), at www.uscourts.gov/sites/default/files/data_tables/jb_b4a_0930.2016.pdf.

come from independent human viewers rather than bots.[14] So how many views are the oral arguments receiving? And for which cases?

The histogram on the following page (from Ninth Circuit's YouTube page at https://www.youtube.com/user/9thcirc) shows the videos receiving different amounts of views from the past year. Half of the videos received 130 views or fewer (shown in dark blue). 95% of the videos received 450 views or fewer (the 45% of videos between 130 views and 450 views are shown in light blue). The remaining 5% of videos received more than 450 views (shown in orange). Only 20 videos in the past year received more than 1,000 views. The median is at 132.5 views.

The Ninth Circuit's videos have not "gone viral" in any sense, though they have a steady following of court watchers. The outliers, the videos gathering more than 1,000 views within the last year, involve cases that received national media attention. Clocking in at an impressive 141,111 views is the Ninth Circuit's most popular oral argument for *State of Washington, et al v. Donald J. Trump et al.*[15] However, for this oral argument, the Ninth Circuit forgoes video footage and instead posted the audio with title cards identifying each speaker and their role. The video footage is available for viewing and downloading elsewhere online (the U.S.

---

[14] Admittedly, YouTube does not scrutinize videos receiving fewer than 300 views for suspicious bot activity and most of the Ninth Circuit's videos are below 300 views. However, considering these relatively low view counts for the Ninth Circuit and the fact that it does not run ads on its videos and therefore has no incentive to convince YouTube that it has enough viewers to be paid high amounts for ads, it is unlikely the Ninth Circuit would use bots to get its view counts up to 100 views. YouTube is after all a site where a video titled "Cats are so funny you will die laughing" garners 47,068,919 views in six months and video-posters

Additionally, YouTube counts as an "independent" view any view lasting longer than 30 seconds. It is possible that the same individual is viewing a video 100 times in a row for longer than 30 seconds each, rather than 100 individuals watching each oral argument. For the purpose of this analysis, I ignore the former possibility (it is a ludicrous, although not totally impossible, scenario, at least for these particular videos. Videos elsewhere on YouTube could provoke dozens of repeat viewings from the same individual but these oral arguments do not involve fluffy puppies or hilarious accidents.)

[15] The view count rose by 20 views within 24 hours, as I wrote this memo, and it will be higher by the next time anyone checks the video.

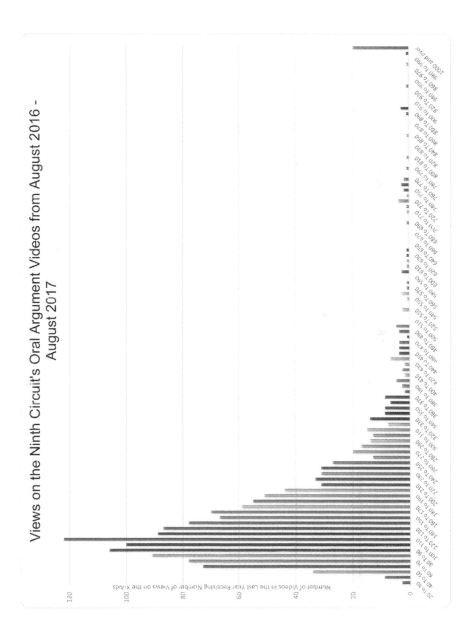

Views on the Ninth Circuit's Oral Argument Videos from August 2016 - August 2017

Courts "Cameras in the Courts" webpage has the entire oral argument posted on its own page and many other YouTube accounts have posted the footage, probably without permission).[16] Despite the absent visuals, the Ninth Circuit's YouTube page was a central destination for the 140,000+ viewers who would never have been able to fit inside the physical courtroom at the same time this past winter.

What other types of oral arguments tend to be the most popular? Within the last year, oral arguments involving well-known individuals (James Cameron, George Bush, and Donald Trump, for example) and well-known companies (the National Football League, Disney, Uber, Samsung, Oracle, Fox Television, and Hyundai) received high view counts. Wacky, one-off cases were also popular. The second most-watched oral argument, with 13,711 views, was a follow-up to the most expensive liability lawsuit against Orange County (a mother who lost custody of her daughters due to fabricated evidence from two social workers sued the county back in 2012 and this year, her daughter sued.) Another popular oral argument involved a monkey's copyright claims after it took a "selfie" (a photograph of itself) and it received 4,026 views.

But big names and wacky cases were not the only draw. Forty-two U.S. Code § 1983 cases, especially those involving police officers either shooting individuals wrongfully or fabricating evidence, had many viewers. A case alleging unreasonable search and seizure after a drunk woman was bitten in the face by a canine unit received 1,026 views, and another involving unsealing confidential information in an officer shooting received 7,937 views. Cases involving violations of the Constitution, particularly the First Amendment, also received high view counts. A challenge to the Montana Code of Judicial Conduct on First Amendment grounds received 486 views. Another lawsuit involving attorney's fees and costs under the Freedom of Information Act received 490 views. Class actions generated much interest as well; the fourth-

---

[16] It is also on C-Span with footage, although here it only generated 8,303 views. This suggests that viewers head first to YouTube for their video needs, despite the inferior video content, rather than C-SPAN. "*State of Hawaii, et al. v. Trump,*" C-SPAN (May 15, 2017), at https://www.c-span.org/video/?427827-1/ninth-circuit-hears-oral-argument-travel-ban.

highest-viewed case last year was a lawsuit against the Bush administration about the illegality of the Iraq War. It received 7,535 views. A lawsuit over the exploding Samsung Galaxy 4 phones received 704 views.

Interestingly, some cases that would ordinarily get channeled to a non-argument track were argued orally and managed to clock in high view counts. A habeas corpus petition challenging a carjacking conviction received 753 views. Board of Immigration Appeals cases, especially those involving torture if the Mexican national were to be deported, were popular. In this context, the shuttling of habeas cases and immigration cases to non-argument track should be reconsidered.

All these highly-viewed cases are reflected in the orange bars on the histogram shown above. I did not keep a systematic record of which cases were less popular; I looked into the 71 most-viewed videos and I left alone the 1,553 other videos. So in selecting by popularity, I do not want to suggest that, say, prisoner petitions are likelier to be watched than other cases I do not describe (and indeed, since prisoner petitions take up a third of the Ninth Circuit's docket, that only a handful of them make it into the most-watched oral arguments suggests that they are vastly underrepresented in oral arguments, or vastly underrepresented in viewers' watching tendencies, or both). Instead, I present this diverse array of cases that viewers chose to watch in order to counter arguments from opponents of televising oral arguments who suggest that the mindless members of the public only watch the most sensational cases, and even then, only intermittently. Viewers certainly go for sensational cases about photogenic macaques, but they also go for a tort case involving asbestos (1,936 views), a case about a union breaching its duty of fair representation (2,853 views), and a case about the good moral character requirement from the U.S. Citizenship and Immigration Services (898 views). The public's interests in oral arguments cannot be fairly represented as restricted only to lurid cases.

Finally, the total views from the oral arguments posted within the last year comes out to 475,526 views for the Ninth Circuit. While this hardly compares to a Key and Peele comedy sketch involving a motivational cat poster, which received 9,884,911 views, these view counts suggest that there are almost half a million court watchers[17] who did not need to pack into the physical seats at the Ninth Circuit's four courthouses but still managed to see the court in action.

To conclude, we the Seventh Circuit can do no better than to copy the Ninth Circuit's system of televising appellate arguments. I repeat my offer to finance the system. I would greatly appreciate an articulate response from the chief judge.

---

[17] Or one court-watcher, half a million times.

Part Three

Winding Up

Chapter One

Tension in the Court

On June 14, just two days before I finished the first draft of this book, I received the following note from the chief judge: "I am sending you the attached memorandum to let you know what changes I have decided to implement in the Staff Attorney's Office, and which I have decided not to adopt. As I say in the memo, this will govern the Office for now; anyone who would like any changes or simply to discuss this further may put this topic on the agenda for our fall court meeting." I include the memo and my response in this part of the book. Here is the memo with just a few short bracketed comments by me in boldface:

Re: Staff Attorney's Office

To: All Seventh Circuit Judges
        Collins Fitzpatrick, Circuit Executive
        Gino Agnello, Clerk of Court
        Michael Fridkin, Senior Staff Attorney
From: Diane P. Wood, Chief Judge
Date: June 14, 2017

For the last several weeks, on Dick Posner's initiative, we have been having a discussion about the Staff Attorney's Office. Dick circulated a lengthy memorandum to all judges on May 31, 2017. That memo contained both descriptive material about the Office and a number of recommendations for improvement. It launched a conversation that has included the staff attorneys themselves and the judges. Both Dick's original memo and the conversation that followed have contributed to my own thinking about this issue. In the interest of resolving some of the questions that have arisen, I am circulating this note to all of you to let you know what I have decided to do. This will govern the office for now. If any member of the court wishes to discuss this matter further at the fall court meeting (date yet to be determined), that is fine; just let me know and I will put it on the agenda.

My decisions are influenced by several things. First is the excellence of our Staff Attorney's Office. I am familiar with the operations of their counterparts in many other cir- cuits, and I can say without hesitation that our program is the best in the country]. Several features contribute to this excellence: the very high quality of the Senior Staff attor- ney [i.e., Michael Fridkin] and his deputies; the outstand- ing qualifications of the young lawyers who serve two-year stints in the Office; our practice of constant personal inter- action between the staff attorneys and every judge on the court [**I wouldn't say *constant***]; and our unparalleled prac- tice of providing full written explanations along with ev- ery Rule 34 order and every short-argument-day resolution that the Office handles. [**A short-argument day is a morn- ing of oral arguments, resulting in opinions and orders no different in kind from the opinions and orders issued in other orally argued cases.**] In addition, we always give a brief summary of our reasons for rejecting or accepting an application for second or successive habeas corpus relief. The Office does all this in a timely manner. Even when it is flooded with applications after a key Supreme Court de- cision, which happened when the *Johnson* (2015) decision was handed down, it has stayed on top of the workload. Many of its sister offices cannot say the same, as I know from the discussion about this that took place at the Meet- ing of the Chief Judges and Circuit Executives at the Judi- cial Conference.

I have also taken into account the discussion (both in memo or email form and in less formal conversations) that we have had. It has clarified for me both Dick's proposals and how they do, or do not, fit in with the way the court operates. Just because we have an excellent Office does not mean that improvement is impossible. To the contrary, we are always looking for ways to do our job better, and so we should all be open to experimentation and change.

In that spirit, I have decided that we should proceed with the following new practices, all of which are either recommended in Dick's memorandum or are consistent with its spirit (as I understand it) [**not really**]:

1.   When the Staff Attorney's Office issues notices of upcoming panel assignments for short-argument days, the notices should remind each judge that he or she is encouraged to invite the staff attorneys to meet in person with the judge to discuss the cases, either before oral arguments or after oral arguments. The supervisory staff attorneys will help find a convenient time for such meetings.

2.   In an effort to improve the match between lawyers willing to take *pro bono* appeals and *pro se* litigants who need appellate representation, we will develop a program under which the staff attorneys will draft brief descriptions of pending *pro se* appeals. Those descriptions can then be posted in a new place on the court's public website, along with an invitation to the bar to volunteer to represent the *pro se* litigant *pro bono* in a particular case.

3.   To improve even more the litigants' understanding of our dispositions, we will experiment with adding one or two explanatory sentences to otherwise one-sentence orders (such as denials of petitions for mandamus, requests for certificates of appealability, or requests for permission to file successive habeas-corpus petitions).

4.   The Staff Attorney's Office will expand its efforts to foster good writing by offering more frequent "writing seminars." We will start by setting up quarterly seminars, at each of which we will invite a judge or volunteer professor to come and discuss effective writing.

Dick's memo contains other suggestions that I am not adopting. The most important of these is his request that he be permitted to review (a) all drafts from staff attorneys *before* the drafts are presented to Rule 34 or short-argument panels, or, more modestly, (b) drafts from staff attorneys who volunteer to have Dick review their work, but again *before* those memoranda are submitted to the assigned panel or individual judge. I am convinced that the insertion of any single judge—whether it is Dick, me, or any other member of the court—between the staff attorney and the judges is incompatible with the operation of a multi-member court, and so I do not endorse that change. If a staff attorney wanted to take a few memos he or she has written in closed cases (*i.e.* the type of written work that one might want to use as a writing sample) and discuss with any willing judge how that memo might have been improved, that staff attorney should follow the same procedure that applies for writing samples.

I'll end where I started: I am proud of our Staff Attorney's Office, and I do not believe that major changes in it are necessary. This is a message that we must convey to the outside world, too, if we are to continue to attract the high-quality people we have come to expect. The fact that some staff attorneys might [**no "might" about it**] need to improve their writing (at least in the eyes of some judges— we do not have a monolithic view about what is best) does not disturb me at all. Everyone, including the judges, can improve, and the steps I have outlined above should help.

This is where things will stand unless or until we have a court meeting at which the court as a whole decides to change it. I appreciate the time and attention that everyone [?] has paid to this matter.

And here is my (Posner's) response to the chief judge (slightly edited for this book), a somewhat elaborated version of my email response to her:

"Respectfully, while point 1 in your memo strikes me as sound, Point 2 is I think unlikely to work, because most law firms don't want to have their lawyers devoting time to pro bono representation, which is unpaid; what needs instead to be done is to identify the firms that do have pro bono programs. Point 3—adding one or two sentences to a one-sentence decision—will have, I predict, little effect. And as for quarterly seminars, they will have no more efficacy for this generation of young lawyers than classroom instruction in college or law school has.

"Also I can't accept the suggestion, flattering to me as it is, that your program rests on my initiative, because nothing in the program tracks suggestions I have made for improving the staff attorney program. That's not to say that your suggested revisions are wrong, just that they're not my suggestions. Nor do I see any indication of who will implement the proposals. I am also concerned about your claim that our staff attorney program is the best in the country, as you do not provide any detail or supporting evidence. I have conducted extensive research, summarized in this book, into the staff attorney programs of all 13 federal courts of appeals, and from that research I infer that a good many of the other circuits have staff attorney programs as good as, or perhaps even superior to, ours. Equal would include for example the Ninth Circuit; I quote its list of "representative duties" of its staff attorneys[1]:

- Review district court and agency records, parties' briefs and other documents filed on appeal, conduct in-depth legal research, and analyze relevant issues.
- Prepare draft dispositions explaining the factual and legal bases for deciding appeals.
- Appear before three-judge panels and orally submit recommended dispositions for ready motions or appeals.
- Analyze motions for reconsideration or petitions for rehearing and recommend disposition to three-judge panels.
- Process emergency and other time sensitive matters in expedited manner for presentation to judges.
- Respond to public inquiries and requests for information or assistance from judges or other court staff.

---

[1] "United States Court of Appeals for the Ninth Circuit: Vacancy Announcement: Position: Staff Attorney," http://cdn.ca9.uscourts./datastore/employment/2017/01/09/17_Staff_Atty.pdf.

- Meet court standards for quality, quantity and timeliness of work.

Continuing with my response to the chief judge: "While the staff attorney programs of the Ninth and several other circuits merely seem closely comparable to ours, the First, Second, Third, Fifth, Tenth, and Eleventh, all discussed earlier in the book, seem more tightly managed than ours, on balance quite possibly superior to ours—and certainly not inferior. My research has elicited no evidence of a national consensus that our staff attorney program is the nation's best. I can't find strong support anywhere for your claim that we have a "practice of constant personal interaction between the staff attorneys and every judge on the court," as well as an "unparalleled practice of providing full written explanations along with every Rule 34 order and every short-argument-day resolution that the Office handles." Regarding the second point, the explanations are limited to the Rule 34 order itself and to whatever order or opinion emerges from a short-argument day's oral arguments. And finally it should be noted that our staff attorney program is one of the smallest of the 13; we have fewer staff attorneys than the First, Second, Fourth, Fifth, Sixth, Ninth, and Eleventh Circuits, and are merely tied with the Third.

"You don't mention any strengths of other staff attorney programs—are you convinced that they're all weakness? That strength is found only in our program? Not only is that unlikely, but it's odd that while insisting that all the other circuits' staff attorney programs are weaker than ours, you cite no weaknesses in those programs. If they have no weaknesses, how can they be weaker than our program, which, according to your list, has no *significant* strengths?

"The closest you come to acknowledging any weakness in our staff attorney program is your statement that 'some [of our] staff attorneys might need to improve their writing (at least in the eyes of some judges)'—an acknowledgment undermined by such words as 'some' and 'might' and 'at least.' I am distressed that you offer no criticism of our treatment of pro se's, though I think I have demonstrated that there is much to criticize. You mention no errors, no bobbles in any cases that come to our judges via staff attorneys, though once again I think I have demonstrated such errors and bobbles are common.

"I am puzzled by your reference to 'the discussion about this that took place at the Meeting of the Chief Judges and Circuit Executives at the Judicial Conference.' (The organizational reference is to the semi-annual Judicial Conferences, of which the chief judges, together with one district judge from each circuit, are the members along with the Chief Justice. The chief judges also meet separately, whether at every, or every other, Judicial Conference—I don't recall which—to discuss matters of mutual interest.) It's not entirely clear what 'about this' is meant to signify, but I'm guessing it concerns your claim that our court has stayed on top of the workload created by the *Johnson* decision and that 'many of its sister offices cannot say the same, as I know from the discussion about this that took place at the Meeting of the Chief Judges and Circuit Executives at the Judicial Conference.' I have it on good authority from a participant in the meeting that there were no such confessions by the chief judges, but of course it's possible that the individual in question ignored or has forgotten them.

"I'm troubled by your not giving the reader a more concrete sense of our staff attorney program, as by telling the reader how many staff attorneys we have, how they are chosen, how paid, how long they stay, or by presenting evidence concerning the staff attorney programs of any of the 12 other federal circuits. You don't tell the reader whether you've spoken to any director of the staff attorney program of another circuit, or for that matter to any staff attorney of another circuit. Indeed you tell the reader virtually nothing about any other staff attorney program—name no names, describe no policies or practices, cite no articles discussing the programs of the other circuits, though such articles are numerous.

"I recall from my days as chief judge the meetings of the circuit chief judges at the Judicial Conferences. They were notably bland. Based on my recollections, I find it hard to believe that the 12 other chief judges, each of whom presides over his court's staff attorney program, would vote our program the best. Imagine him (or her), upon returning to his home circuit, announcing that he's discovered that his court's staff attorney program is inferior to that of the Seventh Circuit? No way! Still, I wasn't there, and may be wrong.

"Although I will not name names, I understand that the discussion of staff attorney programs at the meeting of chief judges at the most recent Judicial Conference was *not* about which court of appeals has the best staff attorneys program but how best to respond to appeals based on the Supreme Court's decision in *Johnson v. United States*, 135 S. Ct. 2551 (1915), and that there were no confessions by the other chief judges that only our court had been able to cope with the additional workload created by *Johnson*. Of course I cannot prove that my understanding is correct.

"I hope the other chief judges didn't feel insulted by being told that our staff attorney program is best, if indeed you told them that. Remember that the Ninth Circuit has between 75 and 80 staff attorneys, the Eleventh Circuit between 60 and 70, and we only 25. Your encomium for our staff attorney program—and I'm not suggesting it isn't your actual, considered view—could be thought to imply that these other circuits are overstaffed, that if they cut their staffs by two-thirds or a half they'd have a chance of equaling us in excellence. That is implausible, especially when one considers that the Ninth Circuit has 43 judges and the Eleventh Circuit 20; we have only 12. After the meeting did the chief judges of these and other circuits go back home and start cutting their staffs? Not likely!

"I conclude that claim that we have the best staff attorney program has not yet been substantiated—that at present the claim is mere *ipse dixit*.[2] That doesn't mean it's wrong, but that it requires more evidence."

* * *

Another claim by the chief judge that I want to note is that the insertion of one and the same judge (me?) between the staff attorney and the panel judges would be incompatible with the operation of a multi-member court. That ignores the fact that any recommendation by a staff attorney, whether or not influenced or even determined by a judge rather than by the staff attorney, can

---

[2] Latin for "he himself said it," implying that his say-so is the only reason to think the statement true.

be ignored by the panel assigned to decide the case to which the staff attorney's memo or draft order or other document pertained. Furthermore the judges of a court of appeals are not fungible with respect to all types of case that the court handles. A judge who is an expert on antitrust law may be quite helpless deciding whether a prison inmate should get a second or third or fourth crack at vacating his conviction or shortening his sentence. I believe that I am the only judge of my court who combines extensive appellate experience (I have greater seniority on our court than any other judge except Judge Bauer, who will turn 91 this year (2017)) with extensive writing experience (my countless books and articles and blog posts and speeches) and, uniquely among this court's judges, a deeply felt commitment to the welfare of the pro se litigants, about half of whom are prison or jail detainees, who crowd our court.

I want to come back for a moment to the third point in the chief judge's email—that to improve even more the litigants' understanding of our dispositions [the word should however be "decisions," not "dispositions"] the court will experiment with adding one or two explanatory sentences to otherwise one-sentence orders (such as denials of petitions for mandamus, requests for certificates of appealability, or requests for permission to file successive habeas-corpus petitions). Her statement was amplified in the following message I received from the staff attorneys' office: "We therefore are experimenting with different ways of using the memoranda. The information we think is appropriate to the memos is (1) the type of case we are sending to you, (2) when the statutory 30-day period expires and an order must issue, (3) why we are presenting the application to this panel of judges, and (4) what documents we are—and, if we are not forwarding exhibits, are not—sending to you."

These points are troubling. In the case of (1), the "you" presumably is the pro se whose claim the court is resolving; this should be stated more clearly. (2) should explain what a statutory period is; but why specify "when ... an order must issue," given that the order is issued simultaneously with the explanatory memo? (3) can be of no interest to the pro se, who will be ignorant of differences among panels (i.e., different judges). (4) is a puzzle, implying as it does (perhaps unintentionally) that only exhibits are forwarded to litigants.

I was therefore not surprised to receive, in a pro se appeal called *Parks v. Knight*, No. 17-2342, along with the appeal and an order rejecting it, a memo that stated only that "Warren Parks asks permission to file a successive collateral attack. A dispositive order must issue by July 29, 2017. I present the application to you [Judges Bauer, Hamilton, and Posner] as members of today's motions panel. I am including a copy of Parks' application and a draft order. Please notify me of your votes and how I can be of further assistance. Thank you." The staff attorney inserted a foot-note after "panel," in which she repeated, word for word, the four points made in the amplified message from the office of the staff attorneys. Yet none of the four points appears in the body of the memorandum, which is empty.

The identical memorandum, except for the name of the pro se, appears in a contemporaneous staff attorney submission, *Weather-spoon v. United States*, No. 17-2320.

What is going on?

* * *

And finally isn't it odd to prefer that a memo or draft order dis-patched to a judge or panel of judges be prepared by a kid (a staff attorney fresh out of law school) than that it be revised and edited by an adult (a judge)?

* * *

I have yet to hear from any judge other than the chief judge why *my* proposed approach to reforming the staff attorney pro-gram (as distinct from the chief judge's), whereby I would review and if necessary revise staff attorney memos, proposed orders, and any other documents prepared by staff attorneys for submission to panels of judges in pro se cases, has been rejected. The chief judge's position is that all the judges of the court are fungible, and there-fore have to have identical responsibilities—so I can't be allowed to play a special role with regard to the staff attorney program, even though I am the *only* judge who has a serious interest in our program and who in addition has studied *all* thirteen federal appellate staff attorney programs in detail. I disagree with the chief judge's position but it is her view and of course she's entitled to it.

No judge other than the chief judge has spoken to me about the rejection of my approach on June 6 except David Hamilton, whom I called a few days later and again on June 20. His idea, much like the chief judge's, was to make a staff attorney's approach to a judge for assistance "voluntary"—"the decision would be the staff attorney's; the judge couldn't insist that the staff attorney bring him or her a draft memo or order for editing." This is not a good idea, because as I explained earlier only the staff attorneys who write well will approach a judge for help (ostensibly), because they know that being good writers they can count on warm letters of recommendation from the judge to their prospective next employer and hence want to get to know an influential judge. Not so the bad writers, who can't be confident that any judge they approach will write a warm letter of recommendation for them.

In a subsequent conversation with me, Judge Hamilton rejected the idea that one judge (me) should screen all staff attorneys' memos, his ground, like the chief judge's, being that such responsibility must be shared among the judges. But why? Are the court's 12 judges fungible, like 12 mice from the same litter?

* * *

It would be good if the chief judge explained the legal basis for the unilateral decisions, concerning the staff attorney program, that she announced in her emailed memo of June 14, as when she said "I am circulating this note to all of you to let you know what I have decided to do. This will govern the office for now." The possibility that she may be (and I emphasize "may be") exceeding her authority as chief judge led me to research chief judges' governance authority. The prevailing conception, I discovered, is that a chief judge's powers are administrative rather than substantive. See, e.g., "Chief Judge," *Wikipedia*, https://en.wikipedia. org/wiki/ChiefJudge; also Wilf, "The Office of the Chief Judge of a Federal Court of Appeals," 53 *Fordham Law Review* 369 (1984). "Chief Judges [of federal courts of appeals] have administrative responsibilities with respect to their circuits, and preside over any panel in which they serve, unless the circuit Justice [the Supreme Court designates a Justice to be a circuit Justice, with certain limited responsibilities to the circuit) is also on the panel," *Wikipedia*. The chief judge is not authorized to make law all by herself. She presides over every panel she sits on, but if the other judges on the panel disagree with her recommended decision in a case, she cannot override them by virtue of being the court's chief judge.

After I wrote the above, I received from my principal research assistant at the University of Chicago Law School, Theresa Yuan, the following comprehensive list of a chief circuit judge's powers (I spare the reader the numerous sources from which she compiled the list):

A circuit chief judge:
- monitors the flow of cases to be sure "flow does not get unduly delayed at one point or another" (for example, judges can direct complaints about not getting enough time to read briefs before argument to the chief judge)
- presides over periodic meetings between [or among] active judges
- supervises the hiring of important staff positions like the Clerk of the Court
- attends the biannual Judicial Conference of the United States meetings (topics of discussion include pay and practices of court reporters and law clerks, codes of conduct, and budget reports, and apparently it takes a few days to read through the stacks of reports that chief judges receive in advance of each Conference)
- attends meetings within the Circuit's Judicial Council (with all active circuit judges and one district judge from each of the circuit's districts)
- ensures that laws, regulations, and court policies are followed
- develops and implements "court plans"
- supervises the clerk's office
- resolves informal disputes
- reviews the court budget

- oversees space acquisition, alternations, construction
- ensures court security
- appoints and serves on court committees
- files reports and plans with the Administrative Office of the U.S. Courts.[3]

Subsequently Ms. Yuan referred me to another, overlapping list of the powers of a chief circuit judge, which I now quote minus the powers that appear on the previous list:

- addressing any complaints of misconduct for the magistrates, bankruptcy judges, district judges, and circuit judges by either dismissing the complaint as frivolous or forming a committee to investigate the complaint monitor court caseloads
- supervise the clerk of court;
- oversee local rule-making
- review court budgets and court spending
- ensure court security and emergency preparedness
- file reports and plans in a timely manner with the circuit judicial council, the AO, and other entities and issuing [should be "issue"] reports and giving [should be "give"] speeches to [should be "about"] the court's operation
- select the membership of the committee on Local Rules and Internal Operating Procedures of the Court of Appeals
- serve as a liaison with outside groups such as the Judicial Conference, the public, the bar, state and local courts and governments, agencies, schools and the media

There's also interaction with the U.S. Marshals Service, the U.S. Attorney's Office, and other federal government agencies.[4]

[Former Second Circuit Chief Judge Wilfred Feinberg is reported to have *said* that the Chief Judge ought to do his or her best

---

[3] I omit certain duties external to the operation of a court of appeals, such as liaising with outside groups such as bar associations and the media.

[4] "On Being Chief Judge," *The Third Branch*, Feb. 2009, p. 4. Notice that even as pruned the two lists overlap, in the sense that some of the items on both lists, though not worded identically, amount to much the same thing.

to increase collegiality between the judges and in doing so, decrease the number of separate opinions. The Judicial Conference's *guide* also recommends this.]

Finally, Chief Judges do *not* have the authority to *specially assign cases.*[5]

The only listed powers that appear to authorize what the chief judge has decided to do with the staff attorney program are "develops and implements "court plans" and "ensures that laws, regulations, and *court policies* are followed" (emphasis added). I am unclear whether developing a court plan implies imposition of it without consultation of the other judges; and ensuring that policies are followed seems remote from inventing policies. And so I am dubious whether a chief judge is authorized simply to impose a policy of his or her invention on her court, but I will not try to resolve the issue.

What about the Judicial Council? The most compendious statement of the proper means of governance of a federal court of appeals is to be found, conveniently enough, in the *Handbook for Appeals to the United States Court of Appeals for the Seventh Circuit* 10 (2017 Edition), where the reader is told that "The circuit Judicial Council consists of the active circuit judges on the court and ten district judges and is empowered to "make all necessary and appropriate orders for the effective and expeditious administration of justice within its circuit." 28 U.S.C. § 332(d)(1). The Judicial Council has overall responsibility for the operation of the court of appeals, the district courts and the bankruptcy courts within the Seventh Circuit, and appoints the circuit executive who works for the council and also is the administrator of the court of appeals. § 332(e).

This doesn't seem exactly right, since the first statutory section states that the circuit Judicial Council "consist[s] of the chief judge of the circuit, who shall preside, and an equal number of circuit judges and district judges of the circuit." § 332(a)(1). But what's important is that neither the Handbook nor the statute supports the proposition that the chief judge has unilateral authority over

---

[5] Elizabeth B. Bazan, "Congressional Oversight of Judges and Justices," Congressional Research Service May 31, 2005.

court programs, authority asserted when she announced that the purpose of her email relating to the staff attorney program is to "let you [i.e., the judges of this court] know what changes I [i.e., she, the chief judge] have decided to implement in the Staff Attorney's Office [should of course be Attorneys', not Attorney's], and which [changes] I have decided not to adopt." This was to be a summer program in which she would "develop a program" under which the staff attorneys would draft brief descriptions of pending *pro se* appeals, and "we will experiment with adding one or two explanatory sentences to otherwise one-sentence orders" and "start by setting up quarterly seminars." It's unclear what exactly she has in mind except with regard to the last point, the seminars. The staff attorneys already draft memos or orders in all pro se appeals; and she provides no clue to the aim or content of the quarterly seminars.

On the basis of the Handbook and (particularly) the statute, I now think the September 26 court meeting that the chief judge has scheduled is properly a subject not for the court alone but for the Judicial Council, with its ten district judges as well as the judges of the appellate court. For district judges have as large a stake in the staff attorney program as the appellate judges and so should be represented in a discussion of major changes in the program. Most of the appeals, pro se and otherwise, to the court of appeals come from the district courts of the circuit; those courts have therefore a strong interest in that court's disposition of the appeals. Change in our staff attorney program could therefore have significant, and quite possibly adverse, effects on the district courts, and that strikes me as a compelling argument for reconstituting the September 26 conference as a conference of the circuit's Judicial Council.

* * *

Moving on: I want to discuss briefly a curiously intersecting event of some weeks (maybe a month or even slightly more) ago. A friend of mine, who happens to be a senior partner in substantial financial companies in New York and Chicago, invited me to give a talk to a meeting of financiers in a Chicago suburb. I agreed but then had to back out, whereupon he asked me whether I'd let him distribute relevant portions of my book (an earlier version of the present draft) to the persons attending the meeting, and I said yes. After the meeting, he reported to me the participants' discussion of the section of my draft in which I expressed disagreement with the chief judge. Here's what he reported:

"Most of the audience had read the assigned chapters on the staff attorney's [should be staff attorneys'] writing program and the cameras in the courtroom. I asked the audience what they thought of the relevant chapters. The audience did not like the discussion about the emails between you and Chief Diane [Wood]. Most of the participants that spoke up had never met you and all were in the investment business rather than lawyers. One person said it [my talk] sounded like the 'rant of an angry old man.' I replied that you were upset because you were only doing the right thing to improve the quality of the court. I asked for a quick vote to see how many agreed with you or agreed with Chief Diane and the group voted overwhelmingly for Chief Diane! I asked why. The view was that you were acting too aggressively in a group setting and [should be but, not and] that your fallback solution of offering voluntary writing assistance to the staff attorneys was the right way to go. They also said that if they had been in Chief Diane's position that they would have done the same thing."

Here's what *I* make of the audience reaction (setting to one side the penultimate sentence, which jibed with the audience's approval of my fallback solution). The audience, remember, consisted of finance experts. They work in firms presided over by one or a team of trained, expert managers. They instinctively equated my chief judge to their bosses, and thought it impertinent for me, as a subordinate judge (and, they guessed correctly, an old one), to be contradicting my chief. Little did they know, I am guessing, that she was not appointed chief judge on the basis of proved managerial competence, for remember that chief judges of federal courts of appeals are chosen strictly on the basis of seniority: when a vacancy occurs, it is filled by the judge in active service who has the most seniority and has not yet reached the age of 70, and that judge, when the chief judgeship of Judge Frank Easterbrook expired, was Judge Wood, who thereupon became the chief. Before becoming a judge of our court she'd been for two years a deputy assistant attorney general in the antitrust division of the Justice Department, which doubtless involved managerial duties and therefore gave her management experience, which she has exercised forcefully though not always in directions that I would have liked to see.

* * *

Moving on once more: One of the curiosities about the chief judge's emails of June that I discussed a little while ago is its references to me. She says, for example, that "I have [i.e., she has] also taken into account the discussion (both in memo or email form and in less formal conversations) that we [she and I] have had. It has clarified for me both Dick's proposals and how they do, or do not, fit in with the way the court operates." And regarding the following new practices that "we [meaning the chief judge] have decided that we [meaning she] should proceed with," she says that "all of [them] are either recommended in Dick's memorandum or are consistent with its spirit (as I understand it)."

Actually the only discussion we ever had regarding the staff attorney program concerned my proposal to screen all the staff attorneys' memos—the proposal that the chief judge turned down shortly after our lunch meeting of June 5 at which she expressed no opposition to the proposal. None of her "new practices" has been endorsed by me—indeed, she has not consulted me about any of them and their description in her email is vague. It strikes me as ironic that she should commend experimentation, having rejected the modest experiment that I wanted to conduct consisting simply of reviewing and where necessary editing staff attorney memos and draft orders en route to submission to panels of our judges in order to assist each panel in deciding how to dispose of a pro se's appeal or other filing and how to furnish the pro se with an intelligible explanation of the panel's ruling. It was an experiment that I had spent months devising with the assistance of Michael Fridkin, the director of the staff attorney program. The chief judge formulated and announced her experiment within days, without suggesting that there had been any input from him, let alone from me.

Although as should be apparent by now I have reservations about some of the chief judge's administrative decisions, she is certainly a competent judge, though I disagree with some of her opinions that I've discussed in this book, such as *Coleman*, and with her siding with Judge Rovner's questionable (as it seems to me) intervention in the *Marberry* case, and with some rather perfunctory orders that she's issued in cases involving pro se litigants. Still, she had an honorable legal career before she became a judge, as a Justice Department lawyer and as a law professor at the University of Chicago and elsewhere, and she continues to make helpful comments on my opinion drafts and those of the other judges. At oral arguments in our court she is (along with Judge Hamilton) the best prepared judge and the most vigorous, tenacious interrogator of the lawyers arguing the cases.

I, being somewhat obstreperous by nature as I acknowledged in Chapter 7, am tempted to repeat Oliver Cromwell's classic denunciation of the Long Parliament when he thought it no longer fit to conduct the nation's affairs: "*You have sat too long here for any good you have been doing. Depart, I say, and let us have done with you. In the name of God, go.*"

Just kidding; it's I who have gone.

* * *

Recently I offered to sit in on an interview that the chief judge had scheduled with two applicants for supervisory staff attorney positions, my offer being based on my considerable knowledge of and experience with staff attorneys. I made clear, however, that I would be entirely content not to open my mouth during the interview, as my principal interest was simply in what the interviewees would reveal, relevant for their fitness for the job, in answer to questions from the chief judge about their interest in and understanding of it. She turned down my offer without giving a reason— as was her right.

Chapter 2

I Encounter the Codes of Conduct

Recall from Chapter 3 my account of how the chief judge had declared that judges, more particularly me, may not make *any public* criticisms of staff attorney documents, as I have done—indeed may not publish any such documents, or, I suppose, parts of them, as I have done in this book in the case of the *Davis, Lewis,* and *Lehn* staff attorney memos along with shorter ones such as *Morris, Nellum, Bonty, Riley, Pope,* and *Dingus.* Her declaration is inconsistent with the treatment of opinion drafts written by law clerks, as those drafts are often the heart, and sometimes the entirety, of opinions issued under the names of the law clerks' judges, because a high percentage of appellate opinions are written in whole or part by judges' law clerks, rather than by judges. Yet it would be absurd to suggest that a judge be forbidden to publish a book or article in which he mentioned or quoted from an opinion of his that had been drafted by a law clerk and merely edited by the judge.

Yet on July 13, 2017, the chief judge sent me a copy of a letter she'd recently written to Chief Judge Rebecca Smith of the Eastern District of Virginia, who chairs the Judicial Conference Committee on Codes of Conduct. The letter repeated the chief judge's earlier criticisms of my intention to publish in a forthcoming book (this book in fact) portions (in a few instances the entirety) of orders or memos written by our staff attorneys. I responded to the criticisms in an email to Chief Judge Smith in which I said (with a few changes that I added subsequently for greater clarity and accuracy):

Dear Chief Judge Smith,

Chief Judge Wood of my court today sent me a copy of her letter of July 10 to you. I would like to offer you my view of the issue she's raised.

To begin with two points that she makes on the second-to-last page of her letter: The first is her statement that "Informal conversations with the other judges on the Seventh Circuit have left no doubt in my mind that Judge Posner's views are not shared by anyone else." I am offended by that statement. She has never told me what she said to them and what they said to her. I should have been part of the conversations. I was not invited to participate in them and did not know about them until she told me after the fact. I do not know their contents. I do know that the exclusion of a judge from a conference of, or conversation among, the judges of our court about issues of concern to all the judges hadn't occurred previously in the 35 years since my appointment to the court.

Second, her letter refers to my receiving royalties on my book. She never asked me whether I am going to receive any royalties. I am not; I will accept no royalties or other compensation; my writing this book has no commercial motivation. I'll say more: when an issue arose recently as to whether the court might not have the money to buy television equipment to enable our oral arguments to be televised, I told Chief Judge Wood that I would be glad to buy the equipment with my own money (up to $200,000, which seems to be the most the equipment would cost, though it would surely cost well over $100,000). I am not in the judge business to make money.

The main issue raised by the chief judge's correspondence with you, Chief Judge Smith, is of course whether it is proper for me to include in my book quotations from staff attorneys' draft orders, memos, etc. I believe it is proper, because those orders, memos, etc. (for simplicity I'll call them all "orders") are public rather than private documents, or at least all the staff attorney documents that I quote or cite in my book are. When a pro se appeals (roughly half the appeals in which staff attorneys are involved are filed by pro se's), the appeal, together with any supporting documentation that the pro se has submitted and the specific relief that he is seeking from the appellate court, is referred to a staff attorney, who prepares an order summarizing the appeal and recommending what the panel of judges assigned to the case should do with it. Without taking time to hear oral argument, the judges issue an order resolving the appeal.

Here is the critical fact: almost always the judges rubber stamp the staff attorney's proposed order—issue it as the order of the court, thereby making it a public document accessible in Google, Westlaw, and other online sites. Sometimes the panel will make changes in the staff attorney's proposed order before issuing the panel decision, but the order will still be public in the sense that part, indeed much, of it will have been incorporated into the public document that is the panel decision, which in a pro se case will almost always be an order rather than an opinion (that is, it will not be published in the Federal Reporter, as the court's opinions are)—and invariably it will be an order based on, even if departing to some extent from, the staff attorney's proposed order.

I do not see how the public can understand staff attorney programs, and orders resolving appeals or other motions by pro se's, without ever having glimpsed any staff attorney orders that in most cases *are* the orders resolving the case, though occasionally there's a panel contribution to (or, though rarely, a panel substitution for) the staff attorney's order.

The chief judge may have been concerned that my book would cause embarrassment to our staff attorneys and make it more difficult for us to hire good ones. I think this unlikely. Remember that the staff attorneys who write the draft orders and memos are hired for two years (their official title, though rarely used, is "Staff Law Clerks"), usually right after their graduation from law school. They are inexperienced writers of judicial documents, and they know it and expect to be edited; at the same time they are excited to be writing documents that usually, with or without *some* changes by the judges or supervisory staff attorneys, *are* the decisional documents—the court's decisions in pro se cases.

Now it would be a very good thing if court staff trained the staff attorneys to write better. Recall that I had suggested to the chief judge back on June 5, 2017, that I review all staff attorney-proposed orders before their submission to the panel of judges charged with deciding the case. I am an extremely experienced writer and editor! I have been writing steadily since my parents gave me my first typewriter, when I turned 13. I was president of the *Harvard Law Review*. I have written more than 65 books and countless articles. I

have written (and I do the writing; I don't work from drafts by law
clerks) more than 3300 judicial opinions since I became a judge. It
is true that the staff attorneys have peer review (i.e., review by each
other) and review by supervisory staff attorneys, but these reviews
generally do not result in significant improvements. Review by me
would, as I would not hesitate to rewrite a badly written memo
or order. I have given examples of such rewriting in this book, in
regard to such cases as *Davis, Lewis, Lehn,* and *Nellum*; I'm about
to come back to the last of these. But the chief judge has spoken;
her rejection of my proffered assistance to the staff was supported
by the other judges; I will leave it at that. But I do think this book
will help the staff attorney program (and the court more broadly),
unless I'm forced to delete all quotations from documents prepared
by staff attorneys!

I wish finally to emphasize that never in the book do I reveal
the name of any staff attorney in a context likely to embarrass him
or her.

Very truly yours,

Richard A. Posner

I received a response from Chief Judge Smith in which she
emphasized that confidential court documents should not be pub-
licized. I replied in an email in which, after thanking her for her
prompt response to my letter, I explained that although I don't
quarrel with the proposition that I should not publish confidential
court documents (although I'll note a reservation shortly), it was
in any event not my *desire* or *intention* to publish such documents.
Rather I had and have in mind publishing staff attorney memos
and draft orders that have already *become* public documents by being incorporated in or published with opinions or orders issued to
the public by a panel of judges.

An example is *United States v. Nellum*, No. 17-1694 [discussed
earlier in this book], in which the nub of the order drafted by the
staff attorney and issued by the judicial panel was that "Nellum
argues only that his prior convictions should not be deemed crimes
of violence. He acknowledges that his contention is contrary to

current precedent," and therefore "IT IS ORDERED that the judgment of the district court is summarily AFFIRMED." Notice that the court's decision was drawn from a staff attorney's memo, which would ordinarily be thought a confidential court document, but the memo became part of the publicly issued decision in the case by being quoted in the decision, and thereby lost its confidential status. This is a common status transformation of a confidential court document into a public document.

I hope, Chief Judge Smith, that this response allays your concerns.

Very truly yours,
Richard A. Posner

I think it did, but I was not left in peace because on August 8 the chief judge dispatched the following email to all the judges of my court:

Dear Judges:

I am writing to share with you an opinion that I requested, and received yesterday morning, from the Judicial Conference's Committee on Codes of Conduct. As you will see on page 2 of the Committee's letter, an email exchange that I had about a month ago with Dick Posner prompted me to seek guidance from the Committee on the question of confidentiality of internal court materials used by a multi-member panel or court, such as a court of appeals, a three-judge district court, or a bankruptcy appellate panel. My view, which I had communicated to Dick, was that internal materials such as bench memoranda, draft opinions, and emails in connection with the deliberative process exchanged between judges or between a judge and a non-judicial employee, are confidential and must not be disclosed, either before a case is resolved or afterwards. Dick wondered where such a rule came from, and so I thought it best to seek clarification.

The problem takes on an especially sharp focus because of the underlying situation from which it arises. For some time now, Dick has been working on a project dealing with our staff attorneys' office. Over the weeks and months, he has told all of us that this project has turned into a draft book. I became concerned when he told me that the draft book included the type of materials I described in the first paragraph of this letter. A few weeks ago, I learned that a draft of the book had been shared with persons outside the judiciary. These disclosures intensified my concern. Later, I received a copy of the book, and I discovered that it did indeed include bench memos, draft orders, emails (often verbatim), and similar materials. More than a few of these passages deal with cases that even now have not yet been disposed of by the court. The Committee concludes that "the anticipated public disclosure of the confidential, internal court communications ... would violate the intent, letter, and spirit of the Code." Letter at 3, 7. The remainder of its letter discusses the various provisions of the Code of Conduct that led it to this conclusion.

For the longer run, the Committee suggests that it might be useful to define more precisely what kinds of materials are not suitable for public consumption. Letter at 6. Comparable definitions exist in the Code of Conduct for Judicial Employees, Canon 3D, and in the Model Confidentiality Statement that the Administrative Office of the U.S. Courts makes available for judges who wish to have their employees formalize their understanding of these rules. See AO Form 306, available on the J-Net. Perhaps the Committee is right, although I wonder whether such a formal step is the most productive way to go forward. We can discuss this topic at our upcoming court meeting.

For the shorter run, however, I commend the Committee's letter to all of you. I'm sure that we all will benefit from its detailed reminder about the scope of our confidentiality obligations and the importance of these rules for the smooth functioning of the court. Most importantly, the Committee's letter leaves no doubt that any release in its current form of Dick's draft book on staff attorneys and televising court proceedings would constitute a serious breach of ethics—one that would do great damage to the court as an institution. But it is not too late to take steps to ameliorate the problem. It is important in this connection to recall that the Committee on Codes of Conduct is not a disciplinary body; it gives advice, in the hopes that any problems can be nipped in the bud. In some ways, it is too late in this case for that to happen, given the dissemination the draft has already received, but there may be some way to recall those copies of the book. With the proper effort, it may still be possible to ensure that any final project stays within the boundaries the Committee has described.

Since everyone on the court has been implicated by the materials in Dick's book [I—Posner— don't know what she means by "implicated"], everyone has an interest in the resolution of this problem. That is why I am sending this letter and the Committee's opinion to all of you. I hope that after reading the Committee's letter, Dick will reconsider the scope of his book and assure the court (1) that he will revise the final book so that it will not include anything that falls within the scope of the internal court documents that must remain confidential, and (2) that he will agree to abide by the Committee's guidance with respect to the treatment of confidential court materials and communications from now on. I look forward to hearing from any or all of you. Sincerely,

Diane P. Wood,
Chief Judge

She's entitled to her views of course, but I sense three questionable features in her note. The first is the statement that internal court documents "must not be disclosed, either before a case is resolved or afterwards." That is *not* what Chief Judge Smith said in her letter to me. She said that such disclosure might violate Opinion No. 55 of the Codes of Conduct. But opinion 55 is an *advisory* opinion, meaning that it is not binding on the recipient. See "Advisory Opinions," *Wikipedia*. Everything in the Codes of Conduct is advisory; nothing in it is mandatory. Furthermore, as I'll note (repeating a comment I made to Chief Judge Smith), once an internal document is disclosed to the public, as is common when a larger document containing that internal document—a judicial opinion

containing an excerpt from a staff attorney's memo, for example—
is published, there is no longer an interest in nondisclosure of that
document.

The second questionable feature in the chief judge's note is her
statement that "Later, I received a copy of the book, and I discovered that it did indeed include bench memos, draft orders, emails
(often verbatim), and similar materials." The "book" she received
could not have been a *book*; it could only have been an earlier, a
preliminary draft of this book, which in fact she acknowledges was
given to her by one of the participants in the financial conference
that I discussed earlier. No one was authorized by me to give her,
or indeed anyone except the financiers (of which she was not one)
participating in the conference, a copy of a preliminary, unpublished draft of my book. Having received it irregularly she might at
least have asked me—she did not—whether she was permitted to
read it, and if so, also permitted to list, and publish her assessment
of, the parts she had read: in short, to eavesdrop on a work in progress. No matter; if asked I would not have forbidden her to read it,
but merely have warned her that it was a preliminary draft.

The third questionable feature in the chief judge's note is that
she appears not to have read Opinion No. 55 very carefully—
though this is completely understandable because it is an unre-
warding read. Here is the text:

Committee on Codes of Conduct:
Advisory Opinion No. 55:
Extrajudicial Writings and Publications

This opinion considers the topic of extrajudicial writing and
publishing. We consider two particular aspects of this issue: (1) the
propriety of a judge writing about cases that the judge has heard;
and (2) the extent of permissible advertising of the judge's publications. While it is difficult to prescribe precise guidelines, the following factors are worthy of consideration by a judge contemplat-
ing these endeavors. If after consideration of these factors a judge
remains uncertain about the propriety of a particular action, the
Committee stands ready to answer specific inquiries.

Writing Generally. As a general matter, the Code of Conduct for United States Judges advises that a "judge may ... write ... on both law-related and nonlegal subjects." Canon 4. Indeed, the Commentary to Canon 4 notes that "[a]s a judicial officer and a person specially learned in the law, a judge is in a unique position to contribute to the law, the legal system, and the administration of justice ... ." The Code's authorization for extrajudicial writing, however, is subject to various limitations. Canon 4 imposes the general caveat that "a judge should not participate in extrajudicial activities that detract from the dignity of the judge's office, interfere with the performance of the judge's official duties, reflect adversely on the judge's impartiality [or] lead to frequent disqualification... . Canon 4G restricts the use of court resources to undertake extrajudicial writing, instructing that a "judge should not to any substantial degree use judicial chambers, resources, or staff to engage in extrajudicial activities permitted by this Canon."

Regarding compensation for extrajudicial writing, Canon 4H states: "A judge may accept compensation and reimbursement of expenses for the law-related and extrajudicial activities permitted by this Code if the source of the payments does not give the appearance of influencing the judge in the judge's judicial duties or otherwise give the appearance of impropriety . . . ." The Code, however, restricts this allowance in the following ways: (1) compensation must be reasonable and not exceed what a non-judge would receive for the same activity; (2) expense reimbursement should be limited to the actual costs reasonably incurred by the judge, and, where appropriate to the occasion, by the judge's spouse or relative; excess payments should be treated as gifts or compensation and not expense reimbursement; and (3) the judge should file the required financial disclosures. Canon 4H(1)-(3).

Writing About Cases the Judge Has Heard. A judge must exercise special caution when writing about a case the judge has heard. To start, a "judge should not make public comment on the merits of a matter pending or impending in any court." Canon 3A(6). However, "the prohibition on public comment on the merits does not extend to public statements made in the course of the judge's official duties, to explanations of court procedures, or to scholarly presentations made for purposes of legal education." *Id.* The Commentary to Canon 3 elaborates on the public comment restriction:

The admonition against public comment about the merits of a pending or impending matter continues until the appellate process is complete. If the public comment involves a case from the judge's own court, the judge should take particular care so that the comment does not denigrate public confidence in the judiciary's integrity and impartiality, which would violate Canon 2A. A judge may comment publicly on proceedings in which the judge is a litigant in a personal capacity, but not on mandamus proceedings when the judge is a litigant in an official capacity (but the judge may respond in accordance with Fed. R. App. P. 21(b)).

Commentary to Canon 3A(6). The Committee offers these additional suggestions, which are not intended to be comprehensive. When writing about a case the judge has heard, even after final disposition, the judge should be especially careful to avoid the potential for exploitation of the judicial position. If referring to a criminal case, the judge should consider whether the comments might afford a basis for collateral attack on the judgment. A judge must avoid writings that are likely to lead to disqualification. In every case, the judge should avoid sensationalism and comments that may result in confusion or misunderstanding of the judicial function or detract from the dignity of the office. Finally, the judge should consider the language, intent, and spirit of the entire Code when deciding to write about a case handled by the judge.

Advertising. The judge should, as far as possible, make certain that advertising for the judge's publications does not violate the language, spirit, or intent of the Code. A judge should be particularly careful to comply with Canon 2B, which, in part, counsels against lending the prestige of the judicial office to advance the private interests of the judge or others. To that end, in contracting for publication it would be advisable for a judge to retain a measure of control over the advertising (including the right to veto inappropriate advertising), so that the advertising does not exploit the judicial position or use the prestige of the judge's office to advance the private interests of the judge or others.

June 2009

Now obviously Opinion 55 is as loose as it is long, leaving little room for the Codes of Conduct committee to accuse a judge of violating it as long as he or she avoids financial activity that yields excessive compensation for his or her judicial work or "inappropriate advertising" of his publications, whatever that means. Even "public comment about the merits of a pending or impending ... case from the judge's own court" is okay as long as "the comment does not denigrate public confidence in the judiciary's integrity and impartiality." "A judge must avoid writings that are likely to lead to disqualification. In every case, the judge should avoid sensationalism and comments that may result in confusion or misunderstanding of the judicial function or detract from the dignity of the office." I agree 100 percent! And "a judge should not participate in extrajudicial activities that detract from the dignity of the judge's office, interfere with the performance of the judge's official duties, reflect adversely on the judge's impartiality [or] lead to frequent disqualification ... and should not to any substantial degree use judicial chambers, resources, or staff to engage in [permitted] extrajudicial activities." Again my agreement is total. I am in compliance with Opinion 55 every inch of the way, even though it's merely an advisory opinion, hence not binding on any judge. I'm not advertising my book, I'm not receiving even a penny per book in compensation, I'm not promoting confusion or misunderstanding. On the contrary, my goals are accuracy and clarity.

The same day that I received the chief judge's missive, I responded to it in an email to all the judges of my court, as follows:

"It would have been better had the chief judge spoken to me about this before messaging the entire court and without, I believe, a full understanding of the situation.

"I would have explained to her that while it is true that I have shown some people copies of a preliminary draft of my book, it is also true that the book when published will contain no *internal* court materials. The primary reason that my preliminary draft contains such materials is that in some instances the court has not yet rendered a decision, although memos or draft orders have been prepared by staff attorneys for submission to the panel of judges who will resolve the case and it is certain that a decision will be rendered before the book is published, and if the decision includes staff attorney materials, those materials will be part of the decision, hence in the public domain. I am reasonably confident, though I cannot be certain because I don't know when my book will be published, that by the time it is published the only "internal" materials will be materials that having been published as part of the court's decision will themselves be public and thus no longer internal. An example would be a staff attorney's memo incorporated—as it often is, as in the *Nellum* case that I cited earlier—into an order or opinion deciding an appeal. So there is no need for me to revise the book.

"And for the further reason that the chief judge gives no example, and I can think of none, where public disclosure of the 'internal' materials in question could harm the court. This is an important point. Judges, courts, are too secretive; I wish someone would give an example of disclosures of internal court materials that harmed our court. The chief judge has given none. Furthermore I have pointed out that Codes of Conduct Opinion No. 55 is, like the other opinions in the Code (the Code indeed is a set of advisory opinions—none is mandatory), adversary, not mandatory, and flexible, not rigid.

"I anticipate the response that I should either not have shown anyone the preliminary draft of my book or have censored anything in the draft that might be considered confidential by a suspicious soul like the chief judge. But it is rare for a writer not to show a preliminary draft of his work to persons who he thinks may have useful suggestions, and I have never heard of such conduct being denounced before today. Furthermore, with only one exception I authorized no recipient of a preliminary draft of my book to lend or give it or a copy to anyone else. The exception was the friend of mine who is a financier and had organized the conference of financiers (no lawyers) that I have mentioned and wanted to give each of them a copy of the preliminary draft of my book (my punishment for having backed out of the conference) and I said okay and therefore gave him a copy that he could make copies of for the participants in the conference. I don't understand—and have not been told—why a recipient gave a copy of the copy to our chief judge. I don't mind that she was given it but I would have liked to have been told in advance.

Dick"

Was that the end? No; for the very next day I received the following note from Chief Judge Smith:

Dear Judge Posner,

The Code [should be Codes] of Conduct]Committee's opinion is clear that, under the Code of Conduct for United States Judges, non-public court documents (internal memoranda, court communications, etc.), ethically should not be made public. If any of these private, internal communications are incorporated into a public order/document, then that public order/document is the public issuance of record, and nothing more. The committee cannot make its decision in this regard any more clear. Neither the Committee's role nor its resources allow for specific review and continuing comment on your upcoming publication and excerpts therefrom.

[In other words Posner, bug off!] But there is one more sentence to her missive: "We [imperial we] suggest that you discuss this matter further with your Chief Judge, and then decide how to proceed with your publication, under our advice to you and to her." But there's no possibility of my having a fruitful conversation on the topic with the chief judge, and anyway the entire issue is now history; for the severe criticism of me by the chief judge, along with my severe response to her severe criticism, was dissolved by our agreeing to abandon both sides of the debate, which seemed to me a good time for me to retire and, like Voltaire's Candide, tend to my own garden—and wish Chief Judge Wood, whom I consider a fine judge despite our disagreements, the very best in her present and future endeavors.

But here is a curious wrinkle, which should scotch all future criticisms of my disclosing, on or after September 2, 2017, information that a critic might think—even if he or she was right in thinking—ran contrary to Opinion 55, the opinion that relates to extrajudicial writing by judges. The wrinkle is this: the opinion concerns only extrajudicial writing by *judges*; I am not a judge; I retired on September 2. I can write anything I please without running afoul of Opinion 55 or any other provision of the Codes of Conduct. But, to repeat, I have neither need nor desire to violate the Codes.

* * *

Moving on: One thing that is clear in my mind as I wind up my judicial career is that some of my colleagues—all of them, for all I know—consider me a maverick. And I can't blame them; on the other hand I have no objection to maverick status. I'd rather be thought a maverick than a timid mouse. ("Timid mouse" is not an oxymoron. Many mice are fiercely destructive; recently mice ate the wires of our dishwasher, rendering the machine unusable. None of the mice were apprehended.) Judges tend to be cautious, patient, resistant to change, respectful of tradition; but these are only tendencies, they are resisted by many judges, and if one scans the roster of the great judges one finds a number of mavericks, many highly regarded as legal pathbreakers, such as Holmes, Brandeis, Cardozo, Jackson, Learned Hand, Henry Friendly, and Roger Traynor; and that is to ignore the living, who include such distinguished mavericks as Judge Alex Kozinski of the Ninth Circuit, for whom I have a very high regard, and three of my favorite federal district judges—John Kane of Denver, and Jed Rakoff and Jack B. Weinstein, both of New York.

We mavericks can be traced back to the legal realists of the 1920s and 1930s, and before that to realist judges such as Holmes. I take legal realism to mean treating a case as a dispute, asking what the best resolution of the dispute in a practical sense would be, and only then asking whether that resolution may be blocked by statutes or rules or precedents that the judge or judges in the case simply can't get around. There are mavericks in the judiciary (as noted in the preceding paragraph) even today, and I am happy to be one.

But even a maverick needs a boost from time to time and I have recently if perhaps eccentrically felt a desire for some support from the arts and have found it in Paul Gauguin. He was of course a great artist, but he was also an author of notable *bon mots*, and let me quote four that are related, albeit distantly, to my situation:

1. "All the joys—animal and human—of a free life are mine. I have escaped everything that is artificial, conventional. I am entering into truth, into nature."
2. "It is so small a thing, the life of a man, and yet there is time to do great things, fragments of a common task."
3. "Follow the masters! But why should one follow them? The only reason they are masters is that they didn't follow anybody!"
4. "If I did what has already been done, I would be a plagiarist and would consider myself unworthy."

* * *

Moving on and changing the subject for the last time: I want to remind the reader of the tiny, innocent germ out of which this book emerged: my agreement, rejected I am sad to say by the chief judge, with staff attorney program director Fridkin that I would review, edit, revise, and evaluate all memos and draft orders prepared by staff attorneys, and that having done so and made sure that the documents would be intelligible to the pro se appellants I would forward each hopefully improved memo or draft order to whatever panel of judges had been assigned to the case. I foresaw no controversy over my volunteering to assist the staff attorney program in this modest way, essentially as Fridkin's assistant (though he isn't even a judge!), without derogating from my normal judicial responsibilities. Unfortunately my plan was rejected by the chief judge. But, as the saying goes, one wins some and loses some. I take solace from the following passage in Shakespeare's *King John*: "This England never did, nor never shall, / Lie at the proud foot of a conqueror." For England read Dick Posner, and for conqueror read Diane Wood.

Chapter Three

A Moment of Peace

I'm coming to the end of this long book, and I don't want to leave an exaggerated impression of my conflicts—now history—with the chief judge. Remember the *Hively* and *Johnson* cases that I discussed very briefly in Chapter 5? They were important cases, especially *Hively* and I'll confine my discussion to it. It was heard en banc—that is, all the judges of our court participated in the oral argument and subsequent vote. Chief Judge Wood was in the majority and assigned the writing of the majority opinion to herself, and she wrote a long opinion. See *Hively v. Ivy Tech Community College*, 853 F.3d 339 (7th Cir. 2017). I had reservations about her opinion and wrote a concurring opinion, but at her request I also joined her opinion despite my misgivings, for it was a very thorough, impressive opinion, and I agreed with the result though not all the analysis and thought it would be picky of me to refuse to join it. Still the difference between our opinions was significant. She relied primarily on Supreme Court and court of appeals decisions; I took a different tack.

Hively, the plaintiff, claimed that because she's a lesbian her employer, the college, had declined to either promote her to full-time employment or renew her part-time employment contract. She sued the college under a provision of Title VII of the Civil Rights Act of 1964 that forbids an employer "to fail or refuse to hire[,] or to discharge[,] any individual, or otherwise to discriminate against any individual ... because of such individual's ... sex ... ." 42 U.S.C. § 2000e-2(a)(1). Now the term "sex" in the statute in 1964 undoubtedly meant "man or woman," i.e., was a synonym for gender, and so a woman who was fired for being a lesbian would not have been thought to have been fired for being a woman. Title VII does not mention discrimination on the basis of sexual orientation as distinct from gender, and so an explanation is needed for how 53 years later the meaning of the statute has changed and the word "sex" in it now connotes sexual orientation as well as gender.

A diehard "originalist" would argue that what was believed in 1964 defines the scope of the statute for as long as the statutory text remains unchanged, and it hasn't been changed. But statutory and constitutional provisions frequently are interpreted on the basis of present need and understanding rather than original meaning. Think for example of Justice Scalia's decisive fifth vote to hold that burning the American flag as a political protest is protected by the free-speech clause of the First Amendment, provided that it's your flag and is not burned in circumstances in which the fire might spread. *Texas v. Johnson*, 491 U.S. 397 (1989); *United States v. Eichman*, 496 U.S. 310 (1990). Burning a flag is not speech in the usual sense and there is no indication that the framers or ratifiers of the First Amendment thought that the word "speech" in the amendment embraced flag burning or other nonverbal methods of communicating.

In other words, the Court amended the statute. And it seemed to me that we likewise could amend Title VII. I thought of what Justice Holmes had written in *Missouri v. Holland*, 252 U.S. 416, 433–34 (1920):

> When we are dealing with words that also are a constituent act, like the Constitution of the United States, we must realize that they have called into life a being the development of which could not have been foreseen completely by the most gifted of its begetters. ... The case before us must be considered in the light of our whole experience and not merely in that of what was said a hundred years ago. The treaty in question does not contravene any prohibitory words to be found in the Constitution. The only question is whether it is forbidden by some invisible radiation from the general terms of the Tenth Amendment. *We must consider what this country has become in deciding what that amendment has reserved* [emphasis added].

My approach was different from, and I think superior to, the approach taken in the majority opinion. That opinion says for example that Congress in 1964 "may not have realized or understood the full scope of the words it chose." That seems very doubtful to me. I am similarly dubious about the majority opinion's reliance on *Oncale v. Sundowner Offshore Services, Inc.*, 523 U.S. 75 (1998), a case of sexual harassment of one man by other men, held by the Supreme Court to violate Title VII's prohibition of sex discrimination, where the Court said that "statutory prohibitions often go beyond the principal evil to cover reasonably comparable evils, and it is ultimately *the provisions of our laws* rather than the principal concerns of our legislators by which we are governed" (*id.* at 79; emphasis added). That could well be thought "originalism," if by "provisions" is meant statutory language. I would prefer to see us acknowledge openly that today we, who are judges rather than members of Congress, are imposing on a half-century-old statute a meaning of "sex discrimination" that the Congress that enacted it would not have accepted. This is something courts do fairly frequently to avoid statutory obsolescence and concomitantly to avoid placing the entire burden of updating old statutes on the legislative branch. We should not leave the impression that we are merely the obedient servants of the 88th Congress (1963–1965), carrying out their wishes. We are not.

Allen Kamp reminds me that Judge Learned Hand in 1913 interpreted the word obscene in the Comstock Act in terms of the "present critical point in the compromise between candor and shame at which the community may have arrived here and now." *United States v. Kennerley*, 209 Fed. 119, 121 (S.D.N.Y. 1913)). Kamp adds: "I thought you would be interested in an earlier use of the interpretive technique that you used in *Hively.* Also, it doesn't make any sense to go back to the original meaning or tradition when we really can't go back even if we wanted to—we can't re-create 1964, Victorian times, 1789, or 1792. We can strip out the laws of a past time, but we can't recreate the entire society that generated those laws even if we wanted to."

L. Steven Platt, a lawyer at the Chicago firm of Robbins, Salomon and Platt, Ltd., wrote me at about the same time, saying my concurring opinion in *Hively* was "brilliant"—an absolute "antidote to statutory textualism"—an illustration of "judicial interpretive updating," which "starts from the premise that you are going to reinterpret the statute. You start by taking away the best argument from the opposition." And shortly afterward I received a very nice email from a Ph.D. candidate at Vilnius University in Lithuania named Karolina Mickute, commending my "vision of pragmatic adjudication," which she says has "inspired her as an academic."

Right on!

Chapter Four

Coda: Whither the Pro Se's?

I worry that by placing as much emphasis as I have on my disagreements with the chief judge I may inadvertently have obscured the most important theme of this book, which is the need for better treatment by the federal courts of pro se litigants, who—to repeat for the last time—are (most of them, though not all[1]) impecunious, and thus cannot afford and so rarely have lawyers, and are further handicapped in their pursuit of legal relief by often inadequate education and low IQ (remember Davis of *Davis v. Moroney*, with his IQ of only 66), and by the indifference of many, indeed probably most, federal judges, who tend to regard pro se litigants as losers and pests, and as a result often in effect delegate the decision of pro se cases to staff attorneys.

I strongly disagree with my former colleague Judge Easterbrook that judges should never assist a pro se as by (as I've urged in this book) showing the pro se how, though his present appeal is a loser, he may have an alternative, lawful route to success. Judge Easterbrook, seconded by many other federal judges, believes that for a judge (including a judge on an appellate panel) to assist a litigant, even an unrepresented litigant in desperate need of guidance, is to discriminate impermissibly against that litigant's adversary. But that belief ignores the imbalance in litigation between a party having legal representation and a party unable, for lack of resources, to obtain legal representation.

I anticipate the objection to my evident "softness" to pro se's that at least the one-half of all pro se litigants who are prison inmates deserve no sympathy, as they are criminals. But that isn't

---

[1] See, discussing both types of pro se litigant, Drew A. Sank, "The Pro Se Phenomenon," 19 *Brigham Young University Journal of Public Law* 373 (2005).

true. Some were convicted in error; some were given unreasonably long prison sentences; some were criminals but have outlived their wanting to become criminals once again and so would no longer *be* criminals were they released.

All the problems of pro se litigants have solutions, requiring little more from the judiciary than empathy and modest effort, starting with recognition that pro se litigants are numerous, are here to stay, do sometimes (maybe more often than judges and staff attorneys think) have valid claims to legal redress, but because of their frequent intellectual and educational limitations and lack of legal representation need help from the judiciary in order to be able to vindicate their rights. We federal judges can and should render the help that pro se's need. We should be much more aggressive in recruiting counsel for pro se's in cases where without legal counsel a pro se has no chance against a defendant or defendants who have legal counsel; and we have seen examples of that in this book. We should use the Flesch test to determine the intelligibility of defense and court documents to pro se plaintiffs. We should do enough research in each pro se case to be able to determine whether the pro se has a potentially winnable case that he blew by filing under the wrong statute or doctrine or rule, and if so we should advise him of the existence of alternative approaches that may still be open to him to pursue. We should improve the staff attorney program, with particular emphasis on improving the intelligibility of the staff attorneys' memos and draft orders. We should enlarge the role of interested judges, such as myself (until my recent retirement!), in the analysis and evaluation of pro se appeals to our court. And rather than bragging about the excellence of our staff attorney program we should endeavor to learn more—much more—about how other courts, with the aid of their staff attorneys, handle pro se litigation.

Above all, the federal judiciary (I don't know enough about state judiciaries to combine them with the federal judiciary in this analysis) needs to do much more than it is doing to provide pro se's, both those in prison and those not, with access to lawyers. The courts (notably the courts of the Seventh Circuit) need to be more aggressive in recruiting lawyers for pro se's, but also in establishing contact with the numerous organizations that cater to the legal needs of pro se's, especially prisoners.[2] These include numerous legal aid clinics, many university affiliated, law firms that have pro bono practices, and organizations that focus on the legal needs of prisoners—such organizations as the—

- Pennsylvania Innocence Project (see *U.S. Law Week*, August 24, 2017, p. 221) ("Pro Bono Help Invaluable to Innocence Project")
- Prison Law Office (California state prisoners)
- Prisoners' Legal Services of Massachusetts
- UC Davis Prison Law Clinic
- Post-Conviction Justice Project (USC Clinic)
- University of Wisconsin Law School's Legal Assistance to Institutionalized Persons Project
- University of Wisconsin Law School's Federal Appeals Project
- ACLU National Prison Project
- Public Counsel's Proskauer Federal Pro Se Clinic
- The Legal Rights Center (Minnesota State courts)
- Equal Justice Initiative of Alabama
- Mid-Atlantic Innocence Project
- Northwestern Pritzker School of Law's MacArthur Justice Center

---

[2] See also Margaret Smilowitz, "What Happens After the Right to Counsel Ends? Using Technology to Assist Petitioners in State Post-Conviction Petitions and Federal Habeas Review," 107 *Journal of Criminal Law and Criminology* 493 (2017); Deane B. Brown, "The Challenge of Pro Bono Legal Service," *Bench & Bar* (Illinois State Bar Association, August 2017), p. 1.

Appendix Four

Judge Gilman's Writing Rules:
Heed Them: Staff Attorneys, Law Clerks, Judges[1]

A. General Principles

1. Consistency. Be consistent with use of words and phrases.

2. Footnotes. No footnotes. Ever.

3. Legal lingo. Avoid legal lingo. (Bad: "He was convicted on two felony firearm counts." Good: "He was convicted on two counts of being a felon in possession of a firearm.")

4. Respect. Be respectful of the parties and other judges. Do not engage in personal attacks or use disparaging language. Criticism is more effective when it is not cloaked in hyperbole.

5. Wordiness. Be concise, not verbose.

B. Sentence Structure

1. Adverbs. Place adverbs before verbs. (Bad: "He assumes erroneously that the list is exhaustive." Good: "He erroneously assumes that the list is exhaustive.")

2. Capitalization. Capitalize the titles of specific documents, but not the generic names of documents. You should capitalize "court" only when referring to the United States Supreme Court or the full name of a court.

---

[1] See page 79, *supra.*

3. **Colons.** Two spaces should follow a colon. The first letter following a colon should be lowercase unless the phrase following the colon is a complete sentence.

4. **Commas.** Generally, insert a comma before the conjunction "but" when it is used in a sentence. But a comma is not necessary in a short sentence. (Example: "The government's argument is sensible but ultimately unpersuasive.") Also insert a comma before "which" when it is used within a sentence as a relative pronoun.

5. **Double negatives.** Avoid sentences with double negatives. (Bad: "This does not mean that he is not disabled." Good: "This does not preclude a finding that he is disabled.")

6. **Em dashes.** You may use an em dash in a sentence to indicate a parenthetical thought. Place an em dash by inserting three hyphens.

7. **First and last words.** No two consecutive sentences should begin or end with the same word.

8. **Hard spaces/hyphens.** As a general rule, Judge G does not like hyphens, numbers, or symbols dangling at the end of a line. Specifically, you will need to place a hard space (by holding down the control button while you strike the space bar) between numbers in an *enumerated series* and the word immediately following the number. For example, if your sentence included a list of factors such as "(1) seriousness of the offense, (2) characteristics of the defendant," you would need to insert one hard space between "(1)" and "seriousness," and a second hard space between "(2)" and "characteristics." You also need to insert a hard space between a *record citation* and the cited page or document number. For instance, if you cite "DE 32 at 5," insert a hard space between "DE" and "32." Similarly, if you cite "JA 289," insert a hard space between "JA" and "289." Place a hard space between *symbols* (such as § or ¶) and their corresponding numbers ("§ 1983"). In addition, insert hard spaces between the periods in an ellipsis to avoid breaking the *ellipsis* over two lines. In Word, a hard space can be created us-

ing ctrl + shift + spacebar (i.e., hitting the spacebar while holding the control and shift keys down). The shortcut in Word-Perfect is ctrl + spacebar. Finally, place a hard hyphen between *number ranges* ("7-10"). In Word, the shortcut is ctrl + shift + -. The Word Perfect shortcut is ctrl + -.

9. ***Headings.*** Capitalize only the first word in a heading or subheading.

10. ***Identifying the lower court.*** When you first describe a lower court in a paragraph, identify the specific court ("bankruptcy court," "district court"). You should then use "the court" throughout the remainder of the paragraph, unless either you mention another court within the same paragraph or use of "the court" would otherwise be confusing.

11. ***Introductory clausitis.*** Do not begin more than two consecutive sentences with an introductory clause.

12. ***Length.*** Shorter sentences are better than longer sentences. Vary the length of sentences.

13. ***Lists.*** Use serial commas in a list of three or more items. (Example: "Despite his disability, Smith could walk, run, and swim.") Do not use semicolons, unless one or more of the individual list items contain commas (semicolons are okay in other contexts, of course).

14. ***Passive voice.*** Feel free to occasionally use the passive voice, especially if the meaning is clear and an awkward present-tense phrasing would otherwise result.

15. ***Possessives.*** Avoid using two or more possessives in a row (for example, do not use "Smith's mother's house").

16. ***Sentence spacing.*** Two spaces should follow the period at the end of each sentence.

17. ***Split infinitives.*** If splitting an infinitive sounds more natural, then split it.

18. ***Transitions.*** Do not begin sentences with "however" or "therefore." (Put these terms in the body of the sentence instead.)

Sentences may, however, begin with "And," "But," and "Moreover."

19. Verb Tense. Be careful to use the correct verb tense. This problem comes up most often with the present tense: you should use the present tense where a fact is still true or where the described thing is still in existence.

C. Word Use

1. Preferred and Disfavored Words

Approximately. Use "approximately" instead of "about." (Example: "The package weighed approximately four grams.") "About" means "regarding" and should be used accordingly.

Attorney fees. Use the phrase "attorney fees," not "attorney's fees," "attorneys' fees," or "attorneys fees."

Because. Do not use "as" as a substitute for "because."

Court/judge. Describe the actions of the lower court ("the district court") rather than the judge ("the district judge"), unless context requires you to refer to the judge individually.

Even though. Use "even though" instead of "despite the fact that."

Finally. Use "finally" instead of "lastly."

In addition. Use "in addition" instead of "additionally."

Pleaded. Use "pleaded" rather than "pled."

Present case. As a general rule, use "in the present case" instead of "here." But use both phrases where one would otherwise appear numerous times in a confined space.

Record. Use "in the record" rather than "on the record."

Regarding. Use "regarding" or "concerning" instead of "as to."

Stated. Stated is a fairly nondescript word. If possible, use another word, such as "reasoned," "concluded," "explained," etc.

Words to avoid. Avoid the words "merely" and "some." Use "clearly" and "thus" sparingly.

2. Word Usage

Abbreviations. Do not put quotation marks around abbreviations, i.e., (ERISA), not ("ERISA").

Caselaw. Judge Gilman prefers to use "caselaw" as one word, not two.

Compound adjectives. Hyphenate most compound adjectives ("independent-source doctrine," "ineffective-assistance-of-counsel claim," "narcotics-detection dog"). But do not hyphenate an adverb ending in -ly. ("properly pled complaint," "particularly described property"). And do not hyphenate compound adjectives that are used most commonly without hyphenation ("district court ruling," "due process clause," "good faith effort," or "summary judgment order").

Court identifiers. Use "this court" when referring to prior decisions of the Sixth Circuit; use "we" when referring to the present case. Never use "we" in a bench memorandum. The "Supreme Court" means the U.S. Supreme Court. References to the supreme court of a state should include the name of that state (e.g., "the Michigan Supreme Court").

Criminal convictions. A defendant is convicted *on* a particular count ("Smith was convicted on count four of the indictment"), but is convicted *of* a specific crime ("Smith was convicted of conspiracy to possess and distribute cocaine").

Dates. Use "October 1998" and not "October, 1998" or even "October of 1998." Also, do not as a matter of course include a comma after a full date, unless the comma would otherwise be appropriate in the sentence. (*For example:* "Unlike the evening of August 30, 2005, the evening of August 31, 2005 was hot and rainy.")

Describing certain court actions. Courts make factual *findings* and reach legal *conclusions*. *Holdings* are dispositive rulings.

Distinctions. Observe the distinctions between the following terms:

that (defining/restrictive)	*which* (nondefining/nonrestrictive)
where (place)	*when* (temporal)
because (causal)	*since* (temporal)
although (contrast)	*while* (temporal)
may (permissive)	*might* (potential)

English words. Use English words whenever possible. (Bad: "Smith alleged, inter alia, that Jones had violated her constitutional rights." Good: "Smith alleged, among other things, that Jones had violated her constitutional rights.")

It. Do not use "it" as an indefinite pronoun. (Bad: "It goes without saying that Bob is a generous man.")

Last names. When referring to parties with the same last name — for instance, Elvis Presley and Priscilla Presley— you can use "the Presleys" to refer to the group, and "Elvis" and "Priscilla" to refer to the individuals.

Latin words and phrases. Common Latin words are not italicized, such as habeas corpus, de novo, sua sponte, etc. Never use the Latin words "supra" or "infra." Use "above" or "below" instead. Uncommon Latin words and phrases, such as *in abstentia*, should be italicized.

Names ending in "s." An individual whose last name ends in "s" takes the possessive form of apostrophe plus "s." But the plural possessive is indicated by only an apostrophe. (*Example*: "John Woods's dog is named Spot." On the other hand, "The Bonds' family dog is named Sandy.")

Numbers. Spell out numbers less than 10, unless there are higher numbers in the same sentence that the lower numbers are being compared to.

Only. Be sure that "only" is modifying the correct word. (Bad: "Relief is only available if both conditions are met." Good: "Relief is available only if both conditions are met." Bad: "The package only contained cocaine." Good: "The package contained only cocaine.")

Party names. Avoid formalistic names for the parties. (Use "Jones" instead of "Plaintiff-Appellant.")

Prefixes. Avoid hyphenating prefixes, unless a visual monstrosity results. ("Postconviction" is fine. "Prepresidential" is not.)

Series. Names or concepts in a series or list should appear in alphabetical order, unless another organizing principle would make more sense given the context.

Standard of review. When explaining the standard of review that the court applies, do not say that the court "reviews for clear error" or "reviews for abuse of discretion." Judge G instead prefers that you say that this court reviews the district court's judgment "under the clear-error standard" or the "abuse-of-discretion standard." In the case of de novo review, however, you may say that this court "reviews de novo a district court's grant of summary judgment."

That. Use the relative pronoun to avoid miscues. (Bad: "The government charged the lease deal sprang from a web of deceit." Good: "The government charged that the lease deal sprang from a web of deceit.") Do not, however, use more than two "that"s in a row in a sentence. Rephrase or eliminate one of the relative pronouns to avoid this result.

D. Citation Style

1. ***Alterations to quoted text.*** When removing alterations from a quotation, such as brackets or an ellipsis, indicate the specific alterations omitted in a parenthetical. Also indicate if you remove any citations or quotation marks within the same parenthetical, and list all of these items in alphabetical order.

   A special note regarding omitted quotation marks. When omitting quotation marks, include the word "internal." In other words, your parenthetical would be "(internal quotation marks omitted)." Also, be careful not to use "quotations" instead of "quotation marks."

   Some examples.

   (brackets and ellipsis omitted)

   (citation and internal quotation marks omitted)

   (brackets, citations, ellipses, footnotes, and internal quotation marks omitted)

2. ***Citing and quoting parentheticals.*** You should use a "citing" parenthetical only if the additional source is particularly relevant (for example, the source is a Supreme Court case, a bedrock Sixth Circuit case, or a case from a specialized court). Use a quoting parenthetical, however, if you are quoting language that is itself quoting another source.

   Note that, per Bluebook Rule 5.3(c), "citation omitted" is appropriate where the citation is being left out of the quoted portion of text. A different situation arises, however, where the quoted language quotes another source, but the citation to this underlying source is *not* itself part of the language that you are quoting. In this situation, Bluebook Rule 5.2(e) recommends using a quoting parenthetical rather than omitting quotation marks and using "internal quotation marks omitted" and "citation omitted" parentheticals. In the 20th edition, Bluebook Rule 1.5(b) no longer recognizes the use of the "internal quotation marks omitted" parenthetical. Bluebook Rule 5.2(f) allows for the omission of internal quotation marks only when the opening mark appears at the beginning of the language that you are quoting and the closing mark appears at the end of the language.

For example, suppose you want to quote the following language from *International Dairy Foods Association v. Boggs*, 622 F.3d 628, 635 (6th Cir. 2010): "By contrast, the decision of whether to grant a motion for a preliminary injunction is 'left to the sound discretion of the district court.' *Deja Vu of Cincinnati, L.L.C. v. Union Twp. Bd. of Trs.*, 411 F.3d 777, 782 (6th Cir. 2005)." According to 5.2(e), you would cite it as follows: "By contrast, the decision of whether to grant a motion for a preliminary injunction is 'left to the sound discretion of the district court.'" *Int'l Dairy Foods Assoc. v. Boggs*, 622 F.3d 628, 635 (6th Cir. 2010) (quoting *Deja Vu of Cincinnati, L.L.C. v. Union Twp. Bd. of Trs.*, 411 F.3d 777, 782 (6th Cir. 2005)).

3. ***Emphasis added (when citing to something in the record).*** When the emphasis-added descriptor does not directly follow a citation, such as in an opinion where you have deleted the record citation for the quotation, treat it as an abridged sentence and place it in parentheses, with the "e" capitalized. (*Example*: [big long block quote] (Emphasis added.)) Note that the period is placed inside of the parentheses.

4. ***Emphasis in original.*** In a rare break from the Blue Book, Judge G prefers that you indicate parenthetically if the emphasis in a quoted source is from the original text.

5. ***Hard spaces.*** Do not split section marks (§) and their section numbers across lines. To avoid this, insert a hard space. This rule also applies to not splitting JA citations from their page numbers, or docket entries from their entry number, or a list of numbers from their accompanying items. In Word, a hard space can be created using ctrl + shift + spacebar (i.e., hitting the spacebar while holding the control and shift keys down). The shortcut in Word Perfect is ctrl + spacebar.

6. ***Other opinions, references to.*** Cite as either "Maj. Op." (when dissenting or when concurring in part and dissenting in part), "Lead Op." (when concurring), or "Dissenting Op." (when writing the majority). *Example*: The majority also states that the Jehovah's Witnesses "may spread their message at stores, on street corners, in restaurants, in parks, and other public forums." (Maj. Op. at 21)

7. ***Parenthetical explanations.*** Include these as often as possible after a case citation unless they would be unnecessarily duplicative of the cited proposition or sentence. Remember not to omit articles such as "the," "a," and "an" from the parenthetical. Begin these parentheticals with a gerund, unless you are quoting a complete sentence.

8. ***Parts, references to.*** When referring to a portion of a memorandum or opinion, place periods after both the Roman numeral and the subpart letter or number. (*Example*: "As discussed above in Parts II.B. and III.A.2., this argument is without merit.") Use the word "Part" instead of the word "Section," and always capitalize "Part."

9. ***Pincites.*** Judge Gilman prefers that you not use pincites when summarizing the facts of an opinion unless you quote directly from the opinion. (*Example*: "The plaintiff in *Smith v. Jones* was a quadriplegic and blind in one eye." This does not require a citation to *Smith*. *But*: "She became a quadriplegic after a reckless driver 'sped through a stop light and collided with her vehicle'" would require a pincite to *Smith*.)

10. ***Record citations.*** Cite the record in parentheses. (*Example*: "When Burt provided a price acceptable to Holland, they shook hands and announced their agreement to the rest of the members at the meeting. (JA 934-35)") No periods should appear either inside or outside of the record citation. Remove citations to the record before submitting an opinion for filing.

11. ***Signals.*** When using the signal "*See, e.g.,*" italicize everything except for the last comma.

12. Small caps. Do not use small caps. Use regular Roman type instead.

13. String cites. Use sparingly and, if used, include explanatory parentheticals.

14. Textual citations. When you refer to a case for the first time in a textual sentence, include the full case citation within that sentence.

15. Two-page rule. A source should be cited in full, even if previously cited in full, where that source has not been referred to in the prior two pages of text. The only exception is when the case cited is well known and repeatedly cited, such as *Miranda* or *Terry*.

16. Unpublished opinions.

For opinions available via online databases only, follow this example: *Lyons v. TVA*, No. 87-5309, 1988 WL 12227, at *1 (6th Cir. Feb. 16, 1988).

For unpublished opinions available both in the Federal Appendix and online, cite to the Federal Appendix: *Lyons v. TVA*, 8 F. App'x 31 (6th Cir. 1998).

For opinions that have been designated for publication but have yet to be assigned to a federal reporter, follow this example: *Roberts v. Ward*, No. 05-6305, — F.3d —, 2006 WL 3392620, at * 2 (6th Cir. Nov. 27, 2006).

17. U.S. Sentencing Guidelines.

When used in text. The first time that you mention the federal sentencing guidelines, refer to them as the United States Sentencing Guidelines. After the first mention, you may thereafter refer to them as "the guidelines." You do not need to provide this shortened form in a parenthetical after the first reference.

When used in a citation. Follow Bluebook Rule 12.9.4 when citing to the guidelines, with the following considerations in mind. The text of a guideline is usually followed by commentary (abbreviated as "cmt.") The commentary includes all explanatory information that follows a guideline, and it often contains subsections for "Application Notes" and "Background" information. When citing to information that appears under the subheading of "Background," cite as U.S.S.G. § 2D1.2 cmt. background. Cite any numbered note in the commentary section—whether it appears under "Application Note" (*see, e.g.,* U.S.S.G. § 3D1.4) or not (*see, e.g.,* U.S.S.G. § 3D1.5)—as U.S.S.G. § [section number] cmt. n.1. And cite to a guidelines appendix as

U.S.S.G. app. C.

Exception: The Bluebook citation format refers to the guidelines as "U.S. Sentencing Guidelines Manual"—e.g.,.S. Sentencing Guidelines Manual § 3D1.1. When citing the guidelines in bench memos and opinions, you should instead use either "United States Sentencing Guidelines" (in the first reference to the guidelines, either in text or a citation) or "U.S.S.G." (if "United States Sentencing Guidelines" has already been referenced in either the text or an earlier citation).

Exception: Specify the guidelines version (i.e. 2010, 2015, etc.) only when relevant to the discussion.

E. General Principles

1. ***Consistency.*** Be consistent with use of words and phrases.

2. ***Footnotes.*** No footnotes. Ever.

3. ***Legal lingo.*** Avoid legal lingo. (Bad: "He was convicted on two felony firearm counts." Good: "He was convicted on two counts of being a felon in possession of a firearm.")

4. ***Respect.*** Be respectful of the parties and other judges. Do not engage in personal attacks or use disparaging language. Criticism is more effective when it is not cloaked in hyperbole.

5. ***Wordiness.*** Be concise, not verbose.

F. Sentence Structure

1. ***Adverbs.*** Place adverbs before verbs. (Bad: "He assumes erroneously that the list is exhaustive." Good: "He erroneously assumes that the list is exhaustive.")

2. ***Capitalization.*** Capitalize the titles of specific documents, but not the generic names of documents. You should capitalize "court" only when referring to the United States Supreme Court or the full name of a court.

3. ***Colons.*** Two spaces should follow a colon. The first letter following a colon should be lowercase unless the phrase following the colon is a complete sentence.

4. ***Commas.*** Generally, insert a comma before the conjunction "but" when it is used in a sentence. But a comma is not necessary in a short sentence. (Example: "The government's argument is sensible but ultimately unpersuasive.") Also insert a comma before "which" when it is used within a sentence as a relative pronoun.

5. ***Double negatives.*** Avoid sentences with double negatives. (Bad: "This does not mean that he is not disabled." Good: "This does not preclude a finding that he is disabled.")

6. ***Em dashes.*** You may use an em dash in a sentence to indicate a parenthetical thought. Place an em dash by inserting three hyphens.

7. ***First and last words.*** No two consecutive sentences should begin or end with the same word.

8. ***Hard spaces/hyphens.*** As a general rule, Judge G does not like hyphens, numbers, or symbols dangling at the end of a line. Specifically, you will need to place a hard space (by holding down the control button while you strike the space bar) between numbers in an *enumerated series* and the word immediately following the number. For example, if your sentence included a list of factors such as "(1) seriousness of the offense,

(2) characteristics of the defendant," you would need to insert one hard space between "(1)" and "seriousness," and a second hard space between "(2)" and "characteristics." You also need to insert a hard space between a *record citation* and the cited page or document number. For instance, if you cite "DE 32 at 5," insert a hard space between "DE" and "32." Similarly, if you cite "JA 289," insert a hard space between "JA" and "289." Place a hard space between *symbols* (such as § or ¶) and their corresponding numbers ("§ 1983"). In addition, insert hard spaces between the periods in an ellipsis to avoid breaking the *ellipsis* over two lines. In Word, a hard space can be created using ctrl + shift + spacebar (i.e., hitting the spacebar while holding the control and shift keys down). The shortcut in Word-Perfect is ctrl + spacebar. Finally, place a hard hyphen between *number ranges* ("7-10"). In Word, the shortcut is ctrl + shift + -. The Word Perfect shortcut is ctrl + -.

9. **Headings.** Capitalize only the first word in a heading or sub-heading.

10. **Identifying the lower court.** When you first describe a lower court in a paragraph, identify the specific court ("bankruptcy court," "district court"). You should then use "the court" throughout the remainder of the paragraph, unless either you mention another court within the same paragraph or use of "the court" would otherwise be confusing.

11. **Introductory clausitis.** Do not begin more than two consecutive sentences with an introductory clause.

12. **Length.** Shorter sentences are better than longer sentences. Vary the length of sentences.

13. **Lists.** Use serial commas in a list of three or more items. (*Example*: "Despite his disability, Smith could walk, run, and swim.") Do not use semicolons, unless one or more of the individual list items contain commas (semicolons are okay in other contexts, of course).

14. *Passive voice.* Feel free to occasionally use the passive voice, especially if the meaning is clear and an awkward present-tense phrasing would otherwise result.

15. *Possessives.* Avoid using two or more possessives in a row (for example, do not use "Smith's mother's house").

16. *Sentence spacing.* Two spaces should follow the period at the end of each sentence.

17. *Split infinitives.* If splitting an infinitive sounds more natural, then split it.

18. *Transitions.* Do not begin sentences with "however" or "therefore." (Put these terms in the body of the sentence instead.) Sentences may, however, begin with "And," "But," and "Moreover."

19. *Verb Tense.* Be careful to use the correct verb tense. This problem comes up most often with the present tense: you should use the present tense where a fact is still true or where the described thing is still in existence.

G. Word Use

1. Preferred and Disfavored Words

Approximately. Use "approximately" instead of "about." (Example: "The package weighed approximately four grams.") "About" means "regarding" and should be used accordingly.

Attorney fees. Use the phrase "attorney fees," not "attorney's fees," "attorneys' fees," or "attorneys fees."

Because. Do not use "as" as a substitute for "because."

Court/judge. Describe the actions of the lower court ("the district court") rather than the judge ("the district judge"), unless context requires you to refer to the judge individually.

Even though. Use "even though" instead of "despite the fact that."

Finally. Use "finally" instead of "lastly."

In addition. Use "in addition" instead of "additionally."

Pleaded. Use "pleaded" rather than "pled."

Present case. As a general rule, use "in the present case" instead of "here." But use both phrases where one would otherwise appear numerous times in a confined space.

Record. Use "in the record" rather than "on the record."

Regarding. Use "regarding" or "concerning" instead of "as to."

Stated. Stated is a fairly nondescript word. If possible, use another word, such as "reasoned," "concluded," "explained," etc.

Words to avoid. Avoid the words "merely" and "some." Use "clearly" and "thus" sparingly.

2. Word Usage

Abbreviations. Do not put quotation marks around abbreviations, i.e., (ERISA), not ("ERISA").

Caselaw. Judge Gilman prefers to use "caselaw" as one word, not two.

Compound adjectives. Hyphenate most compound adjectives ("independent-source doctrine," "ineffective-assistance-of-counsel claim," "narcotics-detection dog"). But do not hyphenate an adverb ending in -ly. ("properly pled complaint," "particularly described property"). And do not hyphenate compound adjectives that are used most commonly without hyphenation ("district court ruling," "due process clause," "good faith effort," or "summary judgment order").

Court identifiers. Use "this court" when referring to prior decisions of the Sixth Circuit; use "we" when referring to the present case. Never use "we" in a bench memorandum. The "Supreme Court" means the U.S. Supreme Court. References to the supreme court of a state should include the name of that state (e.g., "the Michigan Supreme Court").

Criminal convictions. A defendant is convicted *on* a particular count ("Smith was convicted on count four of the indictment"), but is convicted *of* a specific crime ("Smith was convicted of conspiracy to possess and distribute cocaine").

Dates. Use "October 1998" and not "October, 1998" or even "October of 1998." Also, do not as a matter of course include a comma after a full date, unless the comma would otherwise be appropriate in the sentence. (*For example:* "Unlike the evening of August 30, 2005, the evening of August 31, 2005 was hot and rainy.")

Describing certain court actions. Courts make factual *findings* and reach legal *conclusions*. *Holdings* are dispositive rulings.

Distinctions. Observe the distinctions between the following terms:

that (defining/restrictive)	*which* (nondefining/nonrestrictive)
where (place)	*when* (temporal)
because (causal)	*since* (temporal)
although (contrast)	*while* (temporal)
may (permissive)	*might* (potential)

English words. Use English words whenever possible. (Bad: "Smith alleged, inter alia, that Jones had violated her constitutional rights." Good: "Smith alleged, among other things, that Jones had violated her constitutional rights.")

It. Do not use "it" as an indefinite pronoun. (Bad: "It goes without saying that Bob is a generous man.")

Last names. When referring to parties with the same last name — for instance, Elvis Presley and Priscilla Presley— you can use "the Presleys" to refer to the group, and "Elvis" and "Priscilla" to refer to the individuals.

Latin words and phrases. Common Latin words are not italicized, such as habeas corpus, de novo, sua sponte, etc. Never use the Latin words "supra" or "infra." Use "above" or "below" instead. Uncommon Latin words and phrases, such as *in abstentia*, should be italicized.

Names ending in "s." An individual whose last name ends in "s" takes the possessive form of apostrophe plus "s." But the plural possessive is indicated by only an apostrophe. (*Example*: "John Woods's dog is named Spot." On the other hand, "The Bonds' family dog is named Sandy.")

Numbers. Spell out numbers less than 10, unless there are higher numbers in the same sentence that the lower numbers are being compared to.

Only. Be sure that "only" is modifying the correct word. (Bad: "Relief is only available if both conditions are met." Good: "Relief is available only if both conditions are met." Bad: "The package only contained cocaine." Good: "The package contained only cocaine.")

Party names. Avoid formalistic names for the parties. (Use "Jones" instead of "Plaintiff-Appellant.")

Prefixes. Avoid hyphenating prefixes, unless a visual monstrosity results. ("Postconviction" is fine. "Prepresidential" is not.)

Series. Names or concepts in a series or list should appear in alphabetical order, unless another organizing principle would make more sense given the context.

Standard of review. When explaining the standard of review that the court applies, do not say that the court "reviews for clear error" or "reviews for abuse of discretion." Judge G instead prefers that you say that this court reviews the district court's judgment "under the clear-error standard" or the "abuse-of-discretion standard." In the case of de novo review, however, you may say that this court "reviews de novo a district court's grant of summary judgment."

That. Use the relative pronoun to avoid miscues. (Bad: "The government charged the lease deal sprang from a web of deceit." Good: "The government charged that the lease deal sprang from a web of deceit.") Do not, however, use more than two "that"s in a row in a sentence. Rephrase or eliminate one of the relative pronouns to avoid this result.

H. Citation Style

1. *Alterations to quoted text.* When removing alterations from a quotation, such as brackets or an ellipsis, indicate the specific alterations omitted in a parenthetical. Also indicate if you remove any citations or quotation marks within the same parenthetical, and list all of these items in alphabetical order.

   A special note regarding omitted quotation marks. When omitting quotation marks, include the word "internal." In other words, your parenthetical would be "(internal quotation marks omitted)." Also, be careful not to use "quotations" instead of "quotation marks."

   Some examples.

   (brackets and ellipsis omitted)

   (citation and internal quotation marks omitted)

   (brackets, citations, ellipses, footnotes, and internal quotation marks omitted)

2. *Citing and quoting parentheticals.* You should use a "citing" parenthetical only if the additional source is particularly relevant (for example, the source is a Supreme Court case, a bedrock Sixth Circuit case, or a case from a specialized court). Use

a quoting parenthetical, however, if you are quoting language that is itself quoting another source.

Note that, per Bluebook Rule 5.3(c), "citation omitted" is appropriate where the citation is being left out of the quoted portion of text. A different situation arises, however, where the quoted language quotes another source, but the citation to this underlying source is *not* itself part of the language that you are quoting. In this situation, Bluebook Rule 5.2(e) recommends using a quoting parenthetical rather than omitting quotation marks and using "internal quotation marks omitted" and "citation omitted" parentheticals. In the 20th edition, Bluebook Rule 1.5(b) no longer recognizes the use of the "internal quotation marks omitted" parenthetical. Bluebook Rule 5.2(f) allows for the omission of internal quotation marks only when the opening mark appears at the beginning of the language that you are quoting and the closing mark appears at the end of the language.

For example, suppose you want to quote the following language from *International Dairy Foods Association v. Boggs*, 622 F.3d 628, 635 (6th Cir. 2010): "By contrast, the decision of whether to grant a motion for a preliminary injunction is 'left to the sound discretion of the district court.' *Deja Vu of Cincinnati, L.L.C. v. Union Twp. Bd. of Trs.*, 411 F.3d 777, 782 (6th Cir. 2005)." According to 5.2(e), you would cite it as follows: "By contrast, the decision of whether to grant a motion for a preliminary injunction is 'left to the sound discretion of the district court.'" *Int'l Dairy Foods Assoc. v. Boggs*, 622 F.3d 628, 635 (6th Cir. 2010) (quoting *Deja Vu of Cincinnati, L.L.C. v. Union Twp. Bd. of Trs.*, 411 F.3d 777, 782 (6th Cir. 2005)).

3. ***Emphasis added (when citing to something in the record).*** When the emphasis-added descriptor does not directly follow a citation, such as in an opinion where you have deleted the record citation for the quotation, treat it as an abridged sentence and place it in parentheses, with the "e" capitalized. (*Example*: [big long block quote] (Emphasis added.)) Note that the period is placed inside of the parentheses.

4. ***Emphasis in original.*** In a rare break from the Blue Book, Judge G prefers that you indicate parenthetically if the emphasis in a quoted source is from the original text.

5. ***Hard spaces.*** Do not split section marks (§) and their section numbers across lines. To avoid this, insert a hard space. This rule also applies to not splitting JA citations from their page numbers, or docket entries from their entry number, or a list of numbers from their accompanying items. In Word, a hard space can be created using ctrl + shift + spacebar (i.e., hitting the spacebar while holding the control and shift keys down). The shortcut in Word Perfect is ctrl + spacebar.

6. ***Other opinions, references to.*** Cite as either "Maj. Op." (when dissenting or when concurring in part and dissenting in part), "Lead Op." (when concurring), or "Dissenting Op." (when writing the majority). *Example*: The majority also states that the Jehovah's Witnesses "may spread their message at stores, on street corners, in restaurants, in parks, and other public forums." (Maj. Op. at 21)

7. ***Parenthetical explanations.*** Include these as often as possible after a case citation unless they would be unnecessarily duplicative of the cited proposition or sentence. Remember not to omit articles such as "the," "a," and "an" from the parenthetical. Begin these parentheticals with a gerund, unless you are quoting a complete sentence.

8. ***Parts, references to.*** When referring to a portion of a memorandum or opinion, place periods after both the Roman numeral and the subpart letter or number. (*Example*: "As discussed above in Parts II.B. and III.A.2., this argument is without merit.") Use the word "Part" instead of the word "Section," and always capitalize "Part."

9. ***Pincites.*** Judge Gilman prefers that you not use pincites when summarizing the facts of an opinion unless you quote directly from the opinion. (*Example*: "The plaintiff in *Smith v. Jones* was a quadriplegic and blind in one eye." This does not require a citation to *Smith*. *But*: "She became a quadriplegic after a

reckless driver 'sped through a stop light and collided with her vehicle'" would require a pincite to *Smith*.)

10. ***Record citations.*** Cite the record in parentheses. (*Example*: "When Burt provided a price acceptable to Holland, they shook hands and announced their agreement to the rest of the members at the meeting. (JA 934-35)") No periods should appear either inside or outside of the record citation. Remove citations to the record before submitting an opinion for filing.

11. ***Signals.*** When using the signal "*See, e.g.*," italicize everything except for the last comma.

12. ***Small caps.*** Do not use small caps. Use regular Roman type instead.

13. ***String cites.*** Use sparingly and, if used, include explanatory parentheticals.

14. ***Textual citations.*** When you refer to a case for the first time in a textual sentence, include the full case citation within that sentence.

15. ***Two-page rule.*** A source should be cited in full, even if previously cited in full, where that source has not been referred to in the prior two pages of text. The only exception is when the case cited is well known and repeatedly cited, such as *Miranda* or *Terry*.

16. ***Unpublished opinions.***

For opinions available via online databases only, follow this example: *Lyons v. TVA*, No. 87-5309, 1988 WL 12227, at *1 (6th Cir. Feb. 16, 1988).

For unpublished opinions available both in the Federal Appendix and online, cite to the Federal Appendix: *Lyons v. TVA*, 8 F. App'x 31 (6th Cir. 1998).

For opinions that have been designated for publication but have yet to be assigned to a federal reporter, follow this example: *Roberts v. Ward*, No. 05-6305, — F.3d —, 2006 WL 3392620, at * 2 (6th Cir. Nov. 27, 2006).

17. U.S. Sentencing Guidelines.

When used in text. The first time that you mention the federal sentencing guidelines, refer to them as the United States Sentencing Guidelines. After the first mention, you may thereafter refer to them as "the guidelines." You do not need to provide this shortened form in a parenthetical after the first reference.

When used in a citation. Follow Bluebook Rule 12.9.4 when citing to the guidelines, with the following considerations in mind. The text of a guideline is usually followed by commentary (abbreviated as "cmt.") The commentary includes all explanatory information that follows a guideline, and it often contains subsections for "Application Notes" and "Background" information. When citing to information that appears under the subheading of "Background," cite as U.S.S.G. § 2D1.2 cmt. background. Cite any numbered note in the commentary section—whether it appears under "Application Note" (*see, e.g.*, U.S.S.G. § 3D1.4) or not (*see, e.g.*, U.S.S.G. § 3D1.5)—as U.S.S.G. § [section number] cmt. n.1. And cite to a guidelines appendix as

U.S.S.G. app. C.

Exception: The Bluebook citation format refers to the guidelines as "U.S. Sentencing Guidelines Manual"—e.g.,.S. Sentencing Guidelines Manual § 3D1.1. When citing the guidelines in bench memos and opinions, you should instead use either "United States Sentencing Guidelines" (in the first reference to the guidelines, either in text or a citation) or "U.S.S.G." (if "United States Sentencing Guidelines" has already been referenced in either the text or an earlier citation).

Exception: Specify the guidelines version (i.e. 2010, 2015, etc.) only when relevant to the discussion.

Index

–T–

–U–

Made in the USA
Lexington, KY
13 September 2017